JOURNALISM AND DEMOCRACY

An evaluation of the political public sphere

Brian McNair

London and New York

First published 2000
by Routledge
11 New Fetter Lane, London EC4P 4EE

Simutaneously published in the USA and Canada
by Routledge
29 West 35th Street, New York, NY 10001

Routledge is an imprint of the Taylor & Francis Group

© 2000 Brian McNair

Typeset in Sabon by Taylor & Francis Books Ltd
Printed and bound in Great Britain by MPG Books Ltd, Bodmin

British Library Cataloguing in Publication Data
A catalogue record for this book is available from the British Library

Library of Congress Cataloguing in Publication Data
McNair, Brian
Journalism and democracy/Brian McNair
Includes bibliographical references and index
1. Journalism–Political aspects–Great Britain. 2. Press and politics–Great
Britain. 3. Public interest–Great Britain. 4. Democracy. I. Title
PN5124.P6M38   2000
072'.09'045–dc21   99-35507

ISBN 0–415–21279–0 (hbk)
ISBN 0–415–21280–4 (pbk)

CONTENTS

LIST OF TABLES AND FIGURES

Tables

Figures

PREFACE AND
ACKNOWLEDGEMENTS

The role of journalism in the political process has been a topic of public debate – and a focus of political struggle – ever since there have been print media in Britain. Depending on the nature of the prevailing political regime, journalists and their editors have at various times in British history been executed, imprisoned, deported and subject to punitive taxation. In the more liberal times of the late twentieth century, as media coverage of politics has expanded and the relationship of journalists to the democratic process been transformed, the personal stakes for dissenters may not be so high as in the past, but the debate about the media's role in politics has continued, indeed intensified. Few will deny that now, to a greater extent than ever before, the media are politics, and politics are the media. The implications of this merging of the real and mediated accounts of the real are the principal subject of this book.

While written with the widest possible readership in mind, it is directed principally at two groups. The academic community, first – researchers, teachers and students of political communication – will find it, I hope, a useful addition to the rapidly expanding literature on 'mediated democracy'.

Second, it is intended for the practitioners of political communication – the political journalists themselves, some of whom have written and reported nearly as much in recent years about the 'mediatisation' of the political process as they have about policy; and also the public relations professionals, the 'spin doctors' of current media demonology. These two groups – academics, on the one hand, and makers of political communication on the other – often speak in different languages, but they have in common an interest in the state of our mass-mediated democracy; a form of polity, unique to the age of mass communication and now the standard in all advanced capitalist societies, over which journalists and their media organisations stand not merely as reporters and analysts, but as participants in, and producers of what we all – citizens, politicians and their communication advisors, and journalists – experience as political reality.

The prevailing orthodoxy amongst both academic and journalistic writers on British political culture – and this is true irrespective of their place on the ideological spectrum – is that we are living in a time of crisis: the 'crisis of public communication', according to Jay Blumler and Michael Gurevitch (1995); 'the death of news', as the *New Statesman* put it in 1998;[1] the era of 'dumbing down'. All such phrases are intended to suggest that, though we live amidst apparent communicative plenty, we are actually being starved of information – starved, that is, of the *right kind* of information; the kind that we require to function politically and to perform our civic duties. We live in an era of proliferating media outlets, it is generally acknowledged, but their content is increasingly shaped by the low, base needs of commerce and profit rather than the higher motivations of culture and civic duty. In so far as the media are concerned, more most definitely means less.

This book tests these views on the specific terrain of politics. Sir John Birt, whose position as Director General of the BBC in the 1990s frequently found him negotiating controversy between the media and the political system, asked in a 1995 speech if 'the modern media [are] a force for good or for ill' in British politics.[2] That is not a bad way of posing the question which this book addresses. Unpacking it a little, I examine in the following chapters the extent to which the modern political process, in its public, mass-mediated manifestation, can be regarded as the degraded product of market-driven journalistic practice on the one hand, and ever more sophisticated and sinister news management by politicians on the other. Or, contrary to the prevailing critical orthodoxy, are there grounds for claiming that the evolution of mass media in the late twentieth century and into the new millennium has opened up political affairs to the public in a way which is more than superficial? Can we begin to picture, perhaps for the first time in British political history, a truly democratic public sphere, accessible to more people than ever before, uniquely expressive of popular concerns, and capable of watching over the activities of our power elites? No one will dispute that political journalism presents a mediated, manufactured version of political reality: of political life and processes, issues and events. This book evaluates that version of the real, and asks – what are its positive and negative characteristics? How does it match up to what, in an ideal world, we would wish our journalists to write and speak about politics?

I make three qualifications at the outset. First, this is a study of journalism and democracy in a particular society (Britain) at a time of more than usually rapid political, social and cultural change, symbolised most dramatically by the end of Conservative government and the return of the Labour Party to office in May 1997 after eighteen years in opposition. The political and journalistic cultures it describes were and remain fluid and volatile, as one political elite replaced another in government, and as the introduction of new communication technologies has continued to revolutionise the processes of journalistic production.

Secondly, the book appears at a time of fundamental change in the constitution and shape of the political system itself, with Europeanisation on the one hand, and devolution on the other, now fully institutionalised processes. The concepts of Britain and of Britishness, of the United Kingdom and the Englishness of its majority, are mutating in relation to Scottishness, Europeanness, Northern Irishness, Welshness, all of which evolving identities reverberate continually on the political media, both as topics of coverage and as conditions of production. Underpinning constitutional change, however, and for some time to come, there remains an unmistakeably *British* political culture, centred on Westminster and mediated by a 'national' journalism which is consumed throughout the United Kingdom, alongside whatever more local journalisms exist. This book, written by a Scotsman working in a Scottish university, directly addresses the UK-level polity only, and the media which support it.[3]

And third, anything said about the political media of the United Kingdom in this book must be qualified with the recognition that we British are, as a culture, relatively advantaged in the continuing strength and vitality of our public service broadcasting system. After presenting a rather up-beat paper on the future of British broadcast journalism to an academic gathering in Boulder, Colorado,[4] I was reminded by a colleague from New Zealand that not every country had the luxury of a BBC, and could not benefit from the 'levelling up' effect on the quality of other media output which I had argued a strong public service broadcaster to have. In this sense, my conclusions about British political journalism apply in the first instance only to the United Kingdom, and are not necessarily applicable to the political cultures of advanced capitalism in general. Readers in other countries will determine for themselves how relevant the British experience is to their own.

Some acknowledgements. The research and writing time without which the book could not have been produced draw on the *Political Communication and Democracy* project undertaken at the University of Stirling between 1996 and 1998, in collaboration with Philip Schlesinger and David Miller, and funded by the Economic and Social Research Council (award reference L126251022). The University of Stirling also contributed a semester of sabbatical leave to the project, gratefully acknowledged here. Research assistants Will Dinan and Deidre Kevin were crucial supports in the data-gathering and preparation which the project required.

Many academics made helpful comments and suggestions at various points in the gestation and writing of the book, and I would especially like to mention in this context Jay Blumler, Denis McQuail, Ralph Negrine, Bob Franklin, Denis Kavanagh and Alison Preston. The views of those practitioners of political journalism who attended the ESRC-organised seminar on political communication held at Stirling in November 1997 were also welcome.

I am particularly grateful to the many journalists, media managers and political communication professionals who granted interviews for the research, on or off the record. Whether they agree with my conclusions or not, I hope they will find what I have made of their comments useful in the development of their own thinking about the relationship between journalism and democracy.

Many thanks also to Rebecca Barden and Chris Cudmore at Routledge, who guided the book to swift and timely publication.

Brian McNair
September 1999

1

JOURNALISM AND DEMOCRACY

The debate

Modern politics are largely mediated politics, experienced by the great majority of citizens at one remove, through their print and broadcast media of choice. Any study of democracy in contemporary conditions is therefore also a study of how the media report and interpret political events and issues; of how they facilitate the efforts of politicians to persuade their electorates of the correctness of policies and programmes; of how they themselves (i.e., editorial staff, management and proprietors) influence the political process and shape public opinion. The political process, in its public manifestation, reaches citizens as the product of a set of journalistic codes and practices (the prevailing system of newsvalues, styles of interviewing, impartiality and objectivity guidelines), which interact with and are shaped by politicians and their professional communication advisors as they negotiate access to, or otherwise seek to influence the output of, political media in ways favourable to themselves. The accounts of political reality provided by the media are complex constructions embodying the communicative work of both groups, which ideally should, but need not always meet the standards of information accuracy and objectivity expected of political communication in a liberal democracy.

The political media are important because, as Anthony Sampson puts it, 'a mature democracy depends on having an educated electorate, informed and connected through parliament' (1996, p. 47), and it is principally through the media that such an electorate can be formed. That the actions of government and the state, and the efforts of competing parties and interests to exercise political power, should be underpinned and legitimised by critical scrutiny and informed debate facilitated by the institutions of the media is a normative assumption uniting the political spectrum from left to right. Analysts and critics may dispute the extent to which Britain *has* a properly functioning 'public sphere' – as Jurgen Habermas called that communal communicative space in which 'private people come together as a public' (1989, p. 27) – but all agree that such a space should exist, and that the media are at its core. Thus, in debates about the state of the democratic polity journalists figure large, and those who criticise the way in which the public sphere has actually developed focus their attacks on the media.

The 'crisis of public communication' identified by Jay Blumler and Michael Gurevitch in their book of the same name (1995)[1] refers principally to two phenomena: firstly, a decline in the quality of political journalism, driven by what are variously described as processes of commercialisation, tabloidisation, Americanisation and, in the currently fashionable vernacular, 'dumbing down' – in short, the ascendancy of 'infotainment' over 'serious' reportage and analysis of politics. Nick Cohen typifies the argument when he writes of broadcast journalism in the *New Statesman* that 'liberal news – by which I mean impartial coverage of issues of public importance – is in crisis. Its practitioners are nervous and unloved. Its self-confidence has been undermined by the preposterous but dominant intellectual fashion of postmodernism.'[2]

The assertion of crisis alludes, secondly, to a change for the worse in the relationship between journalists and politicians; an unwelcome shift in the balance of power between them, attributed in some variants of the thesis to the rise of the professional political communication specialists – the media consultants, communications managers and spin doctors who today inhabit the corridors and committee rooms of power – and, in others, to the destabilising effects of an overpowerful political media whose practitioners have gotten above themselves.

This book tests these assertions, thus entering a debate which straddles the sometimes separate worlds of the academic analyst and the journalistic commentator, as it blurs the ideological polarities of left and right. One is just as likely to encounter a lament for the decline of political journalism in the pages of the right-wing *Spectator* magazine as in the left-of-centre *New Statesman*, and in the *Guardian* as much as the *Daily Telegraph*. This book is not about the relative merits of different political ideas, then, but rather the capacity of our common media system – our *public* sphere – to service and support the democratic process for the benefit of the people as a whole, in accordance with the principles established to govern their operation at the birth of liberal capitalism in Britain some four centuries ago, and still held to be valid today. It is a debate which transcends politics and unites all species of partisan, all varieties of ideological warrior, in common contemplation of what the emergence of mass communication in the last century of the second millenium means for the present and future quality of our democratic polity. For that reason, the arguments draw on the widest possible range of academic and non-academic sources, as presented in books, articles, speeches and lectures, media interviews and analyses, and in interviews with practitioners of political journalism (and political communication) conducted by the author over a period of two years in 1997 and 1998.

Many significant voices are absent, nonetheless – most notably, those of the public themselves: that great mass of ordinary citizens who comprise the greatest part of the audience for political journalism, and for whose hypothetical collective benefit the whole infernal machinery of political communication functions. What do *they* think of the issues debated so intensely by academics, journalists and politicians on their behalf? In this study I have not sought to access their views directly. I have, however, devoted a chapter to 'the sound of the crowd', by which I mean the noise emanating from those proliferating spaces in the media given over to the facilitation of public access, such as political talk shows, phone-ins and related programme formats. In that chapter, and indeed whenever popular political culture is discussed, I have rejected the assumption of many contributors to this debate that popular means irrational and tabloid means trash; that entertainment cannot at the same time be informative; that serious news cannot at the same time be of human interest. Although my status as an academic defines me as a member of the elite group whose collective criticisms of political journalism are often challenged in the following pages, I am at the same time a fully paid-up member of the mass audience whose democratic rights and civic responsibilities drive the work, and I treat its patterns of media consumption with appropriate respect. I begin from the assumption that today's media audiences are, in historical and cross-cultural perspective, relatively highly educated, well-informed, semiologically sophisticated, *active* consumers of media.

The crisis of the political media

What, then, is the specific nature of the 'crisis'? Reading the pages of academic texts and newspaper articles in recent years, or listening to the reportage and commentaries of the broadcasters, one would have noted at various times all of the following criticisms being made of political journalism.

Dumbing down and the rise of infotainment

Firstly, the quantity of what is usually described as 'serious' political journalism circulating in the public sphere has steadily declined, and its substantive political content been diluted, to the detriment of the democratic process. The political media have been dumbing down, to use the phrase which has now become a routine element of British media commentary.[3] German sociologist Jurgen Habermas, whose considered views on these issues, developed over three decades, underpin most variants of the dumbing down thesis, argues that the public sphere, while it has expanded in the course of the twentieth century to include the population as a whole (acknowledged by all but the most overtly reactionary of commentators to

3

be a positive development), has at the same time been degraded by the growing influence of private, commercial interests on the output of media organisations (1989). In the process, the pursuit of profit has replaced that of serving the public interest as the driving force of journalism. News producers – even those like the BBC which are free of direct commercial pressures – have been required to become more and more oriented towards ratings, subordinating the journalistic obligation to inform to the more audience-friendly task of supplying entertainment. The result of these pressures has been an explosion of *infotainment* – journalism in which entertainment values take precedence over information content, presented at an intellectual level low enough to appeal to the mass audiences which comprise the major media markets ('the lowest common denominator', as critics frequently express it). Lower, too, than a healthy democracy demands. Political journalism is said to be conforming to the pressures of *tabloidisation* observed elsewhere in the media: a term which, used interchangeably with dumbing down and infotainment, functions as shorthand for the offence, as it is often characterised, of catering for popular tastes.

One manifestation of this trend would be the media's contemporary fascination with elite deviance (sexual, financial or moral), as in the cases of Conservative and Labour politicians in Britain throughout the 1990s, and of course Bill Clinton, whose 'sex addiction' was a prominent theme of political journalism in Britain as well as the United States during the 1990s, exemplified by coverage of the Monica Lewinsky scandal in 1998–9. The 'sleaze' agenda (see Chapter 3) which featured prominently in British and American political news for most of that decade was alleged to be driven by market forces rather than public interest, in so far as the relentless commodification of journalism and the ever-increasing competitiveness of the media market put a commercial premium on sensationalism and prurience in coverage of politics.

Political information overload

Another criticism, which at first sight appears to stand in contradiction to the notion of dumbing down, asserts not that there is too little serious politics in the media, but too much. All observers agree that the media – and news media in particular – have expanded exponentially in the late twentieth century, and are likely to continue doing so for some time to come. Coverage of politics has always been at the heart of the British news agenda and, as the space available to news media has increased, so too has coverage of politics. David Walker has suggested that this amounts to a kind of political information overload and that, by boring audiences to distraction, 'the massive scale of coverage merely diminishes public interest in politics'.[4] During and after the 1997 general election, the broadcasters, and the BBC in particular, were accused of overloading their audiences

4

with too much political coverage,[5] resulting in the lower than usual ratings achieved by news programmes during the campaign period (see Chapter 8).

Elitism

Associated with this criticism is the perception that a quantitatively excessive political journalism has at the same time become too *elitist* or *insider-oriented* in its subject-matter; too focused on what commentators often refer to as the 'horse-race' – the *process* of political competition, and the race for electoral victory – and not enough on policy substance. Walker writes of the BBC's political journalism (and the charge would apply equally to most other news organisations) that it suffers from 'a fixation on party politics to the exclusion of matters of power and policy',[6] deriving in large part from excessive journalistic dependence on political sources.

An excess of interpretation

Another trend identified by critics is the tendency towards more interpretation and commentary as a proportion of total output, and the relative decline of straight reportage. Bob Franklin asserts that 'the gallery tradition of reporting parliament is dead' (1997, p. 232), adding his voice to those who interpret this as part of the wider process of tabloidisation/dumbing down of the British media. Ralph Negrine, too, sees the decline of straight parliamentary reporting as evidence of 'the dangers of commercialisation' (1996, p. 76). Media pundit Roy Greenslade suggests that the excessive quantity of political journalism now in circulation has resulted in a tendency to empty pontification,[7] caused by the need to fill the space created for politics in the news and current affairs schedules. Columnist Iain MacWhirter argues that 'the growth of the commentary industry is another manifestation of our degenerating political culture'.[8]

Hyperadversarialism

Degeneration of the political culture is also alleged in the trend towards more adversarial techniques of political interviewing seen in broadcast journalism. Writing of America, but in terms which apply with no less force to the United Kingdom, James Fallows accuses political journalism of *hyperadversarialism* – a combative style in which coverage of politics begins to resemble that sub-genre of natural history broadcasting where the harsh and unending struggle for survival is portrayed as the only point of existence. Journalists, he argues, now place 'a relentless emphasis' on 'the cynical game of politics', undermining the integrity of public life by 'implying day after day that the political sphere is mainly an arena in which ambitious politicians struggle for dominance, rather than a structure in which citizens can deal with wearisome collective problems' (1996, p. 31). Where Habermas identified the deradicalising impact of commercialisation on the late nineteenth century press, Fallows has argued in turn that late twentieth century broadcasting was effectively *depoliticised*, the substance of political debate gradually being replaced by the superficial, entertainment-led spectacle of adversarial game-playing. Political journalism, he argues, has become excessively gladiatorial.

Excessive balance and outmoded impartiality

At other times, however, and in other contexts, political journalism is said to be not opinionated or gladiatorial *enough*, constrained instead by too much balance, artificial notions of neutrality, too-rigidly defined impartiality. During the 1997 general election, for example, critics including the future prime minister Tony Blair accused the BBC's political journalists of sticking too closely to the balance guidelines,[9] and of producing unengaging, formulaic, 'tit-for-tat' news which failed to involve audiences in the democratic process. These criticisms encouraged both of the main British broadcast news providers, the BBC and ITN, to undertake far-reaching post-election reviews of how political journalism should be produced and packaged (see Chapter 8).

Political public relations and the rise of spin

Last, but by no means least of the criticisms of political journalism currently in the public domain is the impact upon its content of public relations in its various forms, such as governmental information management, issues and image management, lobbying, and 'spin'. Post-WWII, writes Habermas in the classic statement of the problem, 'in the advanced countries of the West, they [public relations] have come to dominate the public sphere', and have become 'a key phenomenon for the diagnosis of that realm' (1989, p. 192). The methods and practices of public relations are said to subvert the normative integrity of the public sphere by transforming it into a vehicle for the pursuit of vested interests, and the subordination of the public interest. In America, says Fallows, public relations has moved to 'the centre' of the presidency, and thus to the centre of political journalism (1996).[10] Journalists have become dependent, or at the very least over-reliant, on the professional managers of information and image, to the detriment of the quality of their output, and of the citizens' access to rational information.

Similar criticisms are frequently heard in relation to the United

6

Kingdom, where the professionalisation of political advocacy is almost universally viewed as a negative trend, articulated through what I call in Chapter 7 'the demonology of spin', denounced as another manifestation of Americanisation, to be condemned not only for the way in which spin doctors and other communication professionals seek to massage the news agenda on behalf of political clients, but for the reaction they have provoked from journalists who (as was noted above) are alleged to spend more and more time covering the process of political advocacy – 'the game' – than they do the 'real issues' of political life. Since New Labour's election in May 1997 (and indeed for some time before that when it was re-emerging as an electable force) the British media have been engaged in more or less continuous commentary and speculation about the party's information management system, and its adverse impact on journalists' ability to report politics objectively.

Causes of the crisis

The above criticisms of political media are usually linked to two sets of causes. Advocates of *economic* causation, on the one hand, argue that as political media have become more audience-led they have been subject to processes of *marketisation, commercialisation* and *commodification.* All these terms suggest, accurately enough, that contemporary journalism exists primarily in commodity form, to be sold in a media marketplace alongside other cultural products. Journalists and their editors must therefore compete for market share (as reflected in TV and radio ratings, newspaper and periodical circulations, and shares of advertising revenue). They are inclined to prioritise the popular over the pertinent, the racy over the relevant, the weird over the worthy. Commodification has been accompanied by the proliferation of news 'brands', as competing organisations employ ever more sophisticated marketing techniques to target specific audiences of differing demographic profiles. The emergence of professional news management at the heart of the political process is also seen from this perspective as economically driven, parallelling as it does the expansion of political advertising, value research, and other business techniques which originated as means of influencing, through the media, public opinion about private interests in turn of the century America, and were then exported to the rest of the capitalist world as the twentieth century progressed.

The substantive information content of political journalism is said to be diluted not only by market-driven commercialisation, however (and the implied ascendancy of consumer-friendly style over substance), but by a second group of causes: the negative impact of new technologies on news-gathering and presentation. News is faster, more immediate, more 'live' than ever before, it is commonly agreed. But not necessarily more

7

informative. On the contrary, as one senior broadcast journalist puts it: 'the technology [of news production] enables us to package, graphicise and meld five minutes of old TV information into sixty seconds of new TV time – the whizz and bang of such presentation may be enticing but the content reduction is so acute that normal debate is in danger of being reduced to the absurd.'[11] There is a crisis, then, caused not just by the impact of commercialisation on journalistic style and content, but by the demands of televisual form itself, arising from the constraints which ever-faster, evermore 'real-time' newsgathering possibilities place on the ability of journalists to analyse and explain complex political reality.

Technological evolution is also causally implicated in the rise of public relations and spin. The rapid growth since the early twentieth century of communication consultancy, media advisors and spin doctors to fill what Jay Blumler calls the 'news holes' (1997) created by the technology-driven expansion of journalistic outlets has made the media highly dependent on and thus more vulnerable to manipulation by the spin doctors and the seductions of manufactured political news – those political pseudo-events designed expressly to attract media attention and maximise the favourable publicity received by political actors. Journalistic dependence on political sources for raw material to make into news is identified by many observers as a key element in the contemporary crisis of political communication.

Journalism and the degeneration of the public sphere

From the identification of the above trends and their causes is derived the conclusion that rather than support the democratic process as, in the ideal scheme of things, it should be doing, journalism has become an alienating, cynicism-inducing, narcoticising force in our political culture, turning people off citizenship rather than equipping them to fulfil their democratic potential. Diminishing rates of electoral participation and increasing voter volatility are among the consequences often alleged of this trend. Others include the undermining of democracy through the strengthening of the power of political elites, as when Mannheim asserts of the United States that the rise of television in the latter half of the twentieth century has produced 'a continuing qualitative reduction of the intellectual content of political discourse among the mass of American citizens' (quoted in Denton, 1998, p. 31). This 'may enable an elite which preserves the requisite knowledge, skills, and resources more effectively to manipulate the polity'. American political scientist Doris Graber states that 'the news product has deteriorated when judged as a resource for public opinion formation' (quoted in Blumler and Gurevitch, 1995, p. 66), while Blumler and Gurevitch believe that in Britain 'the political communication process now tends to strain against, rather than with the grain of citizenship' (Ibid., p. 203). Also writing of the UK (and with reference to approximately the same period as is covered in this book) Stephen Coleman suggests that 'designer politics' and 'electoral consumerism' have 'diminished the health of democratic culture, introducing the ethos (and the absence of ethics) of commerce rather than community into the battle for political success' (1998, p. 687).

Pierre Bourdieu's *On Television and Journalism* adds to the critical ranks with the argument (derived from French examples but applicable in most respects to the British case) that entertainment-driven tendencies in political coverage produce 'a cynical view' (1998, p. 5) amongst electors, while Anthony Sampson has written that the role of political journalism in 'providing the chief context for information and understanding for the public' is being undermined by 'the media's ability to confuse news with entertainment' (1996, p. 42). 'As the media have become more pervasive and entertaining', he argues, connecting this trend to the wider crisis of democracy, 'parliament itself is being marginalised in the national debate' (ibid., p. 47). Ex-BBC journalist John Cole writes in his memoirs that the growing emphasis on entertainment in political journalism has 'created a public reluctance to make the effort that is needed for a worthwhile understanding of politics' (1996, p. 450).

Others, by contrast, argue not that contemporary political journalism creates a lazy citizenry and an excessively powerful elite but, on the contrary, an excessively unruly mass and a correspondingly weak governing class – that journalists have become too subversive of authority, too demagogic, too powerful and pro-active in setting agendas over the heads of elected politicians. Political elites are not being shored up in this line of reasoning but are being *destabilised*, and their authority undermined, to the detriment of good government. David Goodhart, for example, asserts that the political media are 'usurping' the authority of government in Britain.[12] The intense media coverage of the Monica Lewinsky scandal in 1998 and 1999 has been argued by some to show that similar processes are evident in the United States (although, of course, President Clinton bounced back from several media-generated ordeals, up to and including his Senate trial for impeachment, and was able to complete his second term of office).

Broadcast journalist Nik Gowing has argued that the 'liveness' and immediacy of foreign news in the era of twenty-four hour 'rolling' coverage presents political decision-makers with a qualitatively new dilemma. Politicians, he writes, 'fear that emotive pictures provided by real-time TV coverage forces them into an impulsive policy response when the reality on the ground is different' (1994, p. 76). Although foreign news coverage 'does not necessarily *dictate* policy responses' (his emphasis), he finds that it can be 'a powerful influence in problem recognition, which in turn helps to shape the foreign policy agenda' (ibid., p. 18). Applying Gowing's analysis to the field of political journalism, and assuming that domestic policy-making and decision-taking are not immune to the impact of these media-generated perceptions and pressures (and there is no reason why they should be), the rationality which normative theory insists should drive public policy debate is potentially undermined by an evolving media environment which places ever-increasing value on the speed and ubiquity of news coverage.

Although they are often in rather dramatic opposition to each other (the media, one might think, cannot be destabilising political elites at one moment, and strengthening their power at the expense of an apathetic, cynical citizenry in another), a number of common assumptions link the approaches underpinning these critical perspectives – approaches which are *pessimistic* in so far as they amount to the argument that the more political journalism we get, the less democratic our society becomes. Those assumptions are:

- that there was in the past some system of democratic government, and of political communication to support it, which was superior to what we now enjoy, and that we are moving away from rather than toward the normative, ideal-type public sphere described in the work of Habermas and other theorists. In this sense, the theses of dumbing down/tabloidisation/Americanisation can be characterised as *narratives of decline*;
- that some modes of political discourse, some styles of journalistic output – usually, it turns out, those favoured and largely monopolised by political and cultural elites (politicians, journalists and academics in particular) – are inherently more rational, and thus more useful to democracy than those now present in much of the media;
- that reason and rationality are terms applying to the substantive content of political debates and their coverage in the media, rather than the modes of their discussion (so that the discussion of a politician's personality, public speaking style or poor taste in haircuts cannot be rational, whereas the discussion of interest rate policy can be nothing but).

If these assumptions are valid, then Britain's political culture is unquestionably undergoing a crisis to which politicians and their communication advisers (who provide the raw materials with which political news is made), journalists (who refine and process those materials for public consumption), and audiences (who buy the newspapers and watch or listen to the broadcasts) have all contributed. If, on the other hand, they are unfounded, or if the evolving economic, social and cultural conditions of turn-of-the-millenium British capitalism make them outmoded, the grounds for pessimism (in so far as the media are concerned, at least) about the health of our democracy may be less firmly based.[13]

Not all critics of the public sphere share the assumptions listed above, it should be said. An alternative approach – *nihilistic* rather than pessimistic – is provided by Jean Baudrillard's thoughts from 1983 on the predicament of 'the silent majority' (a term signifying the widespread perception, if not the empirical fact[14]) that rates of democratic participation have steadily fallen in most liberal democracies. The public sphere, he argues (in a variant of the traditional materialist denunciation of liberal democracy as a sham) is and always has been an elitist bourgeois construct, as are its ideal characteristics of rationality and truth. Designed and built by the radical bourgeoisie of late feudal and early modern Europe (in the course of its political struggle with the feudal aristocracy) to provide democratic participation for its own members in the first instance, it reflects essentially bourgeois values and conditions of existence, and can thus never serve the genuine interests of the people as a whole. Mass apathy and cynicism about politics are, for Baudrillard, a *rational* response to the fact that the people as a whole feel no real involvement in a process which *appears* to give them power but in reality does not. They therefore resist elite efforts to incorporate them into the process of democratic legitimation. The intellectuals in turn respond to this 'silence' by blaming it on the decline of 'rational' political communication in the system. Criticising those who wish always to 'keep the masses *within reason*' (his emphasis), who wish always to 'moralise information: to better inform, to better socialise, to raise the cultural level of the masses', he asserts that 'the masses scandalously resist this imperative of rational communication' (1983, p. 10).

> They are given meaning: they want spectacle. No effort has been able to convert them to the seriousness of the content, nor even to the seriousness of the code. Messages are given to them, [but] they only want some sign, they idolise the play of signs and stereotypes, they idolise any content so long as it resolves itself into a spectacular sequence.

In Baudrillard's hyper-real world, we can infer, the popular political culture of spectacle and drama is not a pacifying entertainment so much as the occasion for *resistance* to a system which remains, despite its democratic facade, bourgeois and exclusive. The liberal intelligentsia's ambition to make the silent majority politically active, by 'injecting them with information' (ibid., p. 25) of a 'rational', 'serious' type , is doomed to failure. By remaining silent, passive, mocking, suggests Baudrillard, in *choosing* to prefer spectacle over substance, the masses subvert a system which they have no interest in legitimising, since legitimation merely leads to perpetuation. Baudrillard's analysis leads to the fatalistic conclusion (and the political dead-end) that there can in the final analysis be no authentically democratic public sphere within capitalism, merely a democratic illusion before which the people stand as a sullen, silent majority, participating only when the spectacle and the drama – like the football or the soaps on the other channel – are sufficiently entertaining to keep them interested.

The evaluation of the public sphere presented in this book argues that neither pessimistic notions of crisis, nor the bleak and depressing nihilism of Baudrillard's writings on the subject (albeit two decades old, and thus not necessarily representative of his current thinking on the subject of mediated democracy), satisfactorily reflect the complexity, unpredictability and frequently contradictory nature of the political media as they function in our time. Where the pessimists see absolute virtue in an ideal public sphere which has never existed – and may never exist outside of the intellectual imagination – Baudrillard raises the couch potato to the status of political radical, and cultural slobbery to that of noble, if passive resistance to bourgeois efforts at incorporation of the masses. The public sphere described in this book is one which, for all its weaknesses, has evolved over time into something altogether more interesting, from the sociological perspective, and more useful as a democratic resource than either variety of critique allows.

The book

The following chapters go on to assess the political public sphere against four criteria, beginning in the next chapter with features which can be classed as *quantitative*, in so far as they address the dimensions of the public sphere as an information resource, measured in numbers of information outlets, size of audiences, and quantities of information in circulation. In subsequent chapters, an attempt is made to assess the *quality* of the information circulated. What is political journalism about? What are its priorities (newsvalues), and what – in its form, content and style – does it tell us about politics? What messages does it convey?[15]

The third criteria of evaluation is the degree of *critical scrutiny* which the public sphere permits to be directed towards political elites; the extent to which the classic 'watchdog' role of the media in liberal democracy is realised.

And the fourth criteria of evaluation, finally, concerns *access*. One of the conditions specified by Habermas for a properly functioning public sphere – and one generally accepted by political scientists – is 'universal access' to the (mainly media) institutions through which politically important information is disseminated, discussed and analysed.[16] Access in this context I take to mean both access *to* information and accessability *of* information. Political information should of course be available to those who want it (the traditional universality of the British public service model being the exemplar), but availability only has value if its content is at the same time comprehensible to those who may wish to make use of it in

12

political decision-making. In this respect access is a product of the form of journalistic discourse, as well as the extent of its availability to the public. Journalist Andrew Marr puts it well when he observes that:

> Good political prose is democratic in effect because it alerts, provoking a response. It wakens us up and engages us in the arguments ... Democracy cannot exist without a common culture ... If political communication becomes over-specialised, or jargon-ridden, it becomes the enemy of that common culture, and the enemy of democratic politics.[17]

In evaluating the political media against these criteria this book sets out to 'map' the public sphere – to identify and describe the various regions of mediated space in which political affairs are reported, analysed, interpreted and discussed; to identify the political media and their audiences, specifying their objectives in relation to their target markets (and how these are expressed in output), and assessing the resources provided for these objectives to be met; to present a political economy of the political media, and to give concrete form to the abstract notion of the public sphere.

The political public sphere does not, of course, comprise a set of institutions and organisations existing in isolation from one another. Print and audiovisual media interact with each other in ways which allow us to think of them as interconnected elements of an organic structure, reproducing over time, adapting to the environmental conditions of their existence in ways which cannot be predicted or pre-planned with any certainty by political actors or media professionals. So the following account is not just a map, but an *anatomy*, addressing how the various journalistic forms which fill the public sphere[18] – the political interview, for example, or the commentary column – originated and have evolved; how political journalism is sourced, and why some events and issues rather than others become news; how frameworks of journalistic interpretation develop and are 'spun'; how the different, often competing elements of the journalistic process relate to each other in all of the above.

2

THE POLITICAL PUBLIC
SPHERE

An anatomy

The journalistic institutions of the contemporary public sphere are information-suppliers in a multi-layered media market, structured by socio-economic audience characteristics such as social class, professional status and educational level. The precise terminology used to distinguish these markets varies between commentators and analysts, and none of the various conventions adopted are entirely adequate. Many refer to the 'quality press' when describing the large-format broadsheet newspapers, for example, which is unsatisfactory in so far as it assumes that 'quality' is synonymous with the style and content of those newspapers especially, and implies that non-broadsheet titles cannot also be of high journalistic quality. Similarly, the largest-selling popular titles have traditionally been called *tabloids*, but since the *Mail* and *Express* titles (at one time both broadsheets) adopted the newsprint size associated with tabloids some years ago the term has become confusing, and increasingly unhelpful in an era when 'tabloidisation' is almost universally used as a critical term of abuse. The designation *red-top tabloid* is a variation used by some analysts to distinguish the racier tabloid titles (*Sun, Mirror, Daily Star*) from the tabloid-sized former broadsheets (*Daily Mail, Daily Express*).

I will use the designations *elite, mid-market,* and *popular* to refer to the three main categories of political media, these designations be ing generally applicable to both broadcast and print outlets. By 'elite' in this context is not implied any qualitative superiority in the content or style of a particular outlet; simply that its audience mainly comprises those whom social statisticians would place above the societal average in terms of income, educational level, or profession.

Print

In the newspaper sector these three groupings correspond to what are referred to in Audit Bureau of Circulation figures as *broadsheet, mid-market* and *tabloid* (although the 'mids', as already noted) are tabloid in form. Table 2.1 shows the market segmentation of British national daily

14

and Sunday newspapers into elite, mid-market and popular titles, with average circulations for each. There are nineteen national titles serving the UK as a whole (coexisting and competing with a much larger number of regional and local titles servicing the Scottish, Northern Irish, Welsh and English markets).

Table 2.1 The political media market

Newspapers	ABC circulation (millions)*	TV and radio	Average audiences (millions)	Periodicals	ABC circulation
Elite					
Times	0.377	Today	1.78	New Statesman	25,648
Sunday Times	1.203	World At One	0.9	Spectator	33,531
Telegraph	1.044	Newsnight	1.0	Prospect	
Sunday Telegraph	0.562	C4 News	0.73	Economist	119,400
Guardian	0.418	PM	0.91		
Observer	0.541				
Independent	0.390	political current affairs programmes (e.g., Despatch Box, Analysis,			
Independent on Sunday	0.385	rolling news and related services (e.g., Sky News, BBC News 24, BBC Parliament)			
Financial Times	0.292				
Mid-market					
Daily Mail	1.689	9 O'Clock News	5.2		
Mail on Sunday	1.960	News At Ten**	5.9		
Express	1.538	Channel 5 News	0.7		
Sunday Express	1.692				
Popular					
Sun	3.588				
News of the World	4.725				
Star	0.808				
Mirror***	3.622				
Sunday Mirror	2.678				
People	2.130				

* Circulation and ratings figures are approximate averages for the first six months of 1998
** *News At Ten* was taken off ITV in March 1999
*** Includes figures for the *Mirror*'s sister paper in Scotland, the *Daily Record*

The broadsheets

The majority of these titles are broadsheets, or *elite* titles – thus defined because they are read largely by socio-economic categories A and B (upper and middle class). These newspapers are the most information-dense of the print media (in terms of wordage), and the most editorially committed to the coverage of politics if judged by content. On a count of days in November 1996 when a political story either headlined, made the front page, or was the subject of an editorial leader, the elite daily titles achieved political newsworthiness ratings (PNRs), as I will call them, of between 68 (*Financial Times*) and 88 (*Daily Telegraph*), while the Sundays were close to 100 (see Table 2.2). PNRs are calculated by dividing the maximum number of occasions (78, for the daily press) when politics could headline, be editorialised, or made the front page of the newspaper, with the actual number, expressed as a percentage). This indicator says nothing about the quality of the coverage, nor the subjects addressed within the broad category of politics (see Chapter 3), but it does illustrate what is widely assumed to be the case – that politics is featured more prominently in the pages of the elite titles than in any other category of newspaper. This is reflected in the allocation of editorial resource within the broadsheets. *The Times*, for example, supports eight political journalists in the lobby alone, as does the *Daily Telegraph*. The *Guardian* and the *Independent* both have six lobby correspondents (see Chapter 3).

The mid-market

By comparison to the broadsheets, the four *mid-market* titles, read mainly by social groups B2 and C1 (middle and upper working class), and with a total circulation of around 3.5m, achieved political newsworthiness ratings in November 1996 of between 42 and 53 (the *Sunday Express* was higher over the sample period, with a PNR of 92). Their market, as their staff perceive it, is 'middle England' (as opposed to middle Britain) – moderately affluent, socially and morally conservative people concerned about, but not obsessed with politics, mainly in so far as it affects their personal incomes and quality of life. As one mid-market political editor puts it:

> We know the context in which we work. [We] have clear views on family, on welfare ... and any journalist working for [us] will be aware of what they are and of what would interest the paper.[1]

The mid-market audience has tended, for most of the post-war period, to be right-of-centre in its voting patterns, and in what its newspapers assume it wants editorially. With the rise of New Labour in the mid-1990s, however, and its successful efforts to capture 'middle Britain', those polit-

Table 2.2 Political newsworthiness ratings in the British media, November 1996

Politics as:	lead story	front page	editorial	PNR*
Times	11	20	23	69
Guardian	16	18	23	73
Telegraph	21	24	24	88
Financial Times	14	19	17	64
Independent	17	18	18	68
Daily Mail	10	12	19	53
Daily Express	6	11	19	44
Sun	4	8	24	46
Mirror	1	3	16	26
Star	0	2	10	15
Sundays				
Sunday Times	3	4	4	92
Observer	3	4	4	92
Sunday Telegraph	3	4	4	92
Independent on Sunday	3	4	3	83
Sunday Express	2	2	1	42
Mail on Sunday	1	2	4	58
News of World	0	0	1	8
People	0	0	0	0
Sunday Mirror	0	1	1	17
Politics as:	leading item			
Today (R4)	8			38
World At One	9			42
Sky News	4			19
C4 News	5			24
9 O'Clock News	3			14
News At Ten	4			19
Newsnight	8			32

* Number of days when politics led a broadcast news bulletin (or, in the case of newspapers, was the subject either of a lead story, front page item, or editorial), expressed as a percentage of the maximum possible number

ical affiliations have been destabilised. Following the 1997 election, for example, and encouraged by a change of ownership, the *Express* shifted quickly from support for the Conservative Party to a more liberal stance, which included campaigning for the legalisation of cannabis. Though not a Labour 'cheerleader', the contrast with the pre-97 *Express* was striking. The *Daily Mail*, also a fiercely pro-Tory newspaper before the 1997 election, metamorphosed thereafter into a considerably less conservative beast, targeting a younger, gender-balanced, more ideologically diverse market than it had traditionally been associated with.

The populars

Finally, the six 'red-top' tabloids, or *populars*, read mainly by C2s and below (unskilled working and underclass)[2] boast a combined circulation of nine million – more than the elite and mid-market titles put together and comprising therefore the majority of the newspaper-buying citizenry. Popular tabloids remain by far the most widely read of print media, and thus central to the evaluation of the political public sphere. The conventional wisdom amongst academic analysts and journalistic observers, as Chapter 1 indicated, has been to dismiss their value as democratic resources, and to scold the demagogic and propagandistic nature of their editorial content (the *Sun*'s coverage of the 1992 election perhaps being the exemplary case).[3] It has also been suggested that these titles are intentionally used to 'distract' their readers from the serious business of politics by their focus on 'pseudo-voyeuristic insights' into the private lives of celebrities, the sexual deviations of randy vicars, and so on (Gripsund, 1992, p. 94). And it is true, as Table 2.2 shows, that in general the populars give less priority to political journalism, if measured in the number of headline and front page articles and editorials printed, than the elite and mid-market media, and that the readers of popular newspapers are assumed – by managers and journalists working on the titles, who cite market research evidence – to be less interested in politics than broadsheet and mid-market readers. The political editor of the *Daily Star* explains his newspaper's lack of political coverage thus:

> We make no bones about it. We're trying to sell newspapers to a certain niche market, and that niche market is primarily interested in television, sport and looking at pretty women, plus competitions, promotions, winning this, winning that. The politics that we run doesn't sell a single extra copy, as far as we're concerned. So our political coverage is very confined.

In November 1996, for example, the four-week period on which Table 2.2 is based, the *Daily Star* achieved a PNR of only 15. The paper never headlined with a political story throughout that period, and only gave politics front page space on the two days when the Conservative government's Budget speech (its last before Labour took power in May 1997) was being delivered and then assessed. Otherwise, celebrity and human interest stories such as the domestic troubles of *Baywatch* star Pamela Anderson took precedence over political matters (this story headlined the *Star* on five consecutive days in November 1996).

The *Star*, however, is not typical of the British popular newspaper in its neglect of politics. On the contrary, both of its larger circulation rivals, the *Sun* and the *Mirror*, are highly politicised media, both in the strength of

the opinions contained in their editorials and in the priority given to politics within their structures of newsvalues. The staff of the *Star* – a 'tits 'n'
bums' tabloid in the classic sense, closer to the quasi-pornographic *Daily
Sport*[4] than any other British newspaper – distinguish themselves from the
former in that they openly acknowledge their disinterest in political affairs
(unless, of course, those affairs are of the sexually explicit variety). The
Star's political editor explains that:

> Although we look a bit like the *Sun* we're actually very different.
> We're not trying to compete with the *Sun*. We have fewer
> resources than the *Sun*. We've found a niche market – mostly
> young men, living in the north. It's a huge generalisation, but
> that's really our market, and we think we know their interests. It's
> a very solid market, much smaller than the *Sun* or the *Mirror*. And
> our experience is that politics should never go on the front page
> unless it's really exceptional. You can measure the audience going
> up and down. We're a paper that relies almost entirely on over-
> the-counter sales. We don't get delivered, so people tend to react
> to what they see on the counter. Put politics on the front page and
> it's usually the kiss of death.

Given all this, it follows that:

> We're not likely ever to break any great political stories, partly
> because we're not really in the market for that kind of thing. And
> it's not likely that if a Cabinet minister had a major story to break
> he'd do it through the medium of the *Daily Star*, quite honestly.
> The *Sun* with ten million readers, or *The Times* are more obvious
> places to come to.

Even a political story with a prominent sexual content is not necessarily of
interest to the *Star*.

> Oddly enough we're not particularly interested in the sleaze
> stories. The Robin Cook story[5] we gave very little room to,
> because it's the editor's instinct that our readers are not very inter-
> ested in Robin Cook. A lot of them won't know who he is, I'm
> afraid. Ours are the sort of readers who probably don't know who
> the members of the Cabinet are beyond the prime minister.

On the other hand, the *Daily Star did* give prominence to the new sports
minister Tony Banks' policy pronouncements on football in the summer of
1997. Here was a story combining sport and politics, linking the political
sphere to the concerns of the *Star*'s niche market in a way which happens

with relative rarity. In this sense, we may categorise the *Star* as an *apolitical popular* newspaper, serving what one commentator characterises as a market of 'unreconstructed politically incorrect northern men'.[6] Although the *Star* does take editorial positions on politics, and has lent its editorial support to one party or another in general elections, it maintains as a rule only minimal political coverage. In contrast to the considerable resources dedicated to politics by most of the media organisations discussed in this chapter, the *Star* maintains no full-time political correspondents, and the political editor is a part-time post, occupied by a journalist whose other responsibilities include writing the captions for the page 3 girls.

Political populars: the Sun

The *Sun*, as the *Daily Star*'s editor concedes, is a very different kind of popular newspaper, in that it features politics prominently in its news agenda. Table 2.2 shows that the *Sun* led with a political story on four days out of twenty-six in November 1996, had a front page political story (but not a headline) on a further four days, and carried a political editorial on twenty-four days, giving a PNR of 46. Bearing in mind that the *Sun*'s political news tends to be placed on the inside pages, and that there was major coverage in the paper during this period of European union, the domestic economy, and other issues high on the political agenda, it is clear that the *Sun*'s market is one which, though perceived by the paper's management to be less educated than those of the mid and elite sectors, is assumed to have an appetite for, and interest in, substantial coverage of politics. The *Sun*'s political editor stresses that 'we try to write stories which will interest our readers, and they are, by and large, stories about people and personalities ...but we obviously have to give the readers an idea of what policies are being introduced'.

The *Sun*, of course, is no passive reporter of politics, providing a disinterested service to its readers. Since its purchase by Rupert Murdoch in the late 1960s it has been engaged in advocacy of the views espoused by its proprietor at any given time, and partisan support of the party, or party faction, most likely to be in a position to implement these views in government. The political editor stresses that 'Rupert Murdoch has always been extremely interested in politics. And indeed I think that politics has been a very big ingredient of the *Sun*'s composition ever since he's owned it.' The well-documented personal interventions of a highly politicised proprietor who perceives himself to be fighting a global battle on behalf of capitalism, the free market and Christian morality (Shawcross, 1992) have been crucial in establishing and maintaining the *Sun*'s commitment to political coverage over three decades, and Murdoch's politics have often been controversial.[7] But however we judge the precise nature of the *Sun*'s contribution to British democracy, the newspaper's attention to politics makes it impossible to dismiss it as a 'tits 'n' bums' tabloid of the *Daily Star* type. The *Sun*, as much as the *Guardian*, the *Telegraph* or *The Times*, treats its readers as important political actors – important enough to be subjected more or less daily to information about, and evaluations of, political events and issues. The style and tone of its coverage is populist and partisan, as one would expect given the nature of its readership and the approach of its proprietor, but this should not by itself imply a qualitative inferiority. On the contrary, as its political editor says, and with some justification, 'over the last few years the reputation of the *Sun* and its political coverage has grown and developed and I think that when people read a political story in the *Sun* these days, they believe it'. The political editor of a leading liberal broadsheet admits to 'a grudging respect for the *Sun*. The *Sun* has style. It's often very funny, and its often very shrewd. I think much of its behaviour is despicable, but it does have redeeming qualities.'

The Mirror

The *Sun*'s main rival, the *Mirror*, is also a *political* popular newspaper, in the sense that it expressly makes a commitment to coverage of politics for its largely working-class readership. Unlike the *Sun*, however, the *Mirror* – for most of the post-war period the only mass circulation left-wing title in the daily newspaper market – has rarely had much difficulty in maintaining its 'quality tabloid' reputation, and only in recent years has been accused of losing its way. In an ITV documentary and *Guardian* feature article, former *Mirror* journalist John Pilger argued that the title – once that rare thing – a paper which campaigned on behalf of 'the people' – had entered a terminal decline. Under pressure from the Murdoch empire (the *Sun* overtook the *Mirror* in circulation in 1978), and undermined by Robert Maxwell's mismanagement and resulting transfer of ownership, it had, critics like Pilger argued, prostituted itself to the god of mammon.[8] Rather than make socialist-inspired sense of the world for its working-class readers, as it had done with singular honour since WWII, the *Mirror* was now reduced to making merely money. This, Pilger argued, extending his attack to the political media as a whole, was symptomatic of 'a wider malaise that is now so serious it threatens to sever the link between democracy and popular journalism'.[9]

Pilger was not alone in his criticisms of the *Mirror*'s declining quality. When former *Sun* editor Kelvin Mackenzie was appointed deputy chief executive of Mirror Group Newspapers in January 1998 he is reported to have told MGN editors, with no irony intended, that he required 'more intelligent papers, better journalism, a greater understanding of politics and the revival of a journalistic culture'.[10] One year later the *Guardian*'s media pundit was attacking the *Mirror*'s inconsistency and lack of direction in political coverage, linking this with the paper's inability to move with 'the spirit of the times' (i.e., the rise of New Labour, and the editorial realignments of the once-Tory press which accompanied it).[11]

As Table 2.2 shows, in contrast to the *Sun*, the *Mirror* led with a political story on only one day in November 1996. A political story was included on its front page on a further two days, and editorials with a political theme were carried on sixteen days. By this measure, the *Sun* could legitimately claim to be, at least during the period of this study, a considerably more 'political' newspaper than the *Mirror*. The latter's stablemates, the *Sunday Mirror* and the *People*, typically devote even less space to politics. Over the four Sundays of November 1996 the *People* had no headlines, front page stories, or editorials about politics, while the *Sunday Mirror* carried only one front page political story and one editorial during the same period.

Periodicals

Political periodicals, though enjoying much smaller circulations than most newspapers, are nevertheless a significant part of the print public sphere. They appear weekly or monthly, functioning primarily as media of comment rather than reportage, and as fora for analysis and debate. Journalists whose main work may be for newspapers find in periodicals an opportunity for a more considered, less news-driven approach to political affairs. The four main political periodicals available in Britain at the time of this mapping exercise – the *Economist*, the *New Statesman*,[12] *Spectator* and *Prospect* – like the satirical periodicals *Private Eye* and *Punch*, are elite media in the sense we are using the term in this chapter, being read by relatively small numbers of As and Bs. There are no mid-market or popular periodicals devoted to politics (in contrast to the thousands of UK periodical titles devoted to lifestyle, sport, motoring, pornography and so on).

Broadcasting

The broadcast journalistic media can be similarly grouped into elite, mid-market and popular 'titles', or programme strands. One can also, in a market rapidly changing its structure because of digitalisation and other technological innovations, distinguish between those broadcast political media which are universally accessible, in the tradition of British public service broadcasting since the 1920s, and those which are delivered by various pay-per-view means – principally Sky but also, since its launch in November 1997, BBC News 24. British cable TV subscribers have access to BBC Parliament (formerly the Parliamentary Channel) which provides nearly twenty hours per day of coverage from constituent assemblies in Britain and Europe. These 'rolling' services are slowly emerging as important elements of the political public sphere, and thus ought not to be excluded from the following discussion, but their democratic role – as defined by their relationship to the mass audience – is clearly very different from those sources of broadcast political journalism which are free at the point of delivery to all citizens and which can claim to be, in that sense at least, 'public service'.

Elite

Occupying one clearly distinguishable segment of the broadcast public sphere, then, are the *elite* outlets: programme strands like *Today*, *The World At One*, *PM* and *The World Tonight* on BBC Radio 4; *Newsnight* on BBC2; *Channel 4 News* on Channel 4; and all the political analysis and discussion formats which appear on the same channels, for the same segments of the audience, such as *The Midnight Hour* (BBC2, now cancelled) and its successor, *Despatch Box*; *Analysis* and *Any Questions* (Radio 4); *A Week In Politics* (C4), and many more. Their place in the public sphere is analogous to that of the broadsheet newspapers and periodicals discussed above. Like the latter, their audiences tend to be the As and Bs of marketing-speak – the most affluent, most educated, best informed sectors of the population (not least because they use the information-rich elite media), generating ratings figures in the hundreds of thousands or the low millions. If the elite audience is numerically relatively small, however, it contains the country's key policy and decision-makers, opinion-formers and issue-definers: elites in the political, business and cultural spheres, as well as university-educated professionals. These media therefore enjoy a political importance which is not measured by their audience size alone.

Mid-market

Paralleling the mid-market print titles in the broadcast sector are the large audience 'flagship' news programmes, such as ITN's *News At Ten* with its 'snappy' style and the 'solid, patriarchal presence of Trevor McDonald'[13] (the programme was taken off ITV in 1999, and replaced by similarly targeted programmes at other times in the prime-time schedule); BBC1's *Nine O'Clock News*,[14] and other peak-time bulletins, such as *Channel 5 News*. The distinction between elite and mid-market in the broadcast sector can be seen in the way in which this latter programme, a relatively new entrant to the information market-place and thus in need of especially clear and effective 'branding', positions itself very differently from, and indeed in competition to, its ITN-produced rivals on Channel 4 and ITV. Tim Gardam, Channel 5's head of news and current affairs, has described its market position in terms which would equally well fit the *Daily Mail*:

> When Channel 5 began, we had to decide what to do with its news ... To work commercially, Channel 5 had to attract a younger audience for its advertisers than ITV could provide. Accordingly it pursued people under 45.

Gardam went on to explain how marketing methods were used to assess what this 'modern mainstream' wanted from its news: specifically, 'the facts and information that would help them to take decisions, and not leave them feeling stupid about the world', delivered with a 'lighter touch', a more consumerist news agenda, and a more informal presentational style, all of which they got, in the form of Kirsty Young's desk-perching matiness.

Although *Channel 5 News* is now viewed as a success by media observers, it is paradigmatic of the on-going debate about British journalism as a whole that initial critical response to the stylistic and presentational informality of the programme was not favourable. The programme was widely denounced as trivial and frivolous, as lacking in seriousness, as not worthy of the great British tradition of public service broadcasting. Like many other recent innovations in British journalism which have subsequently, if grudgingly, found a respected place in the information marketplace (Sky News is another example), it was greeted at first as further evidence of a qualitative deterioration in journalistic culture, another victory for infotainment, another nail in the coffin of the Habermasian ideal-type public sphere.

Audiences for mid-market broadcast news are orders of magnitude larger than those of the elite strands (with the exception of *Channel 5 News* which, as a late entrant to the market on a new channel, is still building audience share, but has already overtaken *Channel 4 News*), and consciously target (or serve) 'the country as a whole', rather than the As and Bs who tend to watch and listen to the former (see Table 2.1). As such, they tend to devote less time, and give less prominence to politics, as Table 2.2 indicates. While elite programmes like *Today* and *Newsnight* achieved PNRs of 38 in November 1996, the *Nine O'Clock News* and *News At Ten* measured only 14 and 19 respectively. In short, politics led the elite bulletins more than twice as often as the mid-market programmes during the sample used in this study. For the latter, as is the case for the mid-market newspapers, politics has a lower place in the hierarchy of news values, although it is still central to the journalistic agenda.

Mid-market current affairs slots include BBC1's *Panorama*, and ITV's *Tonight* (the successor to *World In Action*, taken off the air in 1998) both of which present analyses and investigative reports for a general, rather than a specialist audience, similar in profile to the flagship news bulletins. In trying to maximise audiences following the intensification of televisual competition, both BBC1 and ITV have changed their scheduling, agendas and presentational styles (and been criticised for doing so) in recent years, as exemplified by *Panorama*'s interview with Princess Diana in 1996, and with convicted child-killer Louise Woodward in 1998. The *Tonight* programme, which was launched in April 1999 with interviews with the alleged murderers of Stephen Lawrence, was successfully pitched to ITV controllers in the following terms:

> A new audience is waking up to the appeal of factual programmes on television. Both in Britain and America it is clear that documentary specials, popular factual shows and docu-soaps are key weapons in a network's armoury. A new grammar of factual television has helped revolutionise the audience perception of such shows. Now it is time for current affairs to catch up. A new hour-long series presents an opportunity to reinvent the genre, with one of the most exciting current affairs innovations of the past 20 years. Get it right and ITV will be an essential part of the zeitgeist – reflecting and contributing to the era we live in, interpreting and revealing the facts we need to know.

Popular

Despite these trends in mid-market current affairs broadcasting, it remains the case that there is as yet no direct equivalent of the popular or 'red top' tabloid newspaper in mainstream British political broadcasting. There *are*, it is true, instances of what some interpret as tabloidisation or dumbing down in non-political TV – the new *Tonight* show, for example – and an increasing number of 'confessional' talk shows, many of them imported from the USA, as well as a growth in the number of 'real life' fly-on-the-wall video-documentary formats, mostly involving the police and other public services, as well as 'docu-soaps'.[15] Such programmes have been accused of squeezing out 'serious' current affairs under market-driven ratings pressure, and much of the debate around tabloidisation in broadcasting focuses on the growth of 'infotainment' programming of this type. Whether judged as populist trash or a legitimate democratisation of the current affairs agenda, however, these formats are not presented to viewers as *political journalism*. They rarely cover events in the party political sphere, and if they do (in the context of ministerial philandering, for example, which could conceivably be the hook for a debate about adultery on confessional talk shows like *Vanessa* or *Kilroy*) they are not presented to viewers as a substitute for political journalism, but reflect the blurring of the public and private spheres which is a feature of contemporary journalism throughout the western world.

Reflecting trends in British factual TV more widely, after the general election of 1997 a number of political fly-on-the-wall documentaries were broadcast on British television, following the adventures of new Labour ministers as they took office. Gordon Brown, Robin Cook and Clare Short all had their work filmed and the results broadcast at prime times in the first year of Labour government. These documentaries employed a form usually associated with non-political, infotaining TV, while tackling subjects which the most severe critic of contemporary political journalism would have to concede were worthy and serious. They provided British viewers with revealing glimpses and insights into the workings of government, and provoked considerable criticism of their subjects elsewhere in the media. Indeed, the process of 'demonisation' (see Chapter 7) which eventually required Gordon Brown's adviser, Charles Whelan, to announce his resignation in the wake of the Mandelson–Robinson mortgage scandal may be argued to have begun with this documentary, in which he emerged from behind-the-scenes invisibility to be revealed as a rather arrogant, manipulative figure, contemptuous of the political journalists who appeared to hang on his every word. Infotainment it may have been, but it was also 'critical publicity' in the best Habermasian tradition.

If tabloidisation is not an obvious feature of mainstream British political broadcasting, there have nevertheless been a number of stylistic and generic innovations associated with the fragmentation of the system (and its metamorphosis into narrowcasting) which concern some observers. The 1990s proliferation of British radio channels has allowed, for example, a limited entry of the populist 'shock-jock' phenomenon (an American import) into the broadcast schedules, particularly in the expanding commercial radio sector. One example is Talk Radio's *No Prisoners Taken*, in which notorious lobbyist Derek Draper (the villain of the cash-for-access scandal of November 1998) and right-wing columnist Peter Hitchens, compete in 'rubbishing' each other's and their callers' arguments. Proudly described as 'Rottweiler radio' in its promotional literature, and as 'either appalling or hilarious, depending on how strong your stomach is',[16] the intention to emulate the political shock-jocks of the USA is clear, and the programme may be interpreted as part of a broader trend away from impartiality and toward more opinionated, authorial journalism[17] which is accompanying the establishment of a multi-channel, niche-market system. Going out on a Sunday morning, *No Prisoners Taken* is targeted at the elite and mid-market rather than popular audiences, and premised on a perceived increase in audience demand for confrontational, argumentative political coverage. The programme reflects the recognition by some broadcasters of the limitations of 'impartiality' as a structuring framework for political journalism in a fragmented media environment of many providers.

Rolling political news

British audiences, like those of other countries, have increasing access to a range of satellite and cable news services which are fundamentally changing the structure of the public sphere. Audiences for Sky News, BBC News 24 and BBC Parliament – still limited by the reach (and expense) of new distribution technologies – remain low, but this understates their real and potential influence as political media. Sky News, for example, is estimated to reach on average only *one per cent* of the cable and satellite audience (30–60,000 viewers tuning in on an average evening), itself still a small proportion of the UK's TV viewing audience as a whole, after more than a decade in existence. But the service has a high reputation amongst political and media elites nonetheless. Sky News political editor Adam Boulton is regarded by elite political actors as one of the five or six key 'contextualising' figures in British broadcast political journalism, despite the fact that he is not regularly seen on air by more than a few thousand people per day.

In terms of the categories being applied in this chapter, Sky News positions itself somewhere between elite and mid-market, claiming a role for audiences of both types. As Boulton puts it:

> We have never had a tabloid/broadsheet division. Our bulletins have always mixed pop stories, super models, Diana, whatever, with not just serious news but actually fairly detailed and sophisticated explanation of serious news. That is a difference between us and *News At Ten*, for example, which has a pitch which is sort of mid-market, *Daily Mail*. They won't do complex political stories because they don't think [their audience] are interested. The BBC, likewise, will draw the line, often unsuccessfully, between frivolous Royal stories, or O.J. Simpson or whatever. Whereas we have always seen our canvas going from really quite technical hard news – certainly in politics, we have done some quite sophisticated stories – all the way down to sport, who scored the goals, and so on.

The same can be said for BBC and ITN, of course, in so far as they produce news products tailored to both elite and mid-market audiences (*Newsnight* and the *Nine O'Clock News*, *Channel 4 News* and *Channel 5 News*), with appropriate agendas and styles.

BBC News 24's audience is still so low as to be practically immeasurable, and will remain so until the digitalisation of British broadcasting begins to open it up to wider access sometime early in the new century. To a much greater extent than is the case even for Sky News, its contibution to an improved public sphere is a question for the future rather than the present, and dependent to a large extent on events over which it has no control. In general, both in Britain and abroad, the visibility and popularity of rolling news channels increases when a big story is breaking. Sky News, for example, was able to deal much more fully and flexibly with the resignation of Margaret Thatcher in 1990 than any other UK TV news organisation, and won much praise for its coverage. BBC News 24 had its first major 'breaking story' in April 1998, with the all-night cliff-hanger ending to the Northern Irish peace talks. The channel was also able to give uniquely live and unedited coverage of such events as the bombing of Iraq in December 1998 and the Clinton impeachment trial in January 1999. Just as the Challenger disaster put CNN on the map, journalistically, the speed of growth of the audience for Britain's rolling news channels will be largely related to the chance occurence of events – such as the NATO bombing of Yugoslavia which dominated news agendas in early 1999 – which endow them with the unique selling proposition of being able to be there, live, as it happens, and to stay there with the action for as long as it is going on.

The broadcast magazine

Broadcast equivalents of the political periodicals are few and far between, given that British broadcasting has traditionally refrained from that style of punditry which is the latter's distinguishing feature (see Chapter 4). *A Week In Politics*, presented on Channel 4 by the late Vincent Hanna and print columnist Andrew Rawnsley, was a rare example of the overtly opinionated style (and weekly rhythm) of the periodical press being adapted for television, and there have, as already noted, been similar experiments in national and local radio. In general, however, periodical political journalism is a print media preserve.

Broadcast political satire on the other hand (which rarely contains any journalism, but may still be viewed as part of the public sphere in so far as it presents information and commentary about politics) has included Rory Bremner's weekly C4 stand-up and impersonation programme, comedian Mark Thomas's exposés (the most journalistic of the satirical forms to date, in which politicians are exposed and sometimes humiliated before a late-night C4 audience), and Armando Ianucci's *Saturday Night Armistice* (BBC2). Chris Morris's *Brass Eye* and *The Day Today* series can also be thought of as broadcast political satire, although their targets were really the journalistic media (including political journalists) rather than politicians themselves. They and other satirical forms can be viewed as *meta-media*: not journalism, but referring to journalism, and the political sphere which is journalism's subject with, at their best, ruthless and demystificatory wit. Although empirical data about the effects of such programmes on audiences is not available, they can in their debunking and playful subversion of elites be assumed to be of far greater importance in the construction of public opinion about politics than this short reference implies.

A word of category-caution

Dividing the public sphere as I have done so far in this chapter – employing categories used by the marketing and media industries themselves – works only as a generality, and is no determinant of the media consumption patterns of individuals in any of the above social groupings, who will present numerous exceptions to the rule. At some points the categories are blurred, reflecting the high degree of social mobility and 'de-ideologisation' of contemporary British society. As one commentator observes in relation to the press, 'the social divisions which were once reflected in, and reinforced by, the populist *Mirror* or *Sun* on the one hand and the elitist *Times* or *Daily Telegraph* on the other are disappearing; and as social divisions blur, so do the natural boundaries between the papers' markets'.[18]

Similar qualifications are appropriate to broadcasting. Does Rory Bremner's satire, for example, play to an elite, a mid-market or a popular audience? As an entertainer he may well appeal to all categories, but his political satire frequently assumes a high level of political knowledge, amounting to a series of 'insider' in-jokes which not all of his audience will 'get'. Just as the metaphor of the public sphere is a device by which we aim to give the virtual universe of communicative space-time some shape and structure, so the categories used here – the levels of the public sphere I have identified as elite, mid-market and popular – are to be viewed as convenient guides to audience behaviour rather than constraining strait-jackets: flexible rather than fixed boundaries within and between which citizens have freedom to move. In certain circumstances, such as the death of Diana or the Monica Lewinsky scandal, elite, mid-market and popular political news agendas merge in common exploration of issues which generate cross-category coverage.[19] One might therefore propose a model of the public sphere as shown in Figure 2.1 – a communicative space of increasingly overlapping and intersecting sub-spheres, the tone and linguistic register which are defined by the specific communities which access them, but in which the boundaries between elite, mid-market and popular agendas become ever more fuzzy.

The media and the political agenda

This book is not about media effects, but it is safe to assert that an important impact of journalism is its agenda-setting capacity. News agendas shape public and political agendas, signifying to individuals and organisations which events in the world are socially important at any given time. Good empirical evidence exists to show that the structure of the news agenda (which issues are highlighted, which are marginal) affects public

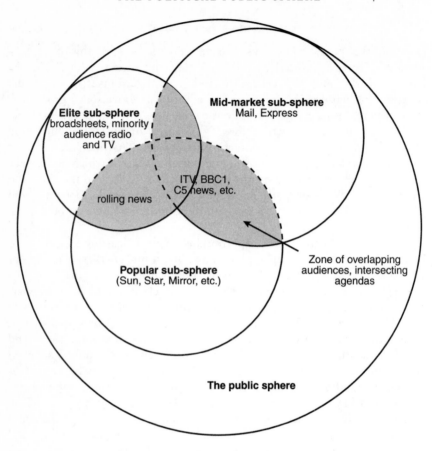

Elite sub-sphere
broadsheets, minority
audience radio
and TV

Mid-market sub-sphere
Mail, Express

ITV, BBC1,
C5 news, etc.

rolling news

Popular sub-sphere
(Sun, Star, Mirror, etc.)

Zone of overlapping
audiences, intersecting
agendas

The public sphere

Figure 2.1   The public sphere: a model

opinion (as measured by polls) and voting behaviour (as reflected in election outcomes).

Within the political public sphere, different media have different
agenda-setting roles. The press, as the prime minister's press secretary
Alistair Campbell complained in February 1999, are the *primary* agenda-
setters, defining the shape of the agenda in the medium and long term.
They have the power to set the *dominant* political agenda, as elaborated
over weeks, months and years, in editorials, columns and other forms of
pro-active, opinionated journalism, amounting to extended narratives of
unity and division, success and failure, rise and fall. In this capacity the
institutions of the press take the lead in establishing the *dominant* interpretative frameworks within which ongoing political events are made sense of.

The press also have an important investigative function, on the back of which major agenda-setting interventions can be mounted, as in the case of the *Guardian*'s cash-for-questions coverage of 1994–97. Documentary TV journalism occasionally performs this role (as, for example, when the *World In Action* programme made damaging revelations about the conduct of Jonathan Aitken MP), but rarely with the impact of the press, or without the issue first having being placed on the agenda by the press.

The broadcasters, legally and conventionally prevented from advocacy and overt commentary of the type routinely indulged in by the press, tend to follow the latter's agenda-setting lead, while focusing on the daily events – the short-term agenda – which they are best equipped to cover. Avoiding partisanship and with minimal commentary and analysis, TV news reports events as they happen – which the press cannot do, of course – while contextualising them in terms of the wider interpretative framework – the dominant agenda – pre-established by the media as a whole, and the press in particular. From the viewpoint of political actors, the broadcasters' is the *priority* agenda, to be addressed and managed immediately, although the dominant agenda may be more electorally important in the medium and long run.

Radio news forms a bridge between the short, medium and long-term agendas. Its interview-based coverage seeks to contextualise live coverage of the daily events of political life within the frames of reference already established in the columns and editorials of the press. Radio journalists (and their TV colleagues, of course) interrogate and explore, on the micro-level, the day-to-day rhetorical battles of the parties, often producing statements from political leaders which feed back into the agenda-setting process at a later stage. Their role is to investigate and interrogate the here-and-now, where the press – more reflective, analytical and evaluative – are intrinsically better equipped to build a cumulative picture of developments from week to week, month to month, and year to year. From this accumulation of information and interpretation the dominant agenda emerges, independently of the communicative work of any single politician, party, or media outlet. Where the short-term news agenda – the priority agenda at any given time – can be manipulated with more or less success by political actors and their professional advisers, the long-term agenda – more important in terms of voting behaviour – has a life and a dynamic of its own.

The political news cycle

All the journalistic outlets described in this chapter have their place in the daily and weekly political news cycles, acting as gateways through which issues come into and out of the media agenda. Although the weekly news cycle has no fixed beginning or end, since the timing of many events is random and unpredictable, key agenda-setting moments are the Sunday interview slots. While not the most widely consumed political media (who, apart from the most dependent political news junkie, is up at eight on a Sunday morning to view *Breakfast With Frost*?), these are the slots taken most seriously by other media, and by members of the political elite themselves, who focus much of their news management efforts on them. Large audience media, such as the *Sun* or GMTV news are also targeted by political news managers, particularly at election time, since they guarantee instant mass exposure and publicity in the absence of the tough interrogative techniques employed on the Sunday programmes and *Today*[20] (see Chapter 5). But the latter will tend to have a greater impact on the news *agenda*.

Sunday newspapers and interview programmes often serve to sum up the preceding week's events, and to identify issues for the next, in the form of exclusive stories (print) and set-piece interviews (broadcast and print) with senior politicians, who often use these fora as opportunities to set the agenda for the following Monday morning.

The daily cycle begins with the first editions of the newspapers, which decide their content and priorities the night before publication. The early morning radio and TV news programmes rely heavily on these first editions to construct *their* agendas, which in turn determine the content of news and analysis throughout the rest of the day. Particularly important in this respect is Radio 4's *Today* programme – nearly three hours of news and analysis which is perceived, both by members of the political elite and other media professionals, as the pivotal moment, the dominant force in shaping the content of the news on any given day. On the programme's fortieth anniversary listeners were reassured that *Today* 'has always prided itself on having the ear of the nation's leaders'. As one Radio 4 presenter put it to the author, *Today* 'marshals the events of the day', often following the lead of professional politicians who – aware of its importance in the news cycle – use the programme as a platform. Although politicians are often confronted by tough interviewing techniques on *Today*, the programme is their opportunity to place policy announcements and responses on the news agenda, from where journalists on later programmes (and the next day's papers) with larger audiences will take their lead.

The World At One, broadcasting four hours later, develops the agenda which *Today* has established, and makes an important contribution to the work of other journalists as they begin to prepare their stories for the next day. In this manner, *The World At One* is a key moment in the political newsgathering cycle. As presenter Nick Clarke puts it:

[*The World At One*] gathers together all the early announcements and whatever has happened during the morning, and it says something about them at a time when the newspapers are gathering together their thinking for the following day. It focuses their attention. It often does the interview they need to hear, or need to have, in the light of the announcement, as opposed to simply making the announcements.

The main evening bulletins, usually going out after parliament has concluded its main business of the day, develop stories with additional analyses, interviews, and inputs from political editors, all of which combine to establish the meaning and significance of events, not for other journalists, who are already working on the next day's stories, but for the mass audience, settling down after work or dinner and wishing to know what has happened that day, and whether or not it should matter to them.

Late evening programmes like *Newsnight* sum up the newsday, assess its implications and meanings, and look forward to the next cycle, often by previewing newspaper front pages, which of course reflect that day's developments and are usually available before midnight. *Newsnight*, for one observer, is 'as central a plank of the political establishment as Prime Minister's Questions, and as indispensable a reference point for newspaper morning conferences as the *Today* programme's 8 o'clock headlines. No other programme can better explain social change, further diplomatic dialogue or unravel the truth behind soundbite headlines'.[21]

Evaluating the public sphere: print and the tabloids

A frequently cited indicator of dumbing down is the alleged decline of 'quality' journalism – by which is meant falling circulations amongst the broadsheets, and the 'tabloidisation' of their content; and increases in popular tabloid circulations. And indeed, circulation trends in the British newspaper market do show a slight overall decline over the five-year period 1993–98 (Figure 2.2). In isolation, these figures might give some grounds for concern, though to cite them as evidence of what one observer calls 'a potential threat to democracy'[22] is overstating the case. Newspapers, after all, now have to compete for time and attention with a vastly greater range of other media than ever before, and it would be surprising if they did not experience some reduction in their overall share of the media market (just as the established public service TV and radio channels, faced with a multi-channel future, must come to terms with some reduction in their audience). Nor does the small decline in newspaper circulation as a whole bear out the dumbing down thesis as it is usually expressed, since it is principally the popular tabloids (usually viewed as the dumbest of the dumb) which show the largest decline in circulation over a five-year period. The majority of elite titles have in fact increased their sales in recent times. Only the *Independent* titles have dropped consistently, a fact which may have more to do with the weak management and poor quality of the newspapers in recent years, and the intensity of competition from their rivals in the broadsheet sector, than any decline in the size of their potential readership. The broadsheet closest to it in editorial alignment, the *Guardian*, maintains a healthy circulation of around 400,000, despite refusing to engage in the price wars unleashed by Rupert Murdoch in the mid-1990s.

Of the mid-market titles, the *Daily Mail* has increased its circulation (overtaking the *Mirror* in late 1998) while the *Express* has declined. Again, the poor quality of the product is as good an explanation for the latter's performance as any assertion of dumbing down, and there is no reason to think that the mid-market sector in general is shrinking.

Assessing recent circulation trends, Roy Greenslade notes with approval that the 'British people remain among the most avid newspaper readers in the world, buying 37 papers per 1,000 inhabitants.'[23] Elsewhere, the same writer concludes that 'in editorial terms, most papers are performing well. They are also providing unprecedented value for buyers.'[24] Overall, circulation trends show that, as the educational level of the British population steadily improves, more people are reading the mid-market and elite titles, with correspondingly less taking the populars. By this, admittedly crude measure, we are not witnessing the dumbing down of British journalism

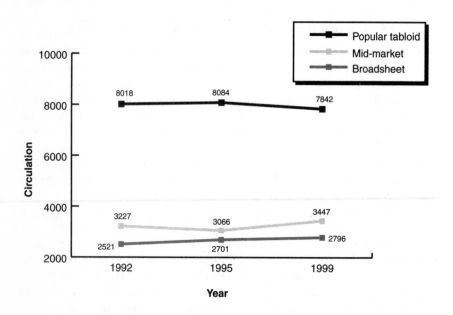

Figure 2.2   Circulation of British national daily newspapers, 1992–99 (000s)

but a steady movement upmarket, as more people are enabled and choose to read more 'difficult' newspapers.[25]

> Rather than dumbing down, the sales figures reveal formerly tabloid readers 'trading up' to buy broadsheet newspapers. Cheaper prices and more accessible presentation have ensured that the broadsheets are no longer 'the posh papers' – but alternatives to the *Daily Mail*.[26]

This trend does not necessarily mean that the *quality* of the public sphere as an information resource is improving, of course, but proponents of dumbing down have at least to account for it.

Some respond to the challenge by shifting their ground, arguing that if the elite titles are not losing market share, this is precisely *because* they are dumbing down in their content, becoming more mid-market in their content and style. Richard Gott, for example, suggests that from the late 1980s 'almost all of the serious newspapers sought to meet the commercial challenge of this post-modern, post-Thatcher era by moving away from serious concerns into the essentially non-political, non-ideological world of lifestyle and "yoof"'.[27] Disregarding for a moment the contentious assumption of a qualitative distinction between serious/political on the one hand, and non-serious/non-political/non-ideological on the other, and with due respect to Gott's status as a former newspaper editor of experience and standing, his reading of the trends is simply wrong. While there has been, in the context of the post-Wapping move towards supplements and magazines as part of a newspaper's package, an expansion of lifestyle journalism to fill the increased space (McNair, 1999c), this has not been at the expense of political coverage, commentary and analysis. On the contrary, as Chapter 4 describes, there has been a significant expansion in the resources devoted by elite newspapers to political journalism, and commentary in particular, in recent years.

Not only have the elite newspapers not gone down market, there has been an observeable movement *up-market* in the content of the popular tabloids. The page 3 girl, for example, a staple of British popular newspapers since the early 1970s, is generally agreed to be old-fashioned and anachronistic (though far from dead). One journalistic observer notes that as the popular tabloids reform their approach:

> The result is a gradual merging of national culture in the middle. Instead of one language for the elite, and another for the working man, a new shared vernacular is taking shape.[28]

The myth of the decline of parliamentary reportage: the Parliamentary Channel and BBC Parliament

Regularly cited as an index of the decline of political journalism in Britain is the virtual disappearance from newspapers of verbatim reports of parliamentary debates and business – 'gallery reportage'. This trend is argued to exemplify the victory of commercial criteria over civic need, and the transformation of the political media into a sphere of apolitical consumption (Franklin, 1997; Negrine, 1996).

It is true that commercial criteria have driven verbatim coverage of parliamentary debates from those newspapers which once featured it. Even when they were the only source of such coverage, relatively few people read these reports. But since the law was changed to allow cameras and microphones into parliament, the broadcasters have been able to do the job of covering debates with much more immediacy and 'authenticity'. The use of parliamentary coverage on TV and radio news, as well as the increased speed of delivery of broadcast news in general, rendered day-old reports of who said what in parliament redundant, and by the late 1980s the majority of readers (according to market research carried out for elite titles like *The Times*) had simply lost interest in this form of print political journalism.

Verbatim reportage of parliamentary debates is available in Hansard, however (which now has a web site on the internet), and beyond the mainstream public service channels British audiences with an interest in unedited parliamentary reportage now have access to several outlets dedicated to its provision, and which together dramatically increase the quantity of such material in the public sphere. Since its establishment in 1992, subscribers to cable TV (as of 1998, about two million homes were cabled in the UK) have had access to extensive live coverage of parliamentary business, first by means of the Parliamentary Channel (TPC) and then, following the BBC's takeover of the service in August 1998, BBC Parliament.

TPC was set up as a non-profit making service by the cable companies, modelling their enterprise on the American C-Span channel which broadcasts live, unedited coverage of US Congressional debates. TPC, managed by the Flextech company, broadcast as of 1998 more than 115 hours per week of Commons, Lords and parliamentary select committee debates, with some European and US coverage too. Although the channel edited and repackaged some material (highlights of European and American debates, for example), the great majority of its output was live and unedited, using feeds from the Parliamentary Recording Unit paid for by TPC and other users such as the BBC, ITN and Sky. Exploiting its relatively non-interventionist, unmediated approach, the Parliamentary Channel marketed itself as 'the ultimate public service broadcaster',[29] providing coverage of politics with the minimum of journalistic commentary or politicians' spin. In an era when the issue of who sets the political news agenda is itself fiercely political, TPC made a virtue out of the fact that in its schedules, uniquely amongst British broadcasters, the politicians were heard to speak without interruption, at length, and to agendas of their own choosing. TPC's audience were characterised by its management as the 'aware and the concerned' – MPs and political journalists, of course, but also a number of As, Bs and C1s who dipped into the service as and when they wanted to, rather in the way that teletext and the internet are used. TPC was also provided free to schools as an educational tool, and the channel had a web site.

That such a service could exist at all was conditional on its non-profit-making status. Freed from commercial constraints, driven not by audience ratings but by a simple editorial commitment to 'gavel to gavel' coverage of parliamentary debates, TPC was a goodwill loss-leader for the British cable companies, in the same way that Sky News was Rupert Murdoch's altruistic, if ultimately self-serving gesture to the relatively high standards of British broadcast journalism (and no less welcome for that). Setting up TPC demonstrated the cable companies' desire and ability to serve the public (though it is less than accurate to think of TPC as a 'public service' in the traditional sense, because it lacked one of the key defining characteristics of British PSB – that it should be universally accessible and free at the point of delivery) by providing a form of political coverage that no other organisation had the airtime or the financial resource to match.

TPC was not a luxurious service, however. Lack of a marketing and promotional budget, and an attitude of indifference from the cable companies meant that, even as the research for this study was taking place in 1997–98, its existence and function were relatively unknown to the British public. Even amongst the many journalists and communication professionals interviewed for this study, relatively few used TPC on a regular basis. In early 1998, frustrated by what it saw as lack of commitment from the cable operators, Flextech announced that it was effectively resigning from management of the service. In August that year, after a number of bids from various consortia, it was announced that TPC would be relaunched as BBC Parliament, financed by the corporation at a cost of some £5 million per annum. The relaunched service would be available first, like TPC, on analogue cable, and from 1999 also on digital terrestrial and satellite.

At the outset audiences (like those for BBC News 24) will be small but, as more British homes are cabled up, and digitalisation increases the scope for the service to expand and diversify (into coverage of the devolved Scottish and Welsh assemblies, for example), BBC Parliament can be expected to emerge as the electronic heir to the 'straight' parliamentary reportage which has disappeared from the print media. BBC Parliament, like TPC before it, goes a further step beyond what even the twenty-four hour rolling news channels can do, devoting itself to parliamentary debates not only at moments of political crisis and 'breaking' stories but in the routine, non-critical moments in the political cycle. It provides routine access to parliamentary politics – and a record of what goes on in our various constituent assemblies – on a qualitatively new scale.[30] What people will do with that resource – the ignorant and the apathetic, as well as 'the aware and the concerned' who currently access it – is a question for the future, but as Jonathan Freedland observes of C-Span, CNN and other services in the United States, we may speculate that BBC Parliament, BBC News 24, and Sky News will come to represent 'the antithesis of the soundbite culture' in twenty-first century Britain (1998, p. 58), and will more than compensate for the decline of straight parliamentary coverage in newspapers.

These services are not free, of course, requiring costly installation of cable, satellite, digital and internet technology, but then neither are the newspapers which once monopolised parliamentary coverage. Subscription to one broadsheet newspaper for one year will cost a reader around £200 at 1999 prices, while access to BBC News 24, BBC Parliament and Sky News is priced at a few pounds per month after initial outlay on infrastructure and hardware.

'Tell me why it matters': the reform of British political broadcasting

Potentially valuable (as democratic resources) as they are, these outlets are still marginal in the public sphere, and while we may speculate on their future contribution as providers of political information, for the time being the vast majority of citizens rely on the mainstream terrestrial broadcasters – the BBC, ITN and the producers of political documentaries and current affairs for both BBC and commercial networks. In these sectors of the broadcast media, dumbing down and commercialisation are argued to be proceeding apace, not least because of the proliferation of new providers of broadcast journalism discussed above, and the increased pressure on ratings which that produces. The success of *Channel 5 News* in its first year of operation, for example, led other broadcast journalism organisations to review their place in the media marketplace, and to move towards giving greater prominence to human interest coverage. In September 1998, after a lengthy preparation of ground, ITV (Channel 3) announced that it would be replacing the thirty-year old *News At Ten* strand (although a version would continue to be transmitted on the new ITV 2 digital channel) with a revamped 6.30 bulletin, at the same time introducing a new weekly current affairs strand based on the American *Sixty Minutes* model. Received by many critics as further evidence of dumbing down in broadcasting, the reform was condemned as a bid 'to shift news to the fringes of prime-time viewing, and reinvent popular current affairs as part of an entertainment mix'.[31] For ITV, on the other hand, this reform of its news and current affairs was a legitimate and necessary response to the success of *Channel 5 News* and other programmes in providing the British TV audience with new styles and agendas. Defending ITN's reform of its scheduling policy and news style in this context, editor-in-chief Richard Tait (1997, p. 23) argued in respect of political journalism, that:

> Far from being part of the so-called 'dumbing down' of television, I believe that making political coverage more interesting will encourage viewers to stay with it rather than head for the real 'dumbing down' of deciding that serious news and current affairs have nothing to offer them and they would be better off with sport and entertainment.

The BBC's *Programme Strategy Review*, published in late 1998, also recognised this need with its announcement that from the spring of 1999 its prime-time bulletins would be substantially revised and 'relaunched' to reflect the findings of extensive focus group research into what viewers wanted. As the director of news and current affairs put it, 'the BBC will re-commit to setting the highest standards of public service journalism with programmes of intelligence, depth and diversity. People are facing a blizzard of news and information. The big question is: does greater volume mean greater understanding? The BBC must give people greater understanding.'[32] Consequently, an 'overhaul of every BBC bulletin and current affairs programme' was to be undertaken,[33] at the end of which politics and other 'complex issues' would be reported with less jargonistic language, and more context – the BBC's watchword would, henceforth, be 'tell me why it matters'. There would, however, be *more* coverage of parliamentary affairs, not less, and more coverage too of European politics, of which there was a serious deficit in Britain throughout the 1990s.

Conclusion

The political public sphere described in this chapter is larger, denser, and accessible to more people than at any previous point in Britain's cultural history, and it continues to expand. By comparison with other countries, and with this country's own not-too-distant past, there is a vast quantity of political information, analysis and interpretation in public circulation at any given time. As one observer notes, political news 'has never been more plentiful, more sophisticated, more the fuel of debate, than now'.[34] While there is no hard evidence to support the opinion of one critic that 'the massive scale of coverage merely diminishes the public interest in politics',[35] there can be no doubt that 'massive' is the appropriate term to describe the political public sphere at the millennial turn.]

Does this represent a substantial improvement in the communicative and informational supports to British democracy, however? It is difficult to see on what grounds one could conclude otherwise: five terrestrial TV channels; Radios 4 and 5; Talk Radio; rolling news on two subscription TV channels; live, unedited coverage of parliament on cable, nineteen national newspapers and hundreds more at regional and local level – all combine to provide a degree of political coverage that no one individual or organisation can absorb in its totality. [The public sphere has become, from the viewpoint of the individual, a communicative space of infinite size, unknowable beyond those small segments of it which we choose to (and have the time to) access.]

Growth has been uneven, however, and if the public sphere is in practical terms infinite, it is also 'lumpy'. In the print sector the popular tabloids have much larger circulations (with the exception of the *Daily Star*) than the mid-market and elite newspapers, but there are many more of the latter – nine elite titles compared to six popular tabloids – and since the former contain more political journalism than any other category of newspaper, it is apparent that print-mediated politics in Britain is, if judged by this simple measure, a predominantly elite pursuit, supported by a numerous and editorially diverse print-media ranging from the *Guardian* on the left to the *Daily Telegraph* on the right. [These are the outlets which devote the greatest share of their editorial resources to political coverage.] Conversely, while the social categories C2 and below contain by far the great majority of voters, they are provided with relatively few print sources of political information as compared with the more affluent, generally better educated groups in society.

There is a well-known economic explanation for this disparity. The elite print market is able to charge relatively high cover prices, and to attract prestige advertising revenue from the manufacturers of luxury consumer goods and services. The *Telegraph* and *The Times* both sell over one million copies per day, but the *Guardian* and the *Financial Times* can make healthy profits on circulations of around 400,000 and 300,000 respectively. Popular newspapers, on the other hand, whose readers are less affluent and therefore less valuable to advertisers, require much larger circulations to be financially viable. There is thus room for fewer tabloid titles. The economics of publishing ensure that there are nearly as many elite newspapers as mid-market and popular titles combined (9:4:6), and that a two-tier information market continues to exist in Britain, divided between affluent and less-affluent, educated and less-educated. [Those with the greatest reserves of money and accumulated knowledge are also those with access to the most information about politics.] True, the inequalities of access and usage which characterise the contemporary public sphere were once much greater than they now are, and I have suggested in this chapter that they are decreasing as general levels of education and affluence increase. But the deep structural inequality which still exists in the distribution of political information is an important qualification to the picture of expansion presented above, although not one which can be addressed by elite paternalism of the sort which sees dumbing down all around.

We are served then, if not by a dumbed-down political journalism, then certainly one which is intellectually top-heavy. By far the greatest proportion of British political journalism – public service and commercial – is provided for, and consumed by, the best-educated, best-informed sections of the population. Circulation trends shows that they want it, and the advertising revenue which they attract more than pays for it. Indeed, to the extent that there *is* a measurable decline in the production and distribution of political journalism, it is in precisely those sectors – the popular tabloids – normally associated with crass commercialisation. If this is accepted, a more important issue than dumbing down emerges – the issue of how to prevent the majority of allegedly apathetic or disinterested citizens from falling ever further behind in the distribution of political information; how to maximise, in the interests of building an efficient and effective democracy for the twenty-first century, the quantity and quality of political information received by those – the large majority – who do not use the print and broadcast media defined here as 'elite'; how to find forms of political media which attract this audience, engage it in its own language, and at the same time furnish it with useful political information; how to harness what Keane calls the 'democratic potential' (1991, p. xii) of the public sphere described in this chapter. The BBC and ITN managers are reforming their news output with precisely these goals in mind, as we have seen. Time will tell if they can be successful in achieving them.

3

POLICY, PROCESS, PERFORMANCE AND SLEAZE

An evaluation of the political news agenda

Size isn't everything, of course, and the 'map' of the public sphere presented in Chapter 2 is less than sufficient to enable an evaluation of its contribution to the democratic process. The *qualitative* features of the journalism which that public sphere contains – its priorities and themes, the accuracy of its information, its styles and idioms – are of at least equal importance in assessing the true extent of the 'crisis of public communication' outlined in Chapter 1. This chapter thus asks a different set of questions. What is political journalism about? Which aspects of political life does it report? Which kinds of political knowledge does it make available to its audiences? And on the basis of the answers to these questions, how valuable is it as a cognitive resource?

Politics as news

Politics has always been a core element in the agenda of liberal journalism (Boston, 1990). It was, indeed, public demand for information about and discussion of power and political affairs which fuelled the development of the modern media as means of reportage, analysis and critical scrutiny, and in the late twentieth century, far from being abandoned on the altar of crass commercialism, coverage of politics has increased. This has not been because of some noble journalistic mission to fulfil the normative ideals of the fourth estate (although many journalists approach their work with that goal). On the contrary, as the organisational pressures on journalists intensified and the technological conditions of coverage improved (the introduction of TV cameras into the House of Commons, for example, or the availability of lightweight recording equipment and 'radio cars' which allowed political interviews to be conducted more or less anywhere, anytime), as the public sphere expanded, and with it the space available for news, politics became a steadily more convenient source of journalistic raw material. A broadcast political editor remarks that for the great majority of British news media:

42

politics is the backbone … If nothing else is happening, you can't get your cameras anywhere, you can always get political reaction, political discussion. News organisations know that they can depend on their fixed investment in political coverage to fill them in on almost any story.

There are periods (and the last two or three years of the Major government was such a time) when, because of special factors like small Commons majorities, or unusually intense intra-party conflict (around the issue of European union in the Tories' case), the drama of party politics makes it particularly newsworthy, but there is never a time when political affairs are without interest to the journalist. Politics is the staple food of journalistic work, supporting thousands of individuals and hundreds of millions of pounds of newsgathering and production resources.

The apparatus of political journalism

British political news-gathering and production is focused on parliament, and the 312 political correspondents housed in the 'gallery'.[1] This figure includes political staff working for regional and local media, news agencies and the BBC World Service, and represents a doubling of the number of political correspondents since 1965 (Tunstall, 1996). It includes those who report political affairs, as well as those who comment upon them in various ways in their capacity as columnists, sketch-writers, and diarists. Two hundred and twenty-seven gallery correspondents are members of the *lobby* – a group of journalists who, in exchange for privileged access to sources of political news, agree to abide by certain rules of attribution laid down by those sources.

The national media mapped in the previous chapter maintain 146 gallery staff, of whom ninety-six are lobby correspondents. These represent the human core of the political public sphere – a cohort of gatherers and processors of information who work on the inside track of the party political and governmental apparatuses, reporting the daily activities of the politicians and the issues which they raise. Their pivotal position means that they are the key definers of political reality in our culture, and for that reason they are the primary targets of the news management activities of the spin doctors (see Chapter 7). The lobby correspondent functions by adherence to a set of rules which effectively constrain the content and style of his or her reportage. Although the New Labour administration has modified some of the inhibiting lobby practices which have been most criticised in the past, such as the requirement to use the formulation 'sources close to …' rather than identify the institutional (if not the individual) source of a piece of information,[2] it remains a system which is both a help and a hindrance to the political journalist – an organisational framework

43

which ensures a regular and predictable supply of newsworthy information, while placing sometimes inconvenient limits on the uses to which that information can be put.

Lobby correspondents are still accused, as they have been for most of the hundred years and more of the system's existence (Cockerell *et al.*, 1984), of maintaining an unhealthily close relationship to the political elites over whom they are supposed to watch; of being over dependent and easily led. Not all political journalists choose to be part of the lobby, therefore (and there is not enough room for all in any case), preferring to establish their own independent newsgathering networks, rather like the war correspondents who refuse to accept the 'pooling' arrangements imposed by the military in a conflict zone. Columnist Hugo Young, for example, despite his reputation as one of the leading 'insider' pundits of the era (see next chapter) is not a member of the lobby. Anthony Bevins has also carved out a reputation as an independent journalist (mainly while working for the *Independent*), if not from the lobby, of which he is a member, but from the (he would assert) incestuous network of official and party sources upon which his colleagues are over reliant.

> It is not my job to remain comfortable, to be liked, to remain in the warmth of the pack ... hunting together and peddling half truths that are landed on my desk by people whose job it is to pedal half truths. It is my job to go out and find other sources. There are lots of documents to be read, lots of politicians to speak to, lots of civil servants to be spoken to.

The resources devoted by media organisations to the coverage of politics vary considerably, with the broadcasters and elite newspaper titles allocating the most. *The Times*, for example employs eight political staff at Westminster, as compared with six on the mid-market *Daily Mail*, and the *Daily Star*'s lonely 'political editor'.

> The *Star* only has one [political journalist – who is also the political editor], and there's a back-up if I'm away. It's not full time. I do other things as well. I *am* the political staff. At the party conferences there'll be two of us. At the general election we bring in more people, but basically it's just the one, and really, my job is just to see that the main political stories are covered, as fairly as possible. We don't go into great depth, because we honestly don't think our readers want to read much about [politics] and if they are interested they'll actually look elsewhere: they'll look at television, or buy some other newspaper.

For the elite and mid-market titles, by contrast, and the 'political' populars too – the *Sun* and the *Mirror* – coverage of politics is the single most resource-consuming 'beat'; what they perceive as their coverage of greatest influence, reflecting management's calculations of readers' interests in the subject, the desire to influence readers' attitudes, and also the newspaper's important commercial asset of being seen to be a credible participant or 'player' in ongoing political debate; an organ to be taken seriously (and thus purchased and read) by politicians and public alike.

Broadcast journalism also prioritises politics in its allocation of resources. The BBC devotes annually over 500 of its available hours (about 5 per cent) to political broadcasting (not including news, *Any Questions* or *Question Time*). Some 500 staff are employed on political coverage, centred organisationally in BBC Westminster, with more than forty managerial staff and some 110 journalists.[3] In addition to the BBC's political editor, eleven political correspondents supply the corporation's national output (in five TV and ten radio news slots). The BBC World Service has its own lobby and political staff, as do the regional divisions of the BBC. ITN, making programmes for Channels 3, 4 and 5 from its headquarters in London's Gray's Inn Road, has fifteen political correspondents, nine of whom are members of the lobby. Sky News has five lobby correspondents.

The scale of editorial resource devoted to political coverage leads some journalists to criticise what they perceive may be an excessive devotion to the minutiae of politics. According to a senior BBC news presenter:

> We have an obsession with politics and politicians, [with] taking the story further, inch by inch, on a daily basis, when we could leave it alone. It becomes an obsession for people who work in news. It's a function of the interest of the journalist in concentrating on politics, but it's also a function, to a small extent, of laziness, in that politicians are constantly available for interview.[4]

For some observers,[5] editorial over-emphasis on – or obsession with – politics is part of the crisis of public communication referred to in Chapter 1. By almost any definition of normative standards, on the other hand, more is better than less, and it must encourage some optimism as to the future evolution of the public sphere that, in the midst of the most fiercely competitive, commercialised media environment ever known in Britain, politics continues to claim such a high proportion of editorial resources. This pattern of resource allocation is partly demand-driven. Partly, it is the consequence of technology-driven organisational factors which have increased the possibilities, and also the convenience of political news; and partly too the effect of a general perception across the journalism industry that in-depth coverage of politics is a standard marker of 'quality' news provision.

The political news agenda[6]

The degree of editorial commitment to politics is reflected in the content of British news and journalism. Table 3.1 shows that politics remains one of the most reported aspects of public life in Britain. In each of the two-week periods in late 1996 reviewed for this study there were more than 700 political stories in the national media (around fifty per day on average). Table 2.2 in the previous chapter showed that politics led the news agenda in November 1996 on as many as twenty-one days (in a calendar month) for some media (the *Daily Telegraph*), and on no days at all for others (the *Daily Star*). Broadcast news outlets headlined with politics less frequently than the print media, but a day without broadcast political news somewhere in a bulletin was extremely rare. In short, politics is at the heart of the contemporary news agenda in both print and broadcast media, and frequently at the head of it – precisely where it ought to be, normatively speaking.

Some critics who might concede this to be true will argue that if politics is high on the news agenda, coverage is inappropriately focused on process and performance rather than policy, on style rather than substance, and on private rather than public affairs. To test that assertion the sample used for this study was broken down by subject, with the following results.

Policy versus process

Of the 1500 or so political stories identified over the four weeks of the sample period,[7] more than 50 per cent (800 items) reported the *issue-based*, policy-advocating activities of party and non-party actors (parties, trade unions, business organisations, and pressure groups such as the pro- and anti-gun lobbies, active in November 1996 as the post-Dunblane firearms legislation approached).[8] By far the greatest proportion of this coverage (more than 80 per cent of items) concerned issues then at the top of the political agenda, such as Scottish and Welsh devolution, and attitudes to European union. A further 244 items reported government activity, while 338 items covered a variety of non-party specific policy issues, particularly debates around European union, which was the most contentious issue of the period (and for the 1992–97 parliament as a whole), at least for the governing party. Coverage of government was also mainly policy oriented, including in the sample period stories about penal reform, anti-gun legislation, and a green paper on the role of information technology in enhancing good government. In the four weeks sampled

46

Table 3.1   The political news agenda

3.1a September 1–14 1996*

Number of items	TV	Radio	Press	Total
Party politics / campaigning				
Labour policy	20	6	170	196
Labour campaign	7	2	29	38
TUC conference	43	4	25	72
CBI conference	2	1	6	9
Conservative policy	7	2	33	42
Conservative campaign	5	2	22	29
Cash-for-questions	2		8	10
SNP policy			5	5
Liberal Democratic policy	4	2	1	7
Liberal Democratic campaign		1		1
Referendum Party			6	1
Campaign (general)	3		20	23
Opinion polls & voting patterns			9	9
Government policy				
Economy		1	3	4
Law and order	2		19	21
Europe	11	6	52	69
Scotland			1	1
Defence			1	1
Issues				
Poverty		1		1
European union	12	6	82	100
Domestic economy	1	1	9	11
Devolution/nationalism	2		15	17
Industrial disputes		1	4	5
Pressure groups		1	13	14
Political communication (process)			21	21
Total				**738**

3.1b November 3–16, 1996

Number of items	TV	Radio	Press	Total
Party politics / campaigning				
Labour policy	7	5	135	147
Labour campaign	5		24	29
CBI conference	2	1	6	9
Conservative policy	11	5	79	95
Conservative campaign			8	8
Cash-for-questions	9	2	43	54
Liberal Democratic policy	2		6	8
Liberal Democratic campaign		1		1
Referendum Party	1		3	4
UK Independence Party			1	1
Campaign (general)		1	5	6
Opinion polls & voting patterns			12	12
Government policy				
Health	2	3	10	15
Economy	2	1	9	12
Law and order	32	8	58	98
Europe	9	3	52	64
Scotland		1	2	3
Media		2	1	3
Issues				
European union	9	5	116	130
Domestic economy	6	4	38	48
Devolution/nationalism	6	1	9	16
Industrial disputes			3	3
Pressure groups	1		4	5
Political communication (process)			10	10
Total				**781**

* Sample: 19 national newspapers; news and interview programmes on 5 TV channels and Radio 4 here, then, policy matters, as determined by the nature of the issues in public debate at the time, were predominant in the coverage.[9]

It is true, however, that not all stories about party politics concern what Tony Benn used to call 'the issues'. A hundred and twenty-three stories in the sample (15 per cent) covered aspects of the ongoing general election campaign (the 'long campaign') which was by then widely acknowledged to have commenced. And not all of these concerned substantive policy issues so much as personality and style. In the first week of September, for example, there was extensive coverage of, and commentary on, the Tories' 'demon eyes' poster campaign – a Saatchi-devised attack ad capitalising on Clare Short's denunciation the previous August of Labour's spin doctors as 'the people who live in the dark',[10] and portraying Tony Blair as a devil in disguise. That week, too, both Norma Major and Cherie Blair were campaigning in the country as their husbands' parties prepared for their annual conferences. Both received extensive coverage, particularly in the mid-market tabloids. In November 1996, there was a rash of stories about Tony Blair's hairstyle and popularity with 'the ladies', based on a MORI poll showing that only 43 per cent of women were satisfied with Blair as leader, compared to 60 per cent of men.[11]

Some thirty-one items (about 2 per cent of stories) were principally about the political *process*, presenting journalistic reflections on the nature of political communication (mainly public relations and 'spin', but including political journalism) itself.[12] In these *meta-discursive* stories (i.e., media coverage of media) journalists addressed ethical and other debates about current trends in the media–politics relationship (in many of which, of course, they were themselves implicated). During the sample period, for example, Bill Clinton's campaign for re-election as US president reached a successful conclusion, prompting much journalistic speculation in the UK about the lessons to be learnt by the British political parties from the American experience. Several stories reported that Clinton's communication adviser George Stephanopoulos 'is set to work for Tony Blair and the Labour Party at the next election'.[13]

Such items are typical of that sub-category of political journalism often criticised for its focus not on policy, nor on the issues which policy presents for debate and decision-making, but on the *process* of political competition. Such coverage is accused, as noted in Chapter 1, of constructing the deeply serious business of democratic politics as a game of party and individual point-scoring, a competition elevated in the structure of political newsvalues over the issues driving it in the first place. In coverage of process, it is argued, the *style* of political performance takes precedence over policy *substance*.

Forget then, for a moment, that even in this more than usually competitive pre-election period, only 15 per cent or so of political news items were concerned with process (in this case, the process of an election campaign which had not yet officially begun) rather than policy, and that the problem, to the extent that there is one, must in quantitative terms be judged to be relatively minor.[14] What of the essential critical point: that stories of this kind contribute significantly to the degeneration of the public sphere by distracting citizens from the substantive concerns of politics and diverting them into superficial judgments about style; that, as one commentator puts it, 'the post-modernist style of politics ... a new and more dangerous corruption than sleaze'[15] is debasing and trivialising the public sphere.

> The triumph of the image, ever more divorced from any discernible reality, represents the corruption of the intellect and the perversion of the spirit. It is an attempt to cheat the public.

For better or worse, politics is now (and probably always has been) as much about competition and process as it is about policy. Politics is nothing (and it is certainly not democratic) if it is not about competition between and within parties around policy; between parties and journalists (with the input of the spin doctors) for access to and control of the means of shaping the public policy agenda through news; and at the level of individual news stories, competition between sources and journalists for definition of what the issues are and how they should be evaluated by the public. Politics is also about competition between individual media organisations for access to the best stories, and for the loyalty of the biggest audiences.

Politics is in all these respects a competitive process, and political journalism naturally reflects this. The journalist is, of course, expected to add value by reporting the political process from a position of critical distance, monitoring the extent to which conduct of the competition follows the rules, how it matches the policy rhetoric, and how it conforms to the normative principles of democracy. And, indeed, this is precisely what one finds in the majority of these stories. Much *process* journalism, whether in the elite, mid-market or popular media, is framed by a critical discourse on the game, as when the *Sun*'s political editor asked of Stephanopoulos' reported relationship with the Labour Party: 'Will gorgeous George end up tainting Tony?'[16]

> The involvement of the President's top spin doctor in a British election campaign may backfire ... against New Labour. *Boyish-faced Mr Stephanopoulos is inextricably linked with the seediest American President in history*. (his emphasis)

There was a time, not that long ago, when the process of political competition was a closed book to the average citizen. The mechanics of political communication, the persuasive-manipulative techniques to which citizens were subjected then as now (if without the refined professionalism of the current scene), remained hidden from all but the journalistic and political elites themselves. Now, coverage of the political process is an important part of an expanded public sphere, and an expanded political journalism, adding to rather than detracting from the breadth and scope of public debate. Reading, watching or listening to journalistic accounts of how political advertising is designed and how patterns of ad-space buying can foretell an election;[17] what focus groups can do for party strategists;[18] how messages are 'spun' and stories manufactured – is not a substitute for information about the content of policy, but it can deepen our under-standing of how political ideas rise and fall in public estimation, and thus adds to the sense-making resources at our disposal. If a certain amount of cynicism is also induced, a further loss of innocence engineered in those who still have an unrealistic faith in the normative ideals of liberal democ-racy, that is an entirely welcome outcome. Citizens are better equipped by such a journalism for the semiological guerrilla warfare which is their best defence against whatever influence politicians, their spin doctors, or the media may try to exert over their political attitudes and behaviours.

Most criticism of process journalism assumes that there is such a thing as pure, transparent, honest policy, distinguishable from and superior to political rhetoric designed for public consumption. But isolating policy statements for the purposes of evaluation is inadequate without a parallel, contextualising analysis of the *process* of their development, contestation and presentation. 'Policy' and 'process' are not separate discourses, in other words, but complementary elements of a public debate in which citi-zens know (and should be reminded, again and again) that appearances (and rhetoric) can be deceptive. A vigorous journalism which acknowl-edges and explores this linkage is to be applauded as a democratic asset rather than condemned as part of some more general dumbing down.

Most process journalism, moreover, is deeply 'serious' in tone and content, consisting of detailed and often quite technical analyses of how focus groups work, or of what George Stephanopoulous achieved for President Clinton and might therefore be able to do for the British Labour Party. Sometimes, of course, process journalism deals with that *bête noire* of the dumbing-down school – human interest – and occasionally in less than serious terms. Extensive coverage of Tony Blair's hair style in November 1996, for example, was tinged with humour and irreverence. As the *Independent*'s John Rentoul reported:

> Westminster was in ferment yesterday over the issue which has
> been troubling close watchers of politics more than any other

since Tony Blair became Leader of the Opposition two years ago – the state of the Labour leader's hair.[19]

The *Daily Telegraph* traced the development of the Blair hairstyle from his well-thatched student days to the somewhat shorter and thinner present, while both the *Independent* and the *Telegraph* ran computerised photographs of a completely bald Blair, and discussion of whether he should go for a 'Perry Como' cut or just 'calming down with some good quality products'.[20] Behind the humour, however (and the assumption that politics can never be entertaining is another questionable premiss of the critics of process journalism) there is often a serious point. If contemporary politics is, to some extent at least, a competitive game, it is a game in which the style and conduct of play matter, as opposed to the substance of policy alone (the score, to continue with the sporting metaphors). Policy rhetoric can never be taken at face value, precisely *because* politicians are competing for power, and may be prepared to sacrifice principle – even truth – for the sake of achieving it. In the era of live news and extreme close-up the style of a political performance, the content of a political image, become available for use as additional and entirely legitimate means of evaluating policy rhetoric. Provided we know how to read style (and most of us acquire, through the media, as part of our education into adult society, a working knowledge of the semiotics of political communication) and are aware of its limitations as criteria of suitability for office, we would be depriving ourselves unnecessarily if we were not to draw upon it in making political judgements.

The coverage of Tony Blair's hair, for example, far from being a journalistic dereliction of duty or a commercially driven surrender to the principles of infotainment, should be seen instead for what it was – one of those rare occasions in the pre-election period when the Labour leader's highly manicured, carefully designed public persona was challenged by the media, and the more serious issue of New Labour's style-consciousness interrogated. Jokes about hair were used as a way into quite deep analysis of the MORI poll on women's attitudes to Blair, and New Labour's attitudes to women. 'That is important', wrote Boris Johnson of the *Telegraph*, 'when you consider that Bill Clinton has just been swept to victory on female votes'.[21] Johnson reported one woman's view that 'when he [Blair] was claiming the mantle of Mrs Thatcher he looked strong and attractive, but his facade has appeared a bit brittle recently. People begin to wonder if it's a performance.' The transition from old to new Labour (and the emergence from relative obscurity of Tony Blair as the saviour of British social democracy) *was* a performance of sorts, most observers agree. Here the integrity and authenticity of the performance was publicly questioned, becoming part of the critical discourse through which readers of the media concerned could evaluate the *substance* of New Labour. Thus

51

does coverage of style frequently become critique of performance *and* policy, and themes of merely 'human interest' acquire genuine political significance.

The prevalence of politics on the news agenda has led, as we saw above, to British journalism being accused of harbouring an 'obsession' with politics; of being excessively interested in the sayings and doings of the political elite, and of alienating ordinary citizens in the process. The head of *Channel 5 News* criticises British television news in general of being over-focused on 'the institutions of power', of producing 'establishment news for the news elite'.[22] Television news has 'for too long been interested in an issue-led, establishment-oriented diet of reports'.[23] The stories of Blair's hair, or 'the war of the wives' (as Norma Major's and Cherie Blair's campaigning activities in 1996–97 were dubbed) emerge from this perspective not as the undermining of democracy, but as a welcome intrusion of human interest into the elite agenda. They are 'tabloid news' in an alternative, more positive sense of that term; as journalist John Dugdale has defined it, 'news led by the audience's interests – less pompous, less pedagogic, less male; more human, more vivacious, more demotic'.[24] For as long as 'tabloid news' thus defined does not squeeze out journalistic consideration of policy issues – and, in the period analysed for this study it certainly did not – there is no reason to assume that journalistic attention to process (whether in its technical or 'human interest' aspects) reduces the effectiveness of the public sphere as a democratic resource. If entertainment and relief from the po-faced seriousness of political professionals is not good enough reason for a certain amount of human interest coverage in our political journalism, and even an occasional shot of 'trivia and fluff',[25] then we should accept that its apparent superficiality is often the cover for quite sophisticated analyses and critiques of politics, the media, democracy, and the relationship between the three.

The sleaze agenda

Some forty years ago Daniel Boorstin noted 'our morbid interest in private lives, in personal gossip, and in the sexual indiscretions of public figures' (1962, p. 255). This, he argued, at a time when the professionalisation of political communication had barely begun to make its mark on journalistic content, was a regrettable, if intelligible, response to the ever more managed nature of political news and the rise of political public relations. 'In a world where the public acts of politicians and celebrities become more and more controversial, we look ever more eagerly for happenings, not brought into being especially for our benefit. We search for those areas of life which may have remained immune to the cancer of pseudo-eventfulness' (ibid.).

Public figures, being only human after all, have always been inclined to indiscretions, even if it is only relatively recently that those indiscretions have become the subject of mainstream political journalism. When Boorstin's *The Image* was published in 1962, John F. Kennedy was enjoying a hyperactive, adulterous sex life around the White House pool without any intrusion from the American press corps (Hersh, 1997) who, if they were not actually participating in the shenanigans, certainly knew about much of what was going on. In Britain, the Profumo scandal was the rule-making exception to a more general journalistic silence on elite deviance. In Profumo's case, but rarely in others, a politician's sexual indiscretions were so widely reported that they became a matter for resignation (and in that particular case there were serious national security implications of the minister's affair with a call girl). In those days, much lamented by some, public figures had private lives which, unless they forced their way into the public domain because of gross incompetence or sheer excess, tended to remain private. The recent history of politics on both sides of the Atlantic has, by contrast, been one in which private indiscretions figure large. The Monica Lewinsky scandal produced the most severe political crisis of the Clinton administration, following on several other scandals of a similar nature. In Britain, the Conservative government of 1992–97 was one in which indiscretions of a sexual and financial kind became so frequent that journalists and commentators began to use the term *sleaze* as shorthand for political coverage of them. Sleaze journalism became a prominent sub-category of British political journalism in the Major years, underpinning the narrative framework of decay and disintegration within which stories about the Conservatives were interpreted after the Black Wednesday crisis of 1992 (see Chapter 8).

During the sample periods referred to in this chapter – not periods when sleaze was at the top of the news agenda by any means – sixty-four items of political journalism were identified as being about sleaze of one kind or another: principally, the cash-for-questions scandal and its reverberations in governmental cover up. Early November 1996, for example, saw extensive coverage of junior minister David Willetts' appearances before the House of Commons Standards and Privileges committee (to defend himself against allegations that he had used his position in government to deflect MPs' and others' attentions from the Neil Hamilton affair). In September that year it was reported that the prime minister John Major was likely to be subpoenaed in the Hamilton versus *Guardian* libel case which the latter's cash-for-questions coverage had provoked. Both stories illustrate how the slow but steady flow of 'sleaze' news was a routine, almost daily feature of political journalism in the final months of Tory government.[26]

Sleaze was also (if by coincidence only) a prominent theme in coverage of the Clinton administration, as already noted, while in Britain the 1997 general election was dominated, and the result largely determined, by two sleaze stories: the ongoing cash-for-questions scandal (further allegations by the *Guardian* newspaper about Neil Hamilton MP which appeared in the first week of the campaign); and the adulterous affair involving Piers Merchant MP. Between them, these two stories – both implicating the Conservative Party – set the news agenda for the crucial first third of the election campaign, reinforcing an already established image of the Tories as the sleaze party, and presenting them with what turned out to be an electoral obstacle too high to overcome. Sleaze alone did not lose the 1997 election for the Conservatives (the inner-party split over Europe, which dominated the final weeks of the campaign, was also an important factor), but it did much to define the political environment within which the campaign was fought, to the displeasure of pro-Conservative commentators like Paul Johnson, who found the media's 'hysterical fury' over sleaze inappropriate, even undemocratic. 'In their pursuit of the "sleaze" issue', wrote Johnson, the media had 'flouted all the decencies and even the law'.[27] Criticisms of sleaze journalism have come not only from the pro-Conservative right, however. Some of those with no interest in defending a particular party have argued that sleaze is not an appropriate topic for political journalism; that journalistic emphasis on sleaze is a manifestation of the descent into tabloidisation of which the media are so regularly accused; further evidence of an anti-democratic preferring of 'trivia and fluff'[28] over serious policy matters, and the ascendancy of a distorted, profit-driven structure of newsvalues which deprives the public of what it really needs to know.

But sleaze journalism can, and with normative democratic principles in mind, *should* be viewed as the welcome by-product of an era when journalistic deference toward political elites has been eroded, and the normative watchdog function of the Fourth Estate is increasingly applied, in conditions of heightened competitiveness, to the secretive, insider networks which if left alone burrow away at and undermine the democratic process. Coverage of the cash-for-questions scandal, even if it did deflect citizens' attentions away from some of that government's genuine achievements in the sphere of economic policy is, within any meaningful definition of critical scrutiny, preferable to media silence and public ignorance about the existence and scale of such abuses. Regardless of the extent to which Hamilton and others implicated in the cash-for-questions scandal were acting as individuals, they were still Tory MPs, and their behaviour quite properly reflected on the professional standards and organisational culture prevailing within the Tory party. To deny that this was, and remains, the appropriate subject matter of political journalism seems perverse.

In the post-Tory era of New Labour in government sleaze continues to be a story, although the narrative framework which gave it such destructive power in the Major years – the decline and imminent departure of a tired and corrupt administration – was absent. Thus, although the Labour government has been accused of sleaze and 'cronyism' in its dealings with the Formula One racing industry, in its relations with Rupert Murdoch, in the financial affairs and associations of Geoffrey Robinson (culminating in the resignation of both Robinson and the trade secretary Peter Mandelson in December 1998), in the provision of access-for-cash, and even in the Lord Chancellor's choice of interior decoration for his official residence, it was not possible for journalists (even those, like the political staff of the *Sunday Times*, who have been most assiduous in pursuing allegations of Labour sleaze post-May 1997) to make sense of them in terms of the framework which was available in the Major years. (This was true as of going to press, although neither the media analyst nor the politician can predict the shape and structure of stories to come.)[29] On the contrary, the preferred journalistic framework for reporting the first half of the first Blair government was the ascendancy of the spin doctors, and a key theme within this framework that of the often surprising failures of political communication which accompanied Labour's seizure of the official information apparatus. Sleaze journalism irritated the Blair government, therefore, but was unlikely to destroy it in the way John Major's government was destroyed.

Sexual sleaze

There is another kind of sleaze journalism, of course, less obviously consistent with normative standards of journalism in a democracy, which exposes private rather than public corruption, personal rather than political or professional failings. There were many examples of such sleaze during the Major years, and since then there have been episodes concerning Robin Cook's love life, Ron Davies' cruising on Clapham Common, Bill Clinton's liking for oral sex in the Oval Office, and a second chapter of the Piers Merchant story. This dimension of sleaze is the most frequently criticised as being unworthy of a quality public sphere, and the most visible indicator of the tabloidisation and dumbing down of political journalism. Here again, however, an alternative interpretation is possible.

Channel 4 News presenter Jon Snow has been among the most outspoken critics of tabloidisation in the political news agenda, warning that it threatens 'the whole fabric of Western democracy'.[30] He criticises a journalistic culture in which, amongst other things, 'the content of politics falls victim to the more easily communicated evidence of human frailty'. And yet, when the bizarre sex life of Piers Merchant MP again exploded into the public domain in October 1997, with torrid tales of live-in lovers, betrayals and media-inspired mental breakdowns, *Channel 4 News* led with the story, just like most of the other media on that day and the next. Second time around, however, unlike the original surfacing of the story in March 1997, there was no general electoral connection, no interpretative framework by which the story could be justified in terms of a wider pattern of 'Tory sleaze' which was destabilising the government. (Five months after the general election, Piers Merchant's affairs were pathetic rather than politically-charged.) In October 1997, to an extent which was not true in the earlier surfacing of the story, Piers Merchant's problems *were* arguably of private rather than public interest. *Channel 4 News* enthusiastically reported them nonetheless, and indeed identified them as the most important news story of that day (October 14). A few months later, as the Monica Lewinsky scandal broke in February 1998, Jon Snow was one of the first British journalists to establish himself in Washington for the duration of what might have been a presidential resignation or impeachment (but, of course, turned out only to be a boost for Clinton's approval ratings). It was Jon Snow and *Channel 4 News*, too, who won the race to be the first British broadcast journalist organisation to interview Monica Lewinsky, for a reported fee of £400,000.[31]

Similarly, Paul Johnson's attack on the role of sleaze journalism in the 1997 general election cited above did not prevent him, and other like-minded conservative commentators, from continually emphasising Bill Clinton's 'sleaziness' in their coverage of late-90s American politics.

While many journalists condemn the prevalence of sleaze, therefore, they often accept its place in a 'quality' news agenda (i.e., their own), and apply to it in such circumstances the full arsenal of reporting and analytical techniques. In doing so they reveal by their journalistic practice, while often denying in their public pronouncements on the matter, that sleaze – sexual as well as financial, private or public – *can* be an important political issue and, even when it is not, as in the Piers Merchant story of October 1997, that it is still sufficiently newsworthy to be given headline coverage, particularly if it concerns the 'other side' of the political divide.

Sleaze journalism – of which, after all, there can only be as much as there are examples of sexual and financial deviance supplied by the politicians – *is* a manifestation of tabloidisation in so far as it imports into the elite sectors of the political public sphere the popular media's centuries-old fascination with sexual deviance and scandal (Boston, 1990; Engel, 1996). And even where that migration has not always been accompanied by the adoption of the sensationalistic expository and revelatory styles which the popular tabloids have traditionally applied to the worlds of entertainment, celebrity and criminality, sleaze journalism *is* clearly infotainment, at least in part, in so far as it provides a vicarious and mildly transgressive pleasure for the audience – pleasure in knowing that the elites who govern us are, like ourselves, fallible, troubled and vulnerable to the seductions of sex or drugs or money. Not gods, then, but mere men and women. For this reason, if for no other, sleaze journalism is an index of the openness and accessibility of late twentieth-century political culture, made possible not just by new technologies of news gathering and the heightened competitiveness of a media market which rewards exposure of elite transgression, but by the gradual fading away of the status and class-based deference which constrained political journalism in the past. Politics was always sleazy, and political power always a temptation to corruption. Now, in contrast to the past, we know about at least some of that sleaze, and some of that corruption, and can factor that knowledge into our voting decisions.[32]

Those who argue that this knowledge is not worth knowing, or that it diverts citizens from consideration of 'serious' issues, underestimate the public's ability to judge when the human frailties exposed in sleaze journalism are relevant to sound political decision-making and when they are not. In the United States, over Monica Lewinsky and her 'presidential kneepads', the people repeatedly signalled that it was the latter (although Republican congressmen and senators disagreed with the popular will, for political reasons of their own). Columnist Andrew Sullivan identifies amongst Americans a 'populist backlash' against what was seen as 'an invasion of the president's private life'.[33] In Britain, by contrast, over cash-for-questions and the many cases of marital infidelity which plagued the party of family values and 'back to basics', the electorate collectively decided that sleaze *was* an important political issue, and the Conservative government paid the price in May 1997. When a succession of Labour ministers as 'outed' in late 1998, by contrast, only one – Ron Davies, alleged to have been mugged while cruising on Clapham Common – was required to resign, not because of his sexuality but his poor judgement in making himself vulnerable to robbery and blackmail. The government of which Davies had been a member was not damaged in opinion polls. Peter Mandelson and Nick Brown, meanwhile, emerged from their 'outings' with their dignities and careers intact because Labour, unlike the Tories, was not vulnerable to charges of moral hypocrisy on the issue of homosexuality (although Mandelson had to resign shortly afterwards in a sleaze scandal of another kind).

My championing of the role of sleaze journalism in a healthy democracy is thus qualified by ethical considerations. Politicians who do not preach moral superiority, and who do not victimise through policy those whom they may define as morally inferior, should not have to fear exposure of sexually deviant or messy private lives, unless (and this of course is often a matter of contention) these undermine their ability to perform public duties.[34] It is not, in many cases, the deviant behaviour which shocks the citizen and erodes trust in the politician, but the disparity between publicly uttered word and private deed. Chris Smith, the first openly gay Cabinet minister, has been one of the success stories of the Blair government. Former Conservative MP Gerry Hayes, on the other hand, married but at the same time linked in the media with a male researcher, was brought down. While Hayes was known to be a liberal on sexual matters, his voluntary association with a party viewed by many as hostile to gay rights, and the contradiction this required between his public and private selves, made him a likely target, if not (in this writer's view, at least) 'fair game'. Not all journalism about political sleaze need be embraced as part of the new mediated democracy, therefore. But in the main, and with the ethical constraints identified above, it can be recognised as a legitimate extension of Habermas' concept of critical scrutiny into the hitherto secret spaces where public image and private reality merge and dissolve.

For sleaze journalism, in the end, is not a discourse only about extra-marital sex, auto-erotic asphyxiation, or cash-for-questions: it is also about *trust*. Anna Coote has noted that 'as traditional differences between left and right break down, so the notion of faith [in politicians] becomes increasingly important: what matters to voters is not what politicians promise, or even what they stand for, but whether they can be trusted. That, in turn, depends on the personality of the politician and the character of the relationship with the voter'.[35] In similar vein, a Dutch scholar suggests that 'in societies where ideologies disappear and differences between political parties become less and less important and visible, for the public much understanding of politics has the structure of narratives centred around individual characters' (Brants, 1998, p. 332). Sleaze journalism is where those issues are exposed and explored, those narratives developed, in the context of a competitive media environment in which, for better or worse, tales of human drama have high exchange value.

Some critics argue, from a different starting point, that the exposure of elite sleaze in the mainstream media is a kind of tokenism: a superficial and ultimately ineffectual cleansing of 'rotten apples' from a system which retains its more fundamental corruptions and injustices. And there is a sense in which contemporary 'sleaze' journalism *can* be viewed as a safety-valve for advanced capitalist societies which, though uniquely affluent and consumption-oriented, continue to be characterised by injustice and inequality; a public demonstration and ritual denunciation of elite deviance which mocks and subverts the 'ruling classes' without actually threatening the structural core of the system. Today's journalism of sexual scandal might even be viewed as akin to those carnivalesque forms of popular culture in which 'the world is turned upside down' (Burke, 1988). In early modern Europe the popular festivals known as carnival are believed to have functioned at one and the same time as entertainment, as affirmation and celebration of community, and as a form of social control, in which exaggerated rituals of role reversal and subversion served ultimately to reinforce social hierarchies. Carnival was permitted by the feudal ruling class because 'they were aware that the society they lived in, with all its inequalities of wealth, status and power, could not survive without a safety-valve, a means for the subordinates to purge their resentments and to compensate for their frustrations' (ibid., p. 201). The denunciations of the powerful which modern sleaze journalism allows may have similar functions in the maintenance of social order and cross-class harmony, although, unlike carnival, they are usually unforeseen, unplanned and uncontrollable by the elite groups whose reputations and positions are damaged by them. The history of political journalism in the late twentieth century, both in Britain and in the United States, showed that sleaze journalism can have serious effects on the exercise of political power, and on the political environment more generally. Whether these effects are in the long run positive or negative, from the democratic perspective, will depend in large part on whether the people succeed, as Andrew Sullivan suggests they can, in imposing their collective judgements of propriety and appropriateness on their media.

Conclusion

Two modes of 'process' and 'sleaze' journalism have been discussed in this chapter: one associated largely with elite media, the other with mid-market and popular. Elite journalism about political process deals mainly with the technical issues of political communication, such as the conduct and influence of marketing, advertising and opinion polling. Coverage of process in the mid-market and popular media is often about hairstyle and other image signifiers. Each type of coverage will have its distinctive idiomatic and stylistic feaures, corresponding to its position in the media marketplace. Similarly, in their coverage of sleaze, elite media tend to focus on such matters as lapses of professional ethics and procedural impropriety by parties or governments, while their popular counterparts prefer exposures of sexual deviance. None of these types of political journalism is unique to the late twentieth century, but as the media environment has evolved they have undoubtedly increased as a proportion of total political output. The normatively preferred agenda of policy over process, and substance over style, still dominates, however. In the period of this study coverage of sexual sleaze was far outweighed by coverage of cash-for-questions and related matters, just as in-depth coverage of the technicalities of the political communication process far outweighed news about such matters as who was 'the sexiest man in politics'.

With increasing frequency in our political culture, however, the boundaries melt away and elite and popular agendas merge, so that elite media report sexual sleaze, the tabloids report on the implications of George Stephanopoulos' advisory role for Labour, the *Financial Times* covers the great 'Blair hair' debate. The emergence in the late twentieth century of a politically sophisticated and media-literate public, de-ideologised and (as its members increasingly see themselves) de-classed, further undermines the elite–mass, educated–uneducated distinctions which have traditionally structured the public sphere. Stylistic variations in coverage of sleaze as between elite, mid-market and popular media continue to exist, but the distinction between 'serious' and 'trivial' information is no longer one which can be taken as the basis for evaluating the public sphere. A proliferation of media outlets, intensifying competitive pressures, and the introduction of new media technologies constantly push back the boundaries of what can be covered and how (live hearings of select committees in the House of Commons, internet dissemination of the Monica Lewinsky story, global broadcasting of the videotape recording of Bill Clinton's grand jury testimony, live coverage of the Senate impeachment trial). In political journalism, as in the culture generally, taste distinctions between high and low are continually eroded. Hartley is correct when he argues that 'the old-fashioned divisions between the public and the private sphere, male and female cultural domains, politics and fashion, news and entertainment, have to be rethought in the context of the postmodern media' (1996, p. 145). The political journalisms of process and sleaze are where those categories most visibly break down.

This process is to be welcomed rather than condemned, in so far as contemporary political journalism, whether elite, mid-market or popular, is healthily suspicious and irreverential of elites, if sometimes obsessive in its pursuit of the game. An earlier form of detached, deferential, more or less verbatim political reportage has gone from the print media (although certainly not from TV and radio, as the previous chapter showed), to be replaced by styles and agendas which, if they are occasionally entertaining, are at the same time more penetrating, more critical, more revealing and demystificatory of power than the polite, status-conscious journalisms of the past. And it is precisely the commercialising influence of the market which has allowed this to happen. Jonathan Freedland praises the ability of the American public sphere to address important political issues through 'human interest' stories, often of a sleazy nature, citing the Lorena Bobbit story and its impact on the domestic violence debate as an example. The Monica Lewinsky scandal is another obvious case, as already noted, of the private sphere serving as a vehicle for the public discussion of serious political issues – sexual harassment and abuse of power relations in the workplace; trust and political ethics. As Freedland puts it, 'the advantage of a political culture which can debate matters of national import through the medium of celebrity scandal is that everyone can take part' (1998, p. 61). As for the USA so too, I would suggest, the UK. To the extent that the journalism of private sleaze raises important issues of public concern relating to the behaviour of individuals in the political sphere, and puts them before a mass audience (in a variety of elite, mid-market and popular discursive modes), it merits space in a 'quality' public sphere.

4

THE INTERPRETATIVE
MOMENT

The journalism of commentary and analysis

One of the most frequently noted,[1] and also most criticised aspects of contemporary political journalism[2] is the remarkable expansion in recent years of the commentary form, what I will call the *interpretative moment* in the news cycle – spaces in the public sphere where evaluation of, and opinion about either the substance, the style, the policy content or the process of political affairs replaces the straight reportage of new information. Critics of this trend do not say that commentary is without value in political journalism – only that it has expanded as a proportion of total output beyond what is required or good for rational political decision-making, and at the expense of straightforwardly informative reportage. In what is, at one level, an extension of the process versus policy debate, one important aspect of the crisis of public communication is said to be the ascendancy of subjective journalistic interpretation over objective fact-reporting. The normative functions of political news are being undermined by a proliferating commentary industry; a plethora of pundits who, drawing their cultural power from the privileged status of the journalist as licensed truth-teller, increasingly flood the public sphere with speculation and conjecture. This chapter assesses the validity of those criticisms.

The rise of political commentary

In its earliest forms, journalism – and 'correspondents' – were merely the conduits of information from one part of the world to another, made necessary (and thus valuable) by the growth of trade and mercantile capital. News acquired commodity-status because of its importance in the pursuit of business (economic) and administrative (political) activities, and has thus always been primarily concerned with the gathering, processing and distribution of economic and political information to those with a use for it. Early in the history of journalism, however, correspondents added to their core function of reportage and information-relay the intellectual labour of interpretation – making sense for their audience of an ever more complex world. Habermas records that 'as early as in the last third of the seventeenth century journals [primitive newspapers containing basic information] were complemented by periodicals containing not primarily information but pedagogical instructions and even criticism and reviews' (1989, p. 25). Around the same time newspapers began to print opinionated essays, usually anonymously in order to avoid prosecution under feudal censorship laws (Silvester, 1997).

These developments coincided with – were an essential part of – the emergence of the bourgeois public sphere in the coffee houses of Britain, France and Germany. Henceforth, newspapers would not simply furnish political and business elites with the information necessary for them to monitor their environments and conduct their business efficiently; they would organise debate on the nature of that environment, and advise and persuade as to the direction of trends within it. They would advocate social and political change, as well as report events. Then, as now, this was recognised to be an essential element of the journalist's role in a liberal democracy.

Since then, and in the latter half of the twentieth century particularly, the interpretative moment in journalism (and especially in political journalism) has occupied an ever greater proportion of output as a whole, in both the print and broadcast sectors, to the point that the sheer size of the 'punditocracy' is argued to be undermining the quality of the public sphere.[3] That there has been a dramatic rise in the number of pundits, and of political commentators in general, is not in dispute. But why now, and what does it mean for the quality of journalistic debate? Jeremy Tunstall observes that 'the emergence of the star journalist in Britain is a topic which awaits its historian' (1996, p. 407). While we wait for that historian to turn up, the following explanations can be advanced.

Commentary and the commodification of journalism

If a primitive journalism of opinion and commentary can be traced back at least as far as the seventeenth century, recognisably modern commentary, in the form of newspaper columns, did not emerge until two centuries later, in response to the growth of mass literacy and commercialised print media. For Silvester, 'the column is an outgrowth of the traditional essay and a refinement of that genre … [it] properly belongs to the age of mass newspaper consumption which started around the middle of the nineteenth century and which established a change in the methods by which the essay was delivered to the reader' (1997, p. xi). Columns began to appear at a time when the developing newspaper market had a use for a more distinctive, personalised journalism, which could entertain as well as inform (commentary columns, in this sense, are perhaps the oldest form of infotainment), and which would thus help to sell newspapers in the increasingly competitive media environment of the late nineteenth century.

Around this time too, as part of the process of press commercialisation and adoption of capitalist manufacturing procedures, the roles of editor and proprietor within newspapers – until the mid-1800s often occupied by the same individual – were demarcated. Editorials, which had until then been fora for the kind of opinionated writing that would come to characterise commentary columns (although contemporary editorials, particularly those of the tabloid press, often retain a carefully cultivated tone of outrage) became 'more sedate and formal ... so the newspaper column became the domain of vigorous, splenetic opinion, sometimes even going against the editorial grain of the particular title in which it ran' (ibid., p. xiii).

The first columnists were not 'political' as such, although they often addressed political subjects. Being market driven and entertainment led (aesthetic pleasure drawn from an individual's prose style being central to their appeal, as it still is), satire and humour were an important element of the columnist's work from the beginning, embellishing his increasingly important interpretative function. The capital and technology fuelled information revolution, which accelerated exponentially in the twentieth century but had already begun to pick up speed in the nineteenth, created an enhanced need and thus a market for overview of, insight into, and commentary on the rapidly expanding flow of information which the expanding literate public had to absorb. Satisfying this need both required authority of and bestowed it on the journalist who undertook the work of column-writing.

By the end of the nineteenth century the journalist 'was taking on new authority as interpreter of public life' (Schudson, 1995, p. 49), and being handsomely rewarded for it. The journalists who wrote commentary acquired enhanced prestige, trusted not only to report about the world accurately, but to interpret and make sense of it in a manner analogous to that of philosophers and artists. Encouraged by such as Walter Lippmann, one of the first political columnists, they gradually took on what Nimmo and Combs describe as 'a new and privileged status within the craft of journalism' (1992, p. 12), becoming as they did so significant social and political actors in their own right – journalists of particular influence, whose *opinions* mattered as much as their reporting skills, and who became a factor in shaping the events being reported.

The subsequent rise of the *political* columnist as a distinct and important sub-category of the commentary industry is principally a phenomenon of the twentieth century, integrally related to the communicative processes and trends which characterised it. The commercialisation of the media, as we have seen, created a market for journalistic opinion, which in the United States, with its system of syndicated newspapers was more fully developed from the outset than in the United Kingdom. In the States the columnist became a commodity in his (and, less frequently, her) own right, selling his columns to newspapers across the country. In Britain, by contrast, the columnist has usually been associated with a particular newspaper, becoming part of its brand (a relationship of association continued in the development of broadcasting 'pundits'). The rise of the political commentator is thus a direct consequence of the commodification of the public sphere, which made it necessary for news organisations to brand their output (give it exchange value in a marketplace containing many other superficially similar brands). The commentator is crucial to securing brand identification and consumer loyalty to a journalistic provider (specific exchange value accruing to an individual 'star' journalist) and political columnists, to this extent, have commercial as well as intellectual functions. If their use-value can be defined as 'interpretation', their exchange-value in a marketplace of many interpreters is predicated on their ability to interpret better than others, or at least with sufficient distinction to attract and hold an audience. So political columnists, like their counterparts in the non-political and human interest arenas of journalistic endeavour, must have aesthetic and technical skills beyond those normally associated with mere reportage. The commentary column is the closest journalism comes to theatre; as Silvester puts it, a 'performance' over and above 'an expression of intellectual argument', in which 'the personality of the writer is a self-referential text along with the subject matter' (1997, p. xi).

The style of the performance differs from one columnist to another, of course, and reflects the particular market (elite, mid or popular) to which the columnist is appealing. Columnists build their reputations, and sell themselves, on the authority of their public voice, which is in turn derived from a combination of intellect, articulacy (in whatever idiom is appropriate to the organ in which it appears), knowledge and contacts (sources). The balance of these elements in the work of particular columnists varies, but viewing the political public sphere overall we can distinguish three basic types of commentary column:

- the *polemical*, dispensing anger and outrage;
- the *analytical-advisory*, characterised by in-depth and considered exploration of current issues and events;
- and the *satirical*, founded on the use of irony and humour.[4]

When successful in establishing a reputation on one or more of these levels (as polemicist, analyst or satirist), the columnist gains a certain editorial autonomy.

The polemical

Silvester cites the late Peter Jenkins' description of the traditional British columnist as 'a star turn with emphasis on turn: the columnist's job was to take an ego trip, to entertain his readers, preferably by annoying them, with strong opinions on each and every subject' (ibid., p. xv). Polemical columnists should have the appropriate mix of readability and righteous anger to win the approval (or at least the respect) of their target audiences. They must persuade their readers that they are 'brilliant' (Peter McKay, *Daily Mail*), or 'incisive' (Bill Greig, *Daily Express*), often by pandering to what are perceived as the prejudices of the readers. When, for example, the *Daily Mail*'s Bruce Anderson refers to an Irish European Union official as 'primitive, bigoted, anti-modern' and 'a champion of the pig-and-potato economy';[5] he calculates that this is what his audience want to read. Provocative, deliberately inflammatory expressions of opinion are the stock-in-trade of this sub-species of column which, in publicly transgressing the conventional boundaries of taste and discretion, hooks the reader (whether or not she agrees with the sentiments expressed) into excited, voyeuristic fascination. Anderson's denigration of Irish eurocrats typifies the approach of a certain kind of columnist (Richard Littlejohn does the same thing in the tabloids), who makes it his business to go against the grain of current thinking – which may be disparagingly referred to by columnists of this type as 'political correctness'.

In general, what one might call perversely polemical commentary is more likely to be found in the mid-market and popular tabloids than in the elite newspapers, although it is certainly not absent from the latter. In the elite print sector, as much as the tabloid, there is commercial value in studied contrariness and cultivated controversy. Columnist Andrew Roberts observes, 'there's definitely a feeling that the more outrageous, the more outre, the more perverse you are, the more likely you are to get a job as a political columnist.' In the post-Tory, New Labour era this columnist sells himself, constructs his public voice, as an

> ideologically committed Tory propagandist. I see myself as a writer who is attempting to provoke and entertain but also, at the same time, to persuade people to look at issues. I like to think that I am putting a reactionary case ... I like to see myself as fighting a possibly doomed, but nevertheless great rearguard action.

In a relatively liberal political environment such as existed in post-Tory Britain, 'reaction' becomes a sellable brand of journalistic opinion, just as 'Red Ken' Livingstone was one of the most popular guest columnists of the Thatcher-era *Sun*: extreme views are distinctive and highly marketable, even when they diverge from the preferred public voice of the organ in which they appear.

This kind of column represents a distinctively British form of what Larry Sabato calls in the American context 'attack journalism' (1981) – polemical, confrontational, sometimes deliberately rude and offensive – all distinctive qualities of British political commentary, and of great importance to the maintenance and development of a democratic political culture in the United Kingdom. There is no comparable tradition of polemical commentary in the United States' print media. Simon Heffer (albeit himself a columnist, and therefore with motivation to praise his profession) observes with good reason that 'in Britain, political journalists are ruthless in their criticism of bad government, and quite often use humour to make their point. In America, the deference shown by the Press to politicians is almost suffocating – and jokes, despite the rich potential of the field, are right off the agenda.'[6] There have been and are still many non-deferential, satirical, mildly subversive political columnists in the United States, such as Hunter Thompson (although he is on the margins of respectable political punditry, his ongoing satirical assault on American politics over a period of thirty years constitutes a major journalistic achievement). The 1998 coverage of the Monica Lewinsky scandal, and in particular that of Matt Drudge – 'a new columnist on a new medium for columnists: the Internet'[7] – who first exposed it, may turn out to be the harbinger of a new and less deferential columnar approach in the United States (it is significant that Matt Drudge claims to have been inspired by the British journalistic tradition).[8] We can, however, accept Heffer's claim that the British tradition of political commentary is distinctively non-deferential and elite-critical: qualities which are, from the democratic perspective, eminently desirable and worth defending.

The analytical-advisory column

The commercial value of good attack journalism is well understood (such arch-polemicists as Richard Littlejohn and Julie Burchill have made fortunes out of little else), but the majority of political columnists prefer a more restrained rhetorical style, signalling their distinctiveness and individuality by intellectual, rather than polemical means. Hugo Young, for example, rather than ranting against 'perceived wisdom' in the manner of a Paul Johnson or an Andrew Roberts, prefers to identify and dissect the previously unexplored angle on a current issue on the political agenda, to run against the pack, above which the columnist soars as an elite sensemaker. A brief example from Young's output illustrates the technique. In mid-November 1996, when the news headlines were full of the Commons' Dunblane-fuelled vote on firearms restrictions and, in the broadsheets, a surprise £4 billion surplus in the country's finances, Young chose in his column to focus on the little-remarked (until then) fact that Labour and the Liberal Democrats were talking about collaboration in government. Even more remarkable, for Young, 'Tony Blair expects to lead, and nobody is screaming blue murder.'[9] From this rather arcane point (as it may have seemed to the casual reader) Young went on to explain, firstly, why the two parties (who had not collaborated so closely for a very long time) were talking (to save valuable post-election parliamentary time by eliminating unnecessary areas of competition); and, secondly, what this *meant* – that Labour were displaying growing maturity and 'fitness' for government; that the Liberal Democrats expected Labour to *be* the government. Through Young's lateral approach the reader learnt something new about the political scene, and a little of what Donald McIntyre of the *Independent* calls 'the real mystery' buried in the minutiae of non-newsworthy political detail.[10]

The satirical column

In their US-focused study of political pundits, Nimmo and Combs distinguish between 'priests' and 'bards'. The former are the insider-intellectuals like Hugo Young and Michael Jones, valued for their insightful analysis rather than their provocative polemic. Bards, on the other hand, are the 'court jesters' that 'ruling elites can tolerate' (1992, p. 67), the satirists of the journalistic profession, who inform about and interpret politics while at the same time debunking and subverting its practitioners. Prominent amongst the print media bards are the parliamentary sketch-writers: Westminster-based correspondents like Matthew Parris, Simon Hoggart and Andrew Rawnsley, heirs to the dying (at least in print) tradition of 'straight' parliamentary reportage who go far beyond objective reportage through the liberal use of satire, irony and humour. In an era when broadcast news can report the facts with much greater speed and immediacy, this is what they *must* do to retain their distinctive places in the information market. They are in every sense of the term 'infotainers', reviewing politics as performance rather than content, although their columns have of course to do more than just entertain. They must maintain a tenable relationship with the 'truth'. As one practitioner puts it,

> You want a readership amongst your peer group, amongst politicians, which means you actually have to touch on a few truths. You can't go completely off on a tangent.

And since parliamentary sketch-writers are of necessity regular spectators of political performance in Westminster, they frequently observe and are able to report significant developments in advance of the straight lobby correspondents. Says Andrew Rawnsley:

The sketch writers during the Thatcher period cottoned on to the fact that Geoffrey Howe was getting more and more pissed off with Thatcher earlier than the conventional Lobby simply because we watched his face when she made a speech and we could tell how deeply disillusioned he was getting. We were onto the fact that he was heading for an early resignation.

The culture of interpretation and information overload

The heightened competitiveness of the British newspaper market since the mid-1980s has led to a sharp increase in the number of columnists employed. Most of these are in non-political areas of coverage such as 'lifestyle' (a fact frequently cited in support of the dumbing-down thesis), but the number of political columnists has also increased. In the single month of November 1996, amongst the nineteen national UK media sampled for this study, there were more than fifty dedicated political columnists employed, and more than 600 political columns printed (in addition to the many thousands of non-political ones). And of course, many other columnists touch on politics as part of a wider brief to comment on any aspect of social and public life which they see as important.

The emergence of a journalistic marketplace for the supply of interpretation reflects increased demand, and the rise of commentary as a form in the twentieth century reflects the expansion of affluent consumerism on which that demand is premissed. It implies the availability of leisure time to read and, in the specific category of political commentary, background knowledge and awareness of the contentious nature of most political affairs. All of this is clearly for the good, if it reflects the growing material and intellectual affluence of the average citizen. But the rise of the political columnist is not just a matter of competitive pressures and the formation of a lucrative market in opinion. The development of media technology in the twentieth century, up to and including the construction of the internet, has made more important the insight and interpretation provided by columnists in the public sphere. Contrary to the apocalyptic predictions of some cultural pessimists, it is clear that for print journalism in general, and columnists in particular, the proliferation of electronic media in the past forty to fifty years has created a new and enhanced communicative function for newspapers and periodicals. Jo Bardoel is among those who have pointed out that in the era of 'information overload', 'real time news' and 'breaking stories', the print media become more than ever a necessary space for the reflection and leisurely consideration of events that cannot be provided by the fiercely time-limited, immediacy- and liveness-obsessed broadcast news media. Columnists in this environment have become, to a greater extent than ever before, essential 'gatekeepers and wellheads, discussion leaders on politics and public policy questions' (1996, p. 285). Elsewhere I have argued that journalistic communication is increasingly 'chaotic' in its structure and effects (McNair, 1998b). The political column is the main space in our crowded and hyperactive media environment where the chaos can be given some order; where the citizen can draw breath and let herself by guided around and through an issue. This assumes the credibility and authority of the columnist, of course, whom we must *trust* to do the guiding, despite or because of his opinions.

Mobilising trust

For political columnists, trust is a function not only of intellectual prowess, or the conventional data-processing skills of the reporter, but of the journalist's 'insider' status – the degree to which she has access to elite political sources willing to divulge privileged information. From this, the columnist constructs an account of 'the "inside" of public matters; not what is secret, but what is latent, the kernel of principle and other significance that exists, recognised or not, "inside" events, policies and manners' (George Will quoted in Silvester, 1997, p. xvi). Constructing credible insider status is probably the most essential skill required of the political columnist, and is usually emphasised in the self-promotion in which most columnists (who are rarely as credible as they would like to be, otherwise they would hardly need to advertise it to their own readers) engage. The *Mail On Sunday*'s Peter Oborne heads his column with the rubric 'Inside Politics', signifying to the reader that here is a journalist who can penetrate the sub-surface levels of the political process, and can reveal them to us as readers. Columnists thus draw attention to their privileged access, and the secrets which, between them, us, and a million other readers, they can divulge. Andrew Rawnsley of the *Observer* typifies this legitimising tactic when he gives his readers the following nugget of privileged information:

> It is easier to agree with the Cabinet Minister who assures me that there is only a remote chance of the Government facing and losing a vote [of confidence] before Christmas.[11]

Michael Jones of the *Sunday Times* shares a confidence with his readers (prior to the Tories' ejection from office in 1997):

> Major, I am told, is preparing to bolster his position ... Major, I am told, will put everything he has into the fight against Blair.[12]

Told by whom? By sources in a position to know, is the unspoken assumption which Jones requires his readers to share. His authority as a columnist depends on our acceptance of his (unstated) claim that he has regular and privileged access to such sources, from whom the essential truth, rather than the surface appearance of things, can be extracted.

The independence of the pundit

Trust and authority in the eyes of the audience also requires independence from elites, and the readiness not to be used as a propagandist, intentionally or otherwise. As *Guardian* columnist Hugo Young puts it:

> Political journalists owe it to their readers to keep open the richest store-house of cynicism. It's our duty, as we say: and sometimes, as we don't say, our pleasure. You should never be left unapprised of the second-guessing, the triple sub-textual meaning, behind what you might otherwise be in danger of supposing is really going on. Not believing politicians is our stock-in-trade, and casting doubt on the bona fides of their words has been magnified, as a branch of the professional task, in direct proportion to the colonisation of our territory by the words-manipulators with whom they now surround themselves.[13]

The column from which this passage is extracted was written immediately after the successful negotiation of the Easter 1998 Northern Ireland peace agreement, welcomed by Young elsewhere in the column quoted above as a rare example of relatively unmanipulated, non-cynicism-inducing politics, the very exceptionality of which proved his point about the need for a distanced, distrusting journalism.

Spin and counter-spin

Young's words alert us to a third explanation for, and an important argument in the defence of, the rise of political commentary. Since the emergence of public relations at the turn of the twentieth century, journalists and their audiences have gradually become aware of the gap between appearance and reality in public affairs; that the former is in many cases a manufactured, somewhat less than truthful version of the latter. When Walter Lippmann wrote in the 1920s that democracy had 'turned a corner' (1954, p. 248) he was referring to the fact that politics would henceforth be about 'the manufacture of consent', assisted by a new professional caste of 'press agents'. Lippmann did not condemn the emergence of public relations which he witnessed taking place in the aftermath of WWI. Indeed, he welcomed it as an organisational convenience for the journalists. But he recognised the added responsibility this trend placed on the journalist's work of analysis, insight and interpretation. I quote him at length here because his words, though eight decades old, have an obvious continuing relevance to current debates.

> Were reporting the simple recovery of obvious facts, the press agent would be little more than a clerk. But since, in respect to most of the big topics of news, the facts are not simple, and not at all obvious, but subject to choice and opinion, it is natural that everyone should wish to make his own choice of facts for the newspapers to print. The publicity man does that. And in doing it, he certainly saves the reporter much trouble, by presenting him a clear picture of a situation out of which he might otherwise make neither head nor tail. But it follows that the picture which the publicity man makes for the reporter is the one he wishes the public to see. He is censor and propagandist, responsible only to his employers, and to the whole truth responsible only as it accords with the employer's conception of his own interests. The development of the publicity man is a clear sign that the facts of modern life do not spontaneously take a shape in which they can be known. They must be *given* a shape by somebody.
>
> (ibid., p. 314–15, my emphasis)

Those somebodies are the press agents on the one hand, and the political journalists on the other, well placed to burrow away 'inside public matters' on behalf of the public (where the press agent is employed by, thus tied to, private interests), peeling away the PR-honed gloss of public rhetoric.

The rise of the political commentator is, then, integrally connected with the rise of the political press agent or 'spin doctor' (and the century-long expansion of political public relations in general), and the need to 'counter-spin' – to deconstruct and critique the messages of the latter as they go about their work of shaping political reality. Both communicative activities are reverse sides of the same sense-making coin. And with the phenomenal rise of spin in the 1980s and 1990s (indeed, going back to the 1960s) the columnist's role in this respect has been greatly enhanced. If politics is increasingly about process and performance, then the pundits are our critics and reviewers, as well as sense-makers. We need them.

These three processes, then – the commercialisation of journalism; the information overload associated with the revolution in communications technology of the last century and a half; and the emergence of political public relations as a science of news management – explain the proliferation of political commentary in the late twentieth century. They also define the essential characteristics of the political column as journalistic form: a distinctive public voice (embodying authority and mobilising trust); sellable to the audience of the newspaper or periodical in which it appears; able to penetrate the relentless flow of new information into the public sphere, giving insight and meaning to the events which it addresses; aware of the process of political rhetoric-making, and its own role in that process.

'Here's someone who can sort it all out for us': the broadcast pundits

As both the most commercialised political medium, and the one in which opinion has long had a prominent place, interpretative journalism in Britain is traditionally associated with the press. Newspapers and periodicals have the additional advantage, from the point of view of making sense of events, that they are not 'flow' media. On the contrary, they 'freeze' politics by transferring it to the printed page, where it can be read at leisure, put aside, re-read, clipped and copied, stored for analysis and remembered. But broadcasting too, as it developed after WWII, has found increasing value in the work of commentary and analysis. Like their print colleagues, the broadcasters, in an information-rich multi-channel media environment such as the one we now inhabit, find an enhanced need to function as sifters and sorters of the data constantly flowing into their newsrooms. This trend is reinforced by the fact that broadcasting has become steadily more commercialised, steadily more like print in its institutional and economic organisation. From the beginning of British competitive broadcasting with the establishment of the ITV network in the 1950s, to the current environment of five terrestrial TV networks, two twenty-four-hour TV news channels, and two speech-based radio channels, the importance of branding has steadily grown. The personality of the broadcast journalist (as presenter, reporter, interviewer or 'specialist' correspondent) has become what one political editor in TV news describes as

> an independent brand factor, irrespective of where the pictures come from or what the truth of the access was.

As with the press columnist, the authority of a broadcaster's political commentary – the level of trust and credibility which it inspires in the audience – is an important element of branding. Unlike the press, however, broadcast commentary must operate within the specific constraints of British broadcasting. It must be presented within a structuring framework not merely of objectivity, but impartiality, as laid down in the rules and guidelines adhered to by all UK-based broadcast news organisations. Even Sky News, despite its status as subsidiary to the otherwise fiercely ideological News Corporation, chooses to compete as a near-impartial news broadcaster against the public service BBC and ITN, since any other approach would risk undermining its reputation and effectiveness as a journalistic organisation, whether or not its cable and satellite subscribers noticed the difference. As was noted in Chapter 2, Sky News has been for Rupert Murdoch a means of gaining entry to the British TV news market and he is probably right in believing that it must, like any other product, conform to the prevailing standards of its chosen market if it is to succeed there. BBC, ITN and Sky News, therefore, to the extent that they broadcast interpretative political journalism, must do so without being seen (or heard) to be taking sides as between parties; whether within individual programmes or in the channel's output as a whole. If impartiality is not perceived to be present, particularly in the case of the more established BBC and ITN, trust is eroded and relationships between politicians and the media quickly deteriorate. Reconciling these elements – the audience's cognitive need for, and thus the market's valuing of, interpretation and commentary on the one hand, and the need to avoid the perception of partiality on the other – has resulted, as we shall see, in the development of interpretative techniques which strike a sometimes uneasy balance between the objective and the subjective.

A second constraint for broadcast commentary is the time frame within which it must operate. Print columnists can foresee the path of political events and analyse them with the benefit of some hindsight (even if it is only a few hours). They can do research and sound out lines of argument before committing their interpretations to print. Broadcasters, on the other hand, are usually live and immediate. Not only that, they are often 'rolling', servicing twenty-four channels like Sky and CNN or, in the case of a typical BBC political correspondent in the era of bi-media, supplying a variety of TV and radio bulletins throughout the day with news and commentary which must be both up-to-the-minute and authoritative. There is little time, in short, for reflection on, or analysis of the meaning of events before the journalist must deliver an opinion. 'A lot of what I do', says one broadcast political editor, 'is fundamentally instant analysis.' An obvious tension is set up by this constraint – to be authoritative and definitive; and to be so right *now*.[14]

The 'stars' of broadcast commentary – those with the greatest licence and authority – are the political editors of the TV news organisations. At the time of writing, these were Robin Oakley of the BBC; Michael Brunson of ITN's ITV news operation; Elinor Goodman of *Channel 4 News*; and Adam Boulton (Sky News). These are the top TV pundits – whom the prime minister's press secretary has described as 'the contextualising voices'[15] of British political journalism (he also included in this category the BBC's chief political correspondent John Sergeant). It would be more accurate to say that they are the most senior and influential of a growing cohort of 'contextualising voices' – those whose experience and abilities give them the most access, on the most favourable terms, to the most powerful politicians in the British system. From this exalted position they go beyond the reportage of politics into the realm of interpretation. Adam Boulton describes himself as

> being like a sports commentator, in as much as I assess the strengths and strategies that they are using, and try to reflect that in what I am covering ... I see myself as someone who is using a set of analytical skills and a range of knowledge to try to distill what is going on at Westminster or within the government. I tell my audience what the government is doing, why the government is doing it, and then, on the available information and context I can give to it, whether it is likely to be successful and what the impact of that will be.

Michael Brunson describes his interpretative work as 'a cross between a judge's summing up and a theatre review. As things have got more and more complicated on the political scene, people seem to appreciate that, at the end of the day, someone just pulls it all together and pulls out the main themes'. The BBC's political editor agrees that 'contextuality' is the defining characteristic of his work. The broadcast political editor's work is not, however, to impose, column-like, a *personal* opinion on the substance of the events of a political news day (i.e., the policy issues), since this would contravene the rules of impartiality. Rather, he is a mediator, using his journalistic and insider-resources to assemble, often at very short notice, an authoritative assessment of a situation. As the Sky News anchor says of Adam Boulton, introducing the political editor's analysis of a just-delivered Budget speech, 'here's someone who can sort it all out for us'. The context provided by these 'contextualising voices', then, is not a property which originates with the journalist directly, but from his objective, privileged viewpoint as a reporter, in respect of the politicians. As Robin Oakley puts it:

> It is not my role to give a judgment on the intrinsic merits of something specific the government or opposition is trying to do. That's where the impartiality and the statutory duties of a public service broadcaster come in.

The constraints imposed by the requirement of impartiality, set against the journalistic compulsion to interpret and comment, are, ironically, one of the main sets of factors leading to the broadcasters' emphasis on *process* rather than *policy*. Where the interpretation of policy leaves broadcasters vulnerable to accusations of journalistic bias, judgements on the process of political competition – the 'horse race' – take place at a distance from policy *per se*, and thus more easily avoid such charges. For this reason, obsession with the 'insider game' is principally that of the broadcasters.

Print pundits, free of the impartiality constraint, have much greater scope to evaluate policy substance. The evaluative components of the broadcasters' political journalism have to avoid judgements on policy, focusing instead on the processes of policy formulation, presentation and governmental decision-making. The broadcast pundit's interpretation is principally of *other*'s views and actions, not his or her own, and is constructed by:

> talking, talking, talking. You spend your whole day, when not putting things together, talking to people, trying to get a fair assessment, down in the lobby, down in the corridors, wherever one can. That's the way you get the sensitive information.

Sensitive information, authoritatively interpreted, is usually communicated to the audience by means of a live interview between presenter and correspondent, in which the latter is clearly signalled as the expert, whose judgements on the events under discussion are not to be challenged. A similar respect is extended to the opinion of specialist correspondents, whose role as sense-makers of events beyond the ken of the audience is analogous to that of the political editor, and will often overlap. The BBC's Northern Ireland correspondent, for example, functions in the great majority of contexts as a political correspondent *and* a pundit, interpreting for the UK audience as a whole the labyrinthine manoeuvrings and heavily coded statements of the participants in Northern Irish politics. The aim of this presentational approach is to extract the value (for audiences and, in the case of commercial organisations, advertisers) of authoritative opinion, and to mobilise trust, while maintaining the separation of fact and opinion (which all objective journalism must be seen to do) within the structure of the item. The legitimacy of the political editor's or specialist correspondent's opinions are located in their identification as experts, reinforced – as with print pundits – by verbal articulations of 'insiderness'. At the same time, their opinions and judgements are presentationally fenced off from the anchor's rigorously maintained neutrality, still the heuristic bedrock of the broadcast news genre in Britain.

There is, however, thanks to the proliferation of broadcast channels and the heightened commercialisation which that brings with it, growing space for less studiedly impartial variations of the 'interpretative moment' in British political broadcasting. Occasional broadcast documentaries by Michael Cockerell and Peter Taylor, and by recognised authors from the world of print journalism such as John Pilger, Andrew Rawnsley and Matthew Parris, function as the televisual equivalent of feature articles in the press. On radio, too, some analytical programme strands – *Analysis*, for example – are authorised to go beyond reportage and into interpretation and even commentary. These forms of authored journalism are made more acceptable to the audiences of public service broadcasting by the late twentieth century's loss of epistemic innocence and declining faith in the possibility of impartiality or objectivity. While adherence to these standards remains an important legitimising strategy in mainstream broadcast news (and the requirement to achieve them a useful mechanism of quality control), some relaxation of the impartiality guidelines is now permitted in contexts where authorship is clearly signalled (the opinions expressed are unambiguously those of their writers or producers), with the broadcasters acting as commissioning publishers. As the number of broadcast outlets has increased, authoritative opinion takes on added brand value, and the dominance of 'tit-for-tat' impartiality is eroded, at least in places.

Channel Four's *A Week in Politics*, for example, presented by Andrew Rawnsley and the late Vincent Hanna, was an early attempt to translate the satirical sketch-writing tradition of print to television, within a constraining framework of broad impartiality as *between* parties. According to Rawnsley, 'we never editorialised in a party political way, but we weren't afraid to take a view on a particular episode of things going right or wrong for a government'. As is the case with non-journalistic satire (Rory Bremner's political impersonations in the 1990s; the *Spitting Image* puppets of the 1980s), *A Week In Politics* could not be seen to demonstrate favouritism towards a particular party, but could show irreverence and disrespect towards the profession of politics in general. Sky News, with its looser adherence to the public service guidelines of the BBC and ITN, has taken a more overtly evaluative, even partisan approach in some of its programmes (for example, when it allowed Labour MP Austin Mitchell and Tory Norman Tebbitt to co-present a political chat show), though not at the expense of its wider reputation for PSB-type impartiality and proprietorial independence.

As the time and space available for broadcast journalism steadily increases, and the commercial value of authoritative but opinionated punditry with it, the twenty-first century will see the further growth of authorial political commentary on TV and radio. The unashamedly biased and confrontational style of the *No Prisoners Taken* strand on Talk Radio (see Chapter 2), with its proud boast that 'you won't like our programme if your idea of balance is a standard-issue BBC liberal presenter trying (and failing) to be impartial'[16] may never be the 'norm' for British public service broadcasting, but it will certainly become more common in the years ahead.

Criticising the commentators

The 'explosion' of the commentary industry – in journalism generally, and political journalism in particular – is often implicated in the 'crisis' of public communication. Three criticisms are advanced. Firstly, that columnists and other commentators are largely responsible for what one observer has called the 'intentionalist fallacy'[17] – an excess of journalistic focus on the motivations of political actors, rather than what they actually have to say in policy terms. This is another version of the policy versus process debate discussed in the previous chapter. To repeat what was argued there: the dichotomy is a false one in so much as there can, in today's political environment, be no meaningful analysis of policy *without* analysis of the process of policy design and presentation. Commentators can hardly be expected not to comment on politics as it is lived in our time and our culture, and to the extent that their columns, sketches, feature articles, documentaries and expert inputs to news programmes are interpretations of 'the game', that is an intelligible response to the promotional, scientifically communicated nature of contemporary political activity. The significant criterion of worth here is not the subject matter of commentary, which is largely determined by events originating in the political sphere and thus outwith the journalists' control, but the quality of the judgements offered, on whatever subject is addressed.

If that point is accepted, a second criticism is more serious, as well as being empirically sustainable. It is that the expansion of political commentary has not been matched by the extra resources to give it analytical depth, nor the emergence of enough sufficiently authoritative journalists. The result is an 'expert journalism' which is frequently less than expert. If the struggle for primary definition of political events (one function of pundits) is a competitive process, it is also one in the pursuit of which media organisations are willing to cut resource corners.

The charge is made particularly against television. Roy Greenslade cites an example where two BBC correspondents – Robin Oakley and Jon Sopel – gave contradictory interpretations on the same bulletin of the same political event, both supposedly authoritative. He also cites the case of a BBC2 *Westminster Live* reporter being too proactive in offering 'his idiosyncratic interpretation of events rather than a straight report of who said what'.[18] It is not the interpretative function of journalism which Greenslade objects to here, but the fact that too much commentary is presented by inexperienced, unauthoritative journalists: 'why should the BBC allow so many youthful reporters to offer their views, and [often] inaccurate analysis on serious political matters?' asks Greenslade.

> The problem is that everyone now wants to be seen as an expert on spin. They delight in deconstructing the supposed meaning and implied sub-text underlying the presumed tactics of every political event and speech. It's great fun, showing off one's expertise, but hardly informative for the public. Perhaps the BBC ought to ask itself: how has the serious mission to explain degenerated into a trivial game to distort?

Roy Greenslade is himself an interpretative journalist – a pundit – whose former employment as a tabloid editor is the principal foundation of his current status as an authority on the media. With due respect to that status, there is little evidence, apart from a few isolated examples, that the BBC's journalists, or those of any other broadcast news organisation in Britain, are routinely engaged in 'trivial games' of the type alleged. What they are, by their own admission, is overstretched and spread too thin. Robin Oakley concedes that there is tension between, on the one hand, the organisational demand for his *authoritative opinion* about what is really going on and, on the other, his ability to form that opinion.

> Where it becomes a problem is that the multiplicity of outlets these days means that, first of all, anybody in a job like mine is facing a constant dilemma between the amount of time he spends newsgathering, talking to MPs in the Members' lobby, and the amount of time he is forced to spend in TV and radio studios, explaining what is going on. Because you can't perform the latter task if you are spending too much time on air. I can find myself doing as many as a dozen live interviews in the course of the day on different radio and television programmes.

The ever-increasing demand for authoritative on-air opinion conflicts with the routine, off-air work of forming it.

Greenslade is right, however, in suggesting that the demand for on-screen authority as a means of competing with other news organisations has tended to produce an overly ritualised, fetishistic form of commentary in which, as he observes, sometimes inexperienced and under-informed reporters are required by their editors (or by demanding presenters) to 'define reality' in ways which later turn out to be at best, highly speculative and at worst, inaccurate and misleading. Expert punditry is increasingly signified to the audience by such artificial means as Reporter Involvement, an editorial policy applied by ITN at the time of writing whereby a correspondent's voice and face is cut into a scene of, for example, the US President answering questions at a pooled news conference. Even if the President has not answered the ITN's reporter's questions directly, or has not addressed him face to face, the viewer *thinks* that he has.

The fetishisation of authority is one of the main ways in which competitive pressures, and the now uniform editorial assumption that journalistic authority is a commercial asset to a news broadcaster, can be said to have weakened the quality of information available in the public sphere. The mere assertion of authority, unsupported by sufficiently accurate or well-informed analysis and interpretation, is a market-driven phenomenon, likely to become more widespread as broadcast news channels continue to proliferate. On the other hand, the sophisticated consumers of the contemporary media environment cannot be expected to ignore those failings. The same process which has made 'authority' such a powerful legitimising device has provided audiences with the viewing and listening skills to recognise when it is absent. There is a commercial incentive, in other words, for broadcast news managers to encourage and support the maintenance of *real* authority (as opposed to the appearance of it) amongst their political correspondents and commentators if they wish to retain their reputations and audience share.

Fifth estate: the excessive power of the pundits

A third criticism of the commentary industry is perhaps the most serious of all – namely, that columnists, leader writers, political editors and specialist correspondents comprise a journalistic elite which has become too powerful, and whose members are usurping the democratically mandated authority of the politicians with their own self-appointed authority. In the United States, argue Nimmo and Combs, pundits 'now constitute a source of opinion-formation and opinion-articulation, agenda-setting and agenda-evaluation, so vast as to make the United States a punditocracy' (1992, p. 8). Punditry, these authors declare, 'now constitutes a fifth estate alongside Montesquieu's three and Burke's fourth. Punditry is a knowledge industry that has grown into a political force' (ibid., p. 20). For these authors the journalist-pundits are at the core of the 'priestly establishment', continuing a long tradition of pundit-bashing which dates back at least as far as Alexander Mackendrick's *The Sweet Smell of Success* (1953). In that film, which is also a biting satire on the journalist–public relations relationship, press agent Sydney Falco remarks of star columnist J.J. Hunsecker, 'He's told Presidents where to go and what to do.' A pivotal scene in the movie depicts Hunsecker sadistically demonstrating his power over an aspiring senator, for whom he has the potential to be a valuable friend or a lethal enemy. The American columnist, as early as the 1950s, was in a position (Mackendrick's film suggests) to make or break political careers, a fact which led Richard Nixon's speech-writer, William Safire (himself a leading columnist) to famously describe pundits as 'those nattering nabobs of negativism'.[19]

In Britain, however, there are no J.J. Hunseckers. American columnists achieved their special power as a consequence of the fact that in the USA, unlike Britain, there was never a 'national' press, but rather a collection of regional and city presses. Columnists, through syndication of their articles to hundreds of newspapers across the territory of the USA (and abroad) provided the closest America came to a national journalism in the print sector. Their heightened influence reflected the fact that in a huge and diverse country, their opinions and interpretations of events comprised a rare and thus particularly valuable form of common culture. In Britain, by contrast, there has always been a variety of national newspapers, each with its own staff of political columnists. British columnists do not have the same elevated status, therefore, as their American counterparts, and enjoy neither their salaries nor their influence. That said, within the British journalistic profession of some 50,000 individuals, the political columnists of the national media are undoubtedly an elite. Tunstall observes that 'the fifteen or twenty leading lobby journalists are clearly significant players in the national political game' (1996, p. 258). About fifteen 'upmarket' print columnists comprise Britain's 'leading political commentators' (ibid., p. 281) who, in the view of some observers, wield excessive power. For the prime minister's press secretary, as was noted above, a mere five broadcast political editors comprise 'the contextualising voices' of Britain's mediated democracy.

For some observers, the existence of a punditocracy presents a threat to the democratic process. The editors of the *New Statesman*, for example, writing in 1994, observed that:

> There are, at most, a hundred or so journalists who fix the prevailing 'consensus' – who determine what views get expressed in print ... Editors, columnists, political editors, a handful of especially respected lobby correspondents, the occasional old-hand independent operator – they were all selected in the first place to be in sympathy with their proprietors' political ethos and they will not have departed from it since. They speak with one voice because, by and large, they are *of* one voice.
>
> Almost entirely London and lobby-based, limited in their social and professional circles ... their opinions are those of a self-reinforcing oligarchy. They test their opinions against the opinions of their peers – other journalists, with the same restricted world-view as themselves – seeking confirmation and approval within those same narrow circles. They run – and hunt – with the pack.
>
> For contact with the outside world they have opinion polls – polls which act only as a mirror, telling the pundits what they have just told their readers.[20]

Political pundits comprise, in short, 'an unelected and unrepresentative elite'. That they are unelected and unrepresentative of their publics is not in doubt, although it does not necessarily follow that their worldviews are as restricted or incestuous as the above criticism implies. Some of the country's leading columnists, such as Hugo Young, are not even members of the lobby, while others (such as the *Independent*'s former political correspondent Anthony Bevins) make much of their independence from the insider network which, they freely admit, can be an encouragement to lazy, pack journalism. And elitist or not, given the nature of British politics as presently constituted, and the logistical realities of our London-based political and media systems, it is hard to imagine what else they might be. Pundits are *by definition* an elite group, as the nature of their work and the mode of its operation demands. We would hardly trust them to be gatekeepers, organisers and intepreters of our political environment were they unable to demonstrate particular skills which the average journalist, let alone the average citizen, did not possess.

The existence of a London-based journalistic elite should also be set against the fact that Britain has strong regional media, which maintain their own pundits dealing with Scottish, Welsh and Northern Irish issues for the audiences whom they serve. I, as a Scotsman, can read the *Scotsman*, the *Herald*, *Scotland On Sunday* or the *Sunday Herald* (to name but four broadsheets sustained by the Scottish market), all of which support extensive Westminster coverage, inflected by the Scottish perspective. Given the existence of strong local media, it is less reprehensible that the London-based pundits of the UK-wide media, addressing UK audiences, are focused on the activities of Westminster government.

The coming years may see changes in the composition and approach of the elite corps of political journalists as power leaks away from London to the new assemblies of Scotland, Northern Ireland and Wales on the one hand, and the European parliament on the other. The London-based pundits interviewed for this study accepted that their coverage of Scottish and Welsh devolution – processes of immense constitutional significance for England as much as Scotland and Wales – has been perfunctory at best. This is a weakness in the public sphere which does not concern the publics of Scotland and Wales, who have their own media focused on the devolution issues, so much as the English, who have an interest in knowing more about the doings and devolvings of their provincial co-citizens than the UK media have traditionally told them.

A similar argument applies to the European issue. Despite its being a major cause of the Tories' 1997 defeat (because it split the party visibly and irreconcilably), even those who wish to know more about the issues find it difficult to acquire quality commentary and interpretation in their mainstream media of choice. As European monetary union approaches (and not withstanding the mass resignation of the European Commission in March 1999 – perhaps the first European political story to be treated as a headlining event by the British press), this continues to be a structural weakness of national British journalism which will have to be repaired, as part of a wider shift in focus away from Westminster, if a healthy Euro-democracy is to be constructed and sustained in the twenty-first century.

We also have the right to expect that recruitment to the British punditocracy should not so obviously favour, as it has traditionally done, public school, Oxbridge-educated white boys. There is still a class bias in political communication (as there is in the higher reaches of the media industries generally), although it is gradually being eroded by more meritocratic structures and career paths. When an anti-establishment, bi-sexual Stalinist with Zionist sympathies like Julie Burchill can become a star columnist for the *Daily Mail*, and a lower-middle-class wide-boy like Richard Littlejohn one of the country's most feared pundits, it is possible to harbour some optimism for the future of the interpretative elite within the journalistic profession.

Pundits have also been markedly unrepresentative in their gender composition, even by the standards of the still male-dominated media. Of the approximately fifty dedicated political columnists working in the national print media during the research phase of this study, only three were women. Of five broadcast political editors, only one was a woman. The gender bias of journalism is steadily declining, however, and recent evidence gathered by the Women In Journalism group suggests that over time it will be eroded further.[21]

Conclusion

The recent expansion in the proportion of print and broadcast journalism given over to political commentary, as opposed to straightforward reportage, is identified by some critics as one manifestation of the decline of political journalism in Britain. This chapter has challenged that interpretation, arguing instead that – with the qualifications outlined above – the 'columnary explosion' (and its broadcast equivalent – the proliferation of pundits and specialist correspondents) is an intelligible journalistic adaptation to an environment which is highly competitive, information-rich and intensively manipulated by political actors. We *need* the interpretative moment in journalism, I have suggested, because the world is too complex, its information flows too rapid, for us to make sense of on our own. With the expansion of the public sphere described above, interpretation has become an even more crucial element of the journalistic function, and nowhere more so than in coverage of political affairs.

Since the need is there, a commentary industry has grown up to service it, in both print and electronic media. In the former, interpretative journalism is heavily laced with partisan opinion and more or less overt ideological propagandising on all aspects of politics. In broadcasting (public service broadcasting, that is), where partisanship is ruled out by convention and law, interpretation is concentrated on the political *process*. Process has become even more important, for both print and broadcast media, because it often involves attempts by politicians to shape and influence journalistic representations of their work. In response to the 'spin' of the spin doctors, journalists have evolved a form of 'spin' of their own. This may be viewed as a negative trend associated with dumbing down or, as I have suggested here, a proper response to the professionalisation of news management.

Without doubt, much of what even the best and most authoritative commentators say and write about politics is baseless speculation, and would not bear revisiting a week, let alone a year later. Nevertheless, in a world of spin and intensified news management, political commentary is the best counter-spin we have. When politics is increasingly a series of performances, we need reviewers. In a world of constantly accelerating information flow, commentary is the 'gatekeeper and wellhead', the essential sense-maker in the virtual Tower of Babel. We need our pundits, and circulation trends suggest we certainly want them, in all their stylistic diversity. Just as long as we are not seduced, awed or intimidated into thinking that they really know as much as they want us to think they know.

5

THE INTERROGATIVE
MOMENT

The British political interview

Situated somewhere in a typology of political journalism between news (although it may often become news) and the 'summing up' stage of interpretation and commentary, is the interview – the public interrogation, in the media, of political actors by journalists. The interview is a key moment in the political news cycle, and the main context in which the journalistic tasks associated with critical publicity and representation of the public can be directly applied to politicians in the media.

In representing the public before politicians the interviewer is required to be an authoritative figure: a licensed interrogator of the powerful, trusted by the audience and respected by the politician. Like the columnist or political editor of the previous chapter, the interviewer's journalistic role goes beyond that of reportage to one of commentary, interpretation and intervention. These are realised not through what the journalist-interviewer writes or says directly about the issues under discussion, however, but in how she positions her subjects to speak, or not to speak about them. In this respect the interviewer's role is like that of a courtroom lawyer questioning a witness. The interview is the *adversarial* moment in the public sphere. After new facts have become available, and the battle for interpretation has begun, the interview is the point at which those who are the subject of the news can attempt to clarify, contradict or add to the facts as reported. In negotiating these efforts the interviewer enjoys something approaching the privileged status of the pundit. And like the pundit, the interviewer must acquire credibility in the eyes of the audience; an authority which legitimises and makes possible the journalistic challenge to those who, as actual or aspiring political leaders, we might also wish to afford some respect. Like the pundit too, the successful political interviewer is a key element in the branding of the organisation for which she works. Her approach must be distinctive in a crowded marketplace of functionally similar interviewing 'brands'.

The drive for interrogative authority and distinctiveness has fuelled an inquisitorial 'arms race' between interviewer and interviewee; an ongoing evolution of interviewing style which, for reasons explored below, has become steadily less deferential and more adversarial – 'hyperadversarial', as James Fallows (1996) puts it. In the process, the performance of the interviewer's role has become a site of particular controversy in current debates about political journalism. Critics ask if the interview form has become excessively gladiatorial and entertainment oriented; if the extraction of rational information is being sacrificed to the spectacle of the journalist–politician contest. Has the interviewer become more important than the interviewed, the dramatic form of the adversarial contest more important than the content which it is supposed to reveal?

Answering 'yes' to these questions are those like Stewart Stevens of the *Mail On Sunday* who, in the dying months of the Major government penned a column deprecating 'the BBC bullyboys' who had 'shed all professional standards as they turn politics into just another branch of the entertainment industry'.[1] Ferdinand Mount argued to the contrary, but with equal distaste for the form, that broadcast political interviews are boring, and that 'television interviewers are not only rude, but also conceited, underbriefed and woefully deficient in historical grasp or intellectual curiosity'[2].

[For its critics, then, the modern political interview is an exemplary illustration of how the pressures of competition and its accompanying commercialisation have overwhelmed the normative tasks of the journalist in a democracy. Interviewers in recent years are alleged to have adopted a stance towards their subjects which is not only inappropriately non-deferential and critical, but hostile and aggressive – the pursuit of confrontation for the sake of market position rather than the exposition of political affairs.] Hyperadversarialism, when taken to extremes, is said to be replacing the interrogation of political actors in the public interest with the entertaining but information-poor spectacle of confrontation, to the detriment of citizens and of the democratic process itself. Andrew Marr complains that the trends listed above have 'encouraged the evolution of a complex ritual of attack and defence' in political interviewing, and that 'the listener hears a false conversation, a sterile unexchange in which the purpose of language – communication – is subverted'.[3] This chapter traces the formal and stylistic development of the political interview, and assesses its contribution to the contemporary public sphere in the light of these arguments.

A typology of the political interview

We might usefully begin by distinguishing between the three basic types of political interview routinely featured in the British media, since they play very different roles in the political process.

The news interview (short form)

The *short-form news interview*, firstly, is usually obtained from a political source as an input to a broadcast or print news story. The story will be illustrated by a quote from the source, acquired during an interview, and driven by the nature of the story itself. Such interviews tend thus to be very brief (seconds rather than minutes), event-led and reactive, often conducted informally as politicians go into or out of buildings and cars, microphones thrust in their faces to capture the quote which will, according to the conventions of journalistic objectivity, validate a point the journalist has made in his piece. New information, or confirmation of previously reported information, is the principal objective of these interviews, although the fact of obtaining a quote, or of its being denied, may be just as newsworthy as the content of what was said.

The news interview (long-form)

The *long-form news interview* is also event-led, but differs from the short-form variant in that the interviewee has usually accepted an invitation to be interviewed, and both sides have the opportunity to prepare themselves for the exchange. The form is restricted to broadcast journalism, since newspapers by their nature do not conduct live interviews. Being longer in duration, this form of interview is not a routine feature of peak-time news bulletins, and is found mainly in the in-depth, minority audience programmes such as *Channel 4 News*, *Today*, *The World At One* and *Newsnight*, where it may vary in length from three to five minutes. Still news-driven, the interviewee's role is usually one of reacting to an event, although interest at this point in the news cycle is more likely to be focused on the issues which the event raises, and the debates which it has generated. The function of such interviews is not primarily to establish facts – although one aim may be to clarify or add to information already in the public domain – but to explore the implications of the facts which will have earlier made the news. An interviewee's access to both short and long-form news interviews is premised on involvement in the story as a government representative or opposition spokesperson, or as someone known to have a special interest or expertise in the subject of the news story.

In a variation known to practitioners as a 'disco', two individuals will be interviewed, one taking the role of accusor to the other's defendant, with the presenter acting as chairperson. The presenter is not necessarily impartial, however, in so far as her role is that of representing the public (or some public body), present in the news studio, against the political establishment (and its particular manifestation in the person of the interviewee). Questioning of a government minister, for example, will tend to be more rigorous and demanding than that of the 'opposing' interviewee, whose side will often be taken by the presenter, regardless of who is right or wrong (although the presence of the 'accuser' in the studio will be premissed on the editorial judgement that she has a measure of credibility). In this context, as in that of the one-on-one interview, the journalist sees herself as defending the public, speaking up for and representing them in her questioning of the powerful. In the words of John Humphrys, a leading British exponent of the art, 'interviewing politicians [is] an important bridge between the electorate and their political leaders. We have to try to distill the national argument, to represent the voters' concerns.'[4]

A distinctive feature of the *Newsnight* strand is the four- or even five-way 'disco', in which the principal elite interviewee is confronted not just with the journalist's questions, but with a range of opposing views. The opposition will also be subject to interrogation by the presenter, but rarely with as much persistence and rigour as experienced by the 'defendant'. When two politicians from different parties are interviewed together, the impartiality of the chair is more narrowly interpreted. If impartiality in public service journalism can be consistent with the journalist's taking the public's side, in cross-party debate/interview items, neutrality between the opposing sides must be seen to be maintained, such as in the application of equally hostile interviewing styles (see below).

The set-piece

The third type of political interview is the *set-piece*, in which senior politicians are interrogated at length, normally by senior journalists who have developed a reputation as authoritative political actors in their own right, and the exchange is as much an event as the news story which may have prompted it. A broadcast variant of the set-piece is the sofa interview, conducted in a studio made up to resemble a living room, or a comparably informal, relaxed environment. Set-pieces of this type may range across a variety of topics on which the interviewee is qualified to speak, or they may focus, forensically and at length, on a single subject. Both print and broadcast media run such interviews with politicians, although the former are subject to processes of editing and pre-interview negotiation which must distinguish them from the often live, relatively unedited broadcast form.

A set-piece interview is an opportunity for political actors to advance or resolve a current news story which is judged sufficiently serious to require a senior intervention. It may be approached as an opportunity for a politician to elaborate a vision and policy agenda more generally. During election campaigns they also act as promotional opportunities for the politician to address the electorate. Unlike party political broadcasts, which the audience knows to be propaganda, the set-piece interview is a rare moment when the politician comes 'naked' into the public sphere, vulnerable and exposed. In a political process which has traditionally excluded the American form of the live candidates' debate, the election set-piece is the opportunity for a surrogate form of face-to-face communication between politician and public, and can be a promotional triumph or a disaster, depending on the interviewee's performance skills. Readiness to be interviewed in this way is now viewed as a basic element of the modern British politician's democratic accountability and 'fitness to govern'.

The evolution of the political interview

The questioning of politicians has been a feature of political journalism since the mid-nineteenth century, when newspapers first began to feature interviews with public figures. American President Martin Van Buren was interviewed by the *New York Herald* in 1839, and Mormon leader Brigham Young in 1859.[5] By the late 1800s in the US 'the interview was so well established that in New York a political figure's refusal to be inter-viewed could become a news item in itself' (Schudson, 1995, p. 48). The form was imported to the United Kingdom in the 1880s where it was denounced, in terms which anticipate the contemporary discourse of dumbing down, as unwelcome 'Americanisation', and 'a monstrous depar-ture from the dignity and propriety of journalism' (Silvester, 1993).

Then, and for the next seventy years or so until the growth of mass audience television in the late 1950s, the political interview functioned principally as an occasion for politicians, with more or less collusion from the media, to gain free publicity – one of the first categories of 'pseudo-event' (Boorstin 1962), whereby the respective needs of the politician for publicity and the journalist for material to report as news were to be neatly combined in a carefully constructed 'mediality' or 'happening' – an event which would not happen, because it would have no point, were it not for the existence of a media outlet to give it exposure. Politicians were not interrogated in these early interviews so much as provided with plat-forms from which to project their desired messages, with the aim of conveying a favourable impression of policy or personality to the readers of the periodical in which the interview appeared. For the interviewer, then as now, professional status and kudos accrued from the rarity of the event, and there was little interest in, or demand for anything approaching the concept of scrutiny or critical publicity.

Early broadcast interviews on radio and television were similarly anodyne, conducted within a framework of strict deference beween jour-nalist and subject, reflecting wider social conventions of exaggerated respect for and submission to authority figures. The sense of occasion, and the audience's general unfamiliarity with the conventions and conditions of the political interview, allowed what seem today to be laughably pompous displays of boot-licking journalistic deference to pass as serious coverage. The gradual decline of this style from the late 1950s onwards was the consequence of three trends.

The growth of the mass audience and the decline of deference

As the previous chapter observed, the growth of a mass media market in the late nineteenth century provided the conditions for the development of ever more authorial forms of journalism (columns, for example) in which personality and opinion were permitted to find expression. Interviews with celebrities like Oscar Wilde were another manifestation of this 'personalisation' of journalism, although the informal, relatively irreverent style of the celebrity interview was rarely applied to political figures. A move away from deference in political interviewing reflected the changing social and cultural environment of the post-WWII years, in which conventional subservience to elites in all walks of life began to be transgressed. A country whose people had just defeated the Nazis and elected a Labour government by a landslide, discarding its heroic wartime leader in the process, was ready by the 1950s for a more robust and open political journalism than it had hitherto been provided with.

Commercialisation and competition

Throughout the late 1940s and early 1950s, however, when the BBC still monopolised British broadcasting, it interviewed governing and opposition politicians in the same deferential tones with which it reported the doings of royalty. This approach changed only when the competitive pressures introduced by the establishment of the Independent Television service in 1955 required it to. When ITN – ITV's provider of news – came on air, anxious to establish its distinctive place in what had become with the establishment of commercial television a broadcast media marketplace, it quickly developed a more aggressive, adversarial style in its journalism, including its interviewing. ITN's leading interviewer, Robin Day, pioneered the shift by asking searching, often critical questions of politics and politicians. His 1958 encounter with Harold Macmillan is viewed by one historian of the form as the 'definitive example' of the new style (Jones 1996, p. 67); a style which strongly influenced BBC journalists like David Frost, who is widely credited with inventing adversarial 'trial by television' in the 1960s.

The emergence of non-deferential, interrogatory political interviewing was thus on one level an organisational response (by the BBC) to a new journalistic competitor (ITN), which had interpreted changing social mores, and its more self-consciously populist position in the market, as sanctioning a new and less formal relationship with the political elite. The interviews which resulted were much more dramatic and interesting as television, and often made the news themselves, as politicians used to the old deference occasionally took offence and made spectacles of themselves on air. Interviewers like Day, Frost and Brian Walden became personalities, and their reputations as tough, confrontational journalists part of their organisations' brand in the market. They became commercial assets to their organisations: 'stars' who over time acquired authority as political actors themselves; valued representatives of the people in facing down politicians' blather. Since that time, the political interview has been the province of a small band of elite political journalists, who typically emerge from more routine news work to become authorised interrogators of the powerful – a special breed of pundit, licensed to go beyond the conventions of impartial reportage and interrogate members of political elites on the public's behalf; to speak for 'us', and to ask the questions which 'we' are assumed to want to ask. The best-known interviewers are watched and listened to by audiences as much for how they conduct interviews, as for what their interviewees might say.

And as the media market has become steadily more competitive, the pressure on interviewers to be distinctive in their style and approach has increased with it. In this market, it is fair to say, deference is the least valued of attributes amongst political interviewers. Today, something approaching the deferential style of early political interviews survives only in those sections of the British press whose publicly declared partisanship inclines them to provide their favoured politicians with space to portray themselves in unremittingly positive terms. On the eve of the 1996 Labour Party conference, for example, both the *Sunday Mirror* and the *People* featured lengthy interviews with Tony Blair, at that time limbering up as a serious contender for the premiership he won seven months later. *The Mirror*'s 'exclusive' interview, like the *People*'s exclusive, is best seen as a form of political advertising rather than journalism – what one might call *vanity interviewing* – allowing only positive statements to be made by or about Blair. In the *Mirror*, for example, he declared without journalistic challenge that 'I will never allow our people to grow old in poverty', while in the *People* Cherie Blair's status as a 'dedicated homemaker and mother' was emphasised.[6]

The conventions of impartiality and neutrality mean that there are few broadcast opportunities available to politicians for uncontested self-promotion of this type. During the sample period used in this study, the only significant example (i.e., one which drew comment from any public body) of excessive deference in a broadcast interview was found on ITN's *News At Ten*, a lapse for which the programme was subsequently criticised by the Independent Television Commission. On July 18 1996 *News At Ten*'s Trevor McDonald conducted a seven-minute interview with then prime minister John Major, which included a reference to the latter's 'extraordinary dedication'. At one point the following question on Northern Ireland was put to the prime minister:

MCDONALD: When you embarked on [the peace process] in Northern Ireland it was a great prize that you set out to achieve. You had a great deal of courage, you invested a lot of prestige in it. Is there anything grand, anything greater you can do now to put it back on track? A kind of Mandela-type gesture, for example?

While John Major may reasonably be thought to have demonstrated political courage in his approach to the conflict in Ulster, and certainly staked much of his own reputation on the success of his policy there, comparisons with Nelson Mandela were judged inappropriate, at least by the Labour Party, who complained to the Independent Television Commission of bias. Adjudicating, the ITC did not find that ITN's impartiality obligations had been breached, but did observe that 'it may have seemed to some viewers that the overall approach was a little too friendly and relaxed for a major set-piece interview with a party leader'.[7]

The decline of parliament and the rise of political public relations

The growing importance of the political interview in a journalistic organisation's branding has been reinforced by what many observers view as the decline of parliament as a decision-making institution, and its replacement by media organisations as the rhetorical foci of our political culture. It is generally accepted by most observers that parliamentary question time, which used to perform the function of critical scrutiny of political rhetoric (albeit for an extremely limited elite audience) has, since the introduction of cameras and microphones to the chamber, become an ever more ritualised, tightly controlled occasion, peppered with sound-bites sculpted with the needs of the media in mind. Since the 1980s, it is true, select committees of the House of Commons have had an increasingly visible interrogatory role, and the expanded coverage of their deliberations on Sky News and BBC Parliament is a welcome addition to the public sphere, but they allow relatively little time for cross-examination and are in any case watched by relatively few people.

As the focus of political discourse in the late twentieth century has gradually moved away from the House of Commons towards the mass media, then, journalists have been called upon to form a surrogate opposition to government, especially those (the Thatcher governments of the 1980s, the Labour government which came to power in 1997) with virtually unassailable parliamentary majorities. Consequently, the interrogations of broadcast journalists – to the extent that they are live, relatively unscripted and unpredictable in their outcome – have taken on an enhanced importance in subjecting politicians to mass democratic accountability. The politicians – who share with journalists and their publics an awareness of this fact – thus approach interviews as at one and the same time a source of positive publicity (if they perform well) and a potential minefield (if they slip up) of journalistic traps which have severely damaged the careers of more than one senior British politician.

With the media now perceived as the key platform for public political speech, politicians have acquired an armoury of defensive communicative techniques, designed and directed by public relations professionals. In response, interviewers have developed new forms of attack. Innovative interrogative techniques are developed, succeed for a time in subjecting politicians to critical scrutiny, and are eventually neutralised by defensive techniques of the interviewee, leading to a further evolution in interviewing strategy.

It is notable that the more self-consciously popular position in the media marketplace of ITN's programmes for ITV has not led, as in the case of popular newspapers, to criticism or mockery of elites, but to a more deferential approach even than that of the BBC, particularly to elites of the right. In this respect Trevor McDonald's apparent affection for John Major was consisent with the stance of his predecessors such as Alistair Burnett, who was renowned in the early 1980s for having been distinctively 'gung-ho' in coverage of the Falklands conflict, by comparison at least with the BBC. *News At Ten*'s political interviews remained in the 1990s, as we have seen, a prime-time news space where senior Conservative politicians could still receive a degree of deference which at times threatened to cross the line between impartiality and bias.

Superficially similar to the ITN style criticised by the ITC in July 1996, but much more effective as an instrument of critical scrutiny, has been the friendliness and cordiality of David Frost's Sunday morning programme. Frost's 'sofa' interviews give the appearance of deference, while ensnaring the disarmed subject into revealing some significant, and potentially damaging new information. In 1987 Neil Kinnock lost the general election on Frost's programme by responding without sufficient care to an apparently throwaway question about defence. Tony Blair – 'Tony' to Frost – avoided this fate, but the following exchange – taking place towards the end of the 1997 general election campaign – gives a flavour of how a relaxed and matey approach need not mean deference.

FROST: And now, we're delighted to welcome the leader of the Labour Party, Tony Blair. Good morning Tony. There are all these headlines about Labour landslides and so on, I suppose the one thing you'll be hoping for is that there won't be a rogue poll on Thursday.

BLAIR: Well, I think the polls just go up and down. I've always said to people all the way through ... there's only one poll that counts and that's the one on election day.

FROST: But that could be the rogue poll.

BLAIR: Well, it could be but I think in the end, for most people, they're looking at the issues rather than looking at the polls ...[continues by stressing the need for Labour supporters not to be complacent and to make sure they vote on election day]

Frost then goes from this friendly opening banter straight into the highly sensitive rail privatisation issue, with a heavily sarcastic comment drawing attention to Labour's abandonment of earlier policy.

FROST: And yesterday you spent a morning with Richard Branson [who stood to be a major beneficiary of rail privatisation as planned by the Tories], and he must have been amazed when you got out your 1995 speech at conference and read to him the words: 'To anyone thinking of grabbing our railways, built up over the years so they can make a quick profit as our network is broken up and sold off, I say this. There will be a publicly owned and publicly accountable railway system under a Labour government.' He must have been a bit shocked by that.

BLAIR: Well, no, the situation's changed, obviously, because the railways have been sold off and the money's been accounted for. [Blair goes on to explain why Labour won't reverse Tory decisions on rail privatisation]

More important for our purposes than the details of the policy under discussion in the exchange is the fact that beneath the superficial softness of Frost's approach lurks a hard interrogative core, and the accusation of, at best, an inconsistency requiring explanation, at worst, hypocrisy and double standards. Blair is immediately put on the defensive, though the style of the interview dictates that he must not appear to be *too* defensive. Frost's exaggerated respect for his subjects requires them to respond politely.

Of another exponent of cordiality in political interviews, one experienced practitioner observes that:

The interviewer who got the most out of Mrs Thatcher, ever, was Jimmy Young on Radio 2. Those would be 'soft' interviews, for a particular audience, but there's absolutely no doubt that I heard more interesting stuff from Mrs Thatcher with Jimmy Young than I ever did with Robin Day.

A step away from cordiality and towards confrontation is represented by what we can characterise as the forensic style of interviewing, where the apparent friendliness of Frost and Young is replaced by a dogged persistence in getting to the 'truth' of the issue, chiefly by contesting the rhetoric used by the politician. The interviewer–interviewee relationship in such exchanges is relatively cold and businesslike, the former being positioned like a detective before a suspect. Robin Day and Brian Walden pioneered the style, with firm, repetitive questioning which gradually boxed the subject into making a reply or, if the question was not answered, highlighted its evasiveness.

From forensic interviewing, it is a small step to more direct confrontation and the journalistic readiness to respond to semantic evasion with varying degrees of sarcasm and even rudeness. The style in which this is done may vary from the adversarial – in which the interviewer behaves like a lawyer in a court case – through the irreverently sceptical, to the overtly dismissive. On the BBC's *Today* programme James Naughtie may respond to a politician's comment with such sceptical expressions as 'Surely ...?', 'Isn't it a bit rich ...?', and 'Oh come on!' *Newsnight*'s Jeremy Paxman has a reputation for confronting his subjects with verbal put-downs and body language which signify with unavoidable clarity his contempt for the answers he is hearing. He sardonically communicates with facial expressions what the rules of impartiality would forbid him to say in plain English, though he has on more than one occasion been tempted to push his luck. During the general election of 1997, for example, Paxman interviewed the then Liberal Democrat leader Paddy Ashdown about his party's manifesto in a style which no viewer could have failed to recognise as patronising in the extreme.

PAXMAN: Now, we also know that you want to cut public spending below 40 per cent of GDP ...

ASHDOWN: No, we said that was a target which was achievable towards the end of the next parliament.

PAXMAN: ... a target. Hmmm. You've just told us you want to put five pence on a packet of cigarettes. We know you want to put up the basic rate of income tax. We know you want to put up the top rate of income tax. We know you want to bring in a carbon tax. Is this aspiration some sort of a joke?

(BBC2, *Newsnight*, March 19 1997)

Ashdown takes this dismissal of his party's entire platform as 'some sort of a joke' without flinching, and the interview goes on, Paxman asking more questions of Lib Dem policy and appearing to listen politely while Ashdown answers. Then, just as the Liberal leader may have thought he was being allowed to seriously elaborate his party's views, the interviewer's eyes rolled:

PAXMAN: To come back to planet earth for a while, there is no chance of you forming a government.

This may be the closest to hyperadversarialism British political interviewing has come. Not only is the politician treated with obvious contempt, but the entire basis of his programme, the *raison d'être* of his party's campaign, is subjected to public mockery. If the journalistic message which emerges – you, Paddy Ashdown, are not a serious politician, and your party is not a serious party – does not violate the flexible conventions of impartiality which constrain the British broadcast interviewer, then it is hard to imagine what would.

Such 'interview abuse' of politicians is rare, however, and even rarer at election time. Even by the standards of Jeremy Paxman this was an exceptionally sneering interview, by a journalist whose brand of interrogation is uniquely sarcastic, cynical, and often entertainingly confrontational, to the point where it has itself become the subject of satire elsewhere in the public sphere.[8] On a continuum ranging from deferential to mocking, interviews with broadcasters representing all of the main news outlets suggest that confrontation 'for its own sake' is not the preferred approach to engaging with politicians. Adversarial questioning, when it occurs, is defended as a necessary response to the increasing facility with which politicians approach their interrogators. As leading BBC interviewer Nick Clarke puts it:

I think this whole business about adversarial interviewing is exaggerated. I don't think there's nearly as much of it as people think, but you only have to hear one, and you think you've heard them all. I don't think the world is necessarily as people hear it. They hear what they want to hear.

I am certainly not interested in adversarial interviews for their own sake. I don't do them. Which is not to say that interviews don't sometimes take the form of a verbal contest. That can happen. But I would like to think that that only happens with me if it is required by the substance. In other words, not for its own sake, but only because I think something is not being answered, which I think really should be answered, and I want to make sure that if it is not answered, at least everybody understands that has happened.

New Labour, new interviewing style

The development of the political interview, as we have seen, can be understood as a kind of communicative arms race: as the political actor's defences become tougher and more sophisticated in response to society's (and society's representative, the political interviewer's) declining deference, the journalist must devise new ways of getting round them. The logical conclusion of this process of escalation was reached when, at the height of the Formula One funding controversy of November 1997, the Labour government refused to provide anyone for interrogation on BBC's *Newsnight* programme. This refusal to play the politician–journalist game by the rules established under successive Conservative governments, a favoured 'source tactic' of New Labour's first six months in office, was countered by a shot of an empty chair, and Jeremy Paxman's observation to viewers that, once again, 'no ministerial bottom' could be found to fill it.

The demystificatory playfulness of Paxman's comment may be the logical end-point in the stylistic evolution of the broadcast political interview – an empty chair; a significantly absent interviewee; the game halted in its tracks by the refusal of one of the contestants to play. On the other hand, the importance of the 'star' interviewer in a news outlet's branding, and of the politicians' need for publicity, makes it certain that there will be further innovations. The dialectical nature of the journalist–politician relationship, in which each is continually adapting to the tactics and strategies of the other, makes further evolution of political interviewing style inevitable. As one practitioner puts it:

> There is a kind of undefined culture of television and people try out interview styles, and for a period of time, they have a great impact. Then what happens is, collectively, politicians work out how to answer those particular problems. All the time, through the culture of people doing it, politicians watching it, being subjected to interviews themselves, people learn how to adapt to techniques.

Interviewing styles are continually evolving, then, and at any given time, a variety of interviewing strategies are available to journalists, each with advantages and disadvantages suited to specific situations, and revealing different types of information. Adversarial interviews are by no means the only type which can elicit useful information. On the contrary, as we have seen, the deceptive cordiality of David Frost may uncover facts which the in-your-face adversarialism of Jeremy Paxman antagonises the politician into keeping hidden.

Do interviews work?

For John Humphrys, one of the journalists most frequently accused of hyper-adversarialism, the evolution of the political process has given the interview – specifically, its broadcast form – an enhanced role. Firstly, as was suggested earlier, the growing intensity and professionalism of polit-ical news management – itself a response to the growing intensity and professionalism of interviewing – requires the journalist to interrogate the politician's statements with ever greater rigour, to critically analyse the gap between political action and rhetoric. Humphrys' colleague at the BBC, documentary-maker Michael Cockerell, observes approvingly that 'his [Humphrys'] aim is to strip away the public relations gloss and use his own sharp teeth to counter rehearsed soundbites ...to reveal the gap between a government's rhetoric and what is going on behind the scenes.'[9] After the 1997 general election, when Humphrys was under sustained attack from the Labour government for using precisely the same tech-niques as had aroused the wrath of the Tories, he took the opportunity of a press interview to make the obvious, but nonetheless important point that 'sometimes [politicians] don't tell the truth. And one of the jobs of the interviewer is to give the listener or the viewer the opportunity to judge for themselves whether they are telling the truth or not.'[10] Of Paxman, one observer writes that 'he can't change the system. But he can expose the fact that someone doesn't answer the question.'[11] A senior BBC interviewer puts it thus:

> My role is to ask the questions that people at home would like to ask if they met politicians, to constantly question those people who put themselves in positions of power. I think it is very impor-tant to ask all the questions that the public might want to ask, and to be very probing.

Political documentary-maker Michael Cockerell puts it this way:

> How do we judge politicians? What are the things we want from them? We want honesty, integrity, decisiveness, vision, courage, ability under pressure. It does seem to me that at least some of those characteristics are on display quite well in a television or radio interview, in a way that they are not on display when they [the politicians] are closeted by their desks in Whitehall, or just putting out press releases. I think it is an indicator of their calibre.

In the context of debates about the capacity of the public sphere to func-tion as a source of useful (to the citizen) political information, this is the key defence of the adversarial interviewing style, and one with which few will disagree. But does adversarialism achieve what its advocates claim? Can the aim of stripping away the rhetorical gloss of the presentationally adept political actor ever be achieved within the limitations of the broadcast interview? Some argue that the organisational and formal constraints of television interviewing in general, rather than the limitations of any particular style, suggest not. Journalists David Leigh and Ed Vulliamy, in their book-length account of the cash-for-questions scandal, argue that television interviews are 'ineffective' in addressing complex questions of public affairs. Not only does limited time constrain the depth of the discussion which can take place, they suggest, but the pressure of deadlines makes TV 'a particularly effective medium for an accomplished liar when the story is complex and partly hidden' (1997, p. 234). Like TV magicians, crooked politicians can deceive and dissemble behind the invisibility of TV's construction.

The particular story they have in mind here is the subject of their own book, the cash-for-questions affair which embroiled Neil Hamilton and the *Guardian* newspaper in a complex legal case for much of 1996. Their comments about the limitations of television interviewing are addressed specifically to a *Newsnight* item involving Paxman, Hamilton and the *Guardian* editor Alan Rusbridger, broadcast at the end of a day in which Hamilton had withdrawn his libel action against the newspaper, thus undermining his protestations of innocence in the cash-for-questions scandal. Commenting on the item in January 1997, Rusbridger too used it as an example of the limitations of the broadcast interview, arguing that TV journalists, by comparison with their print counterparts, are poorly briefed on stories which may explode into the headlines after months of slow development. Rusbridger also noted that TV journalists are tied to the conventions of impartiality, thus preventing the exposure of lies (assuming that they know lies are being told). In this item, Rusbridger argued, 'even with as tenacious and well-informed an interrogator as Jeremy Paxman, Hamilton emerged relatively unscathed and the story was not greatly advanced'.[12] However, careful analysis of the Hamilton/Rusbridger interview/debate supports a less dismissive view of the limitations of televisual form than is implied by the criticisms of Leigh, Vulliamy and Rusbridger.

First of all, the item to which they refer lasted twenty minutes and eight seconds – nearly half of *Newsnight*'s running time – beginning with a lengthy background report. *Newsnight*'s producers may reasonably have assumed an audience familiar with the Hamilton/*Guardian* libel case, and the cash-for-questions issue at its core, but were nevertheless obliged to put the breaking news of the day – the collapse of the libel case – in context. While the BBC could not call Hamilton a liar – and the fact that he was a liar had not, after all, been proved in court – what followed could have done little else but leave an unfamiliar viewer with an unflattering picture of Hamilton, parliament and the process of political lobbying which produced the cash-for-questions scandal.

REPORTER: It's a seedy view of parliament [which the reporter does nothing to refute]. MPs on the take, money pouring in from outside interests in exchange for pulling strings. Cash for asking parliamentary questions. The Tory MP who's just dropped his libel case says he's not guilty, but now, faced with a fresh barrage of allegations, he's going to have to persuade the House, and the country, that he's telling the truth ...The *Guardian* today called him a liar and a cheat. He denies it.

HAMILTON: I'm not a liar, no, and I would have liked the opportunity to vindicate myself in the courts. The problem was that I'd run out of money. As a result of technical, legal problems on Friday we found ourselves without a legal team.

REPORTER: The legal technicalities Mr Hamilton referred to ... were in fact the emergence of a clear contradiction between what he remembers and the memory of his co-litigant, the parliamentary lobbyist Ian Greer.

[The reporter elaborates further on this contradiction, before giving further details of the allegations, and the role of the Nolan Committee in resolving the issue.]

(BBC2 *Newsnight*, November 1 1996)

In the subsequent 'disco' Paxman took the role of chair, first taking the role of 'Devil's advocate' and challenging Rusbridger on the *Guardian*'s ethics.

PAXMAN: How do you justify a headline like that – 'A liar and a cheat'?
RUSBRIDGER: It's the truth.
PAXMAN: Doesn't this begin to look like a vendetta?

The greatest proportion of the interview, however, and the most persistent questioning, was targeted at Hamilton, whose answers and demeanour appeared (to this viewer, at least) evasive and defensive. Space does not allow a full transcript of the interview to be reproduced here, but there can be no doubt that Hamilton, in responding to Paxman's adversarial style, revealed much about himself, and the obvious holes in his account of events, which would have provided a viewer new to the story with much food for thought. The item was not a substitute for the hundreds of thousands of words written in the broadsheet press about cash-for-questions, nor for the detailed reportage of the story which appeared throughout the media over a three year-period, but neither was it the victory for political corruption over lazy, under-resourced journalism claimed by Rusbridger and his colleagues. This *Newsnight* item, like many before and after it, contributed a uniquely revealing moment of personal drama and face-to-face confrontation to a complex and confusing story, which no print outlet could have matched.

This example does not preclude the possibility that some broadcast interviewers, in some circumstances, are ill-informed and poorly briefed about the subjects under interrogation, but the suggestion that the form is in and of itself inferior – 'an effective medium for an accomplished liar' – seems unfair. The interrogative moment in the political process is a particular kind of journalistic space, different to that provided by a broadsheet like the *Guardian*, with its detailed reportage and analysis. To repeat: it is not a substitute for, but a complement to the latter, in which the depth and cumulative informational power of good print journalism is reinforced by the impact on the attentive viewer of the verbal duelling and body language which can be featured in live broadcast journalism. As a well-known practitioner of the form Sheena McDonald puts it, 'for all its inherent weaknesses, the well-researched and plotted interview can always illumine and inform. The answers may be arid, repetitive and evasive, but we see them [politicians] for what they are, and mark the trajectory of the questioning. The best interviewers simultaneously draw out and analyse.'[13] Even if the subject resists such 'drawing out', as many do, the enduring popularity of the broadcast interview form reflects the fact that we can learn just as much about a politician from one guilty silence as from ten thousand words of reportage of a verbatim statement to a House of Commons committee.

Interviews and the manufacture of political news

Political interviews are often criticised not only for their alleged shallowness and inability to reveal information of genuine value, but for their role in what I will describe as the *manufacture* of news and the *inflation* of political crises.

The proliferation of journalistic media since the late nineteenth century has created, in addition to the commentary explosion examined in the previous chapter, a much increased demand for material which can be packaged as news. The political interview is ideally suited for such packaging. The long-form and set-piece varieties in particular are rare moments when the most senior politicians (prime ministers, chancellors, leaders of the opposition) are exposed to detailed interrogation of their policies and rhetorics. Because the outcome of these exchanges is often unpredictable, especially if they occur in the context of live broadcasts, new information can be revealed about the interviewee's policy, personality or performance skills. They can thus be news events in their own right, over and above what light they may shed on other events *in* the news. Indeed, journalistic evaluations of the success of set-piece interviews (and of political interviews in general) are based largely on the extent to which they make the news and set the agenda. The set-piece and sofa interviews which feature prominently on British television on Sunday mornings are important news sources for other journalistic organisations (see Chapter 2), and an interview will be regarded as successful if it makes the news later in the day, or sets the agenda for the following week. Despite the fact that audiences for these exchanges may be low, they function as a major source of stories for prime-time news bulletins later in the day, and for the week to come. Sunday is a quiet news day in normal circumstances, but political journalists are still on duty. Thus, set-piece interviews of the type conducted by David Frost, John Humphrys or Jonathan Dimbleby are approached from the outset as news events with agenda-setting potential, by both journalists and politicians. For that reason, the questioning is often framed to elicit short, unambiguous answers which can then be packaged as sound-bites and reported as 'news' by story-hungry journalists at a later stage in the cycle. If the interviewer is successful in extracting sound-bites, he and his programme also become news.

During election campaigns interviews feed into the daily process of agenda-building, and often provide key points of focus for the identification and definition of a campaigner's (individual or party) strengths and weaknesses. In 1987 David Frost's interview with Neil Kinnock was the turning point in a campaign which, until that moment, there might have been some chance of Labour winning. Not only were Kinnock's comments damaging in themselves, but they allowed the Tories to put the issue of defence – on which Labour were at that time anti-nuclear defence and thus vulnerable – at the top of the election news agenda, a development from which their opponents could only benefit. In 1987, too, David Dimbleby's interview with Margaret Thatcher for the *Nine O'Clock News* threatened to damage the Conservative campaign by revealing her contempt for Britain's 'whingers', 'drooling and drivelling that they care', as she infamously put it. In the event, the controversial passage was cut from the bulletin, and shown only at a point late in the campaign when it could make no significant difference to the outcome. Between elections interviews play a similar role in the political process, though rarely with such potentially disastrous consequences for the interviewees.

One consequence of this sense of journalistic expectation, and the desire for it to be fulfilled, is that set-piece and long-form news interviews are frequently the origin of what with hindsight will turn out to have been over-exaggerated political 'crises'. One observer notes that 'a political correspondent is always scheduled to work on a Sunday. His or her presence in the newsroom, laden down with interviews, means the news machine is forcing reports onto the airwaves and into the newspapers.'[14] Statements which in most circumstances would not be newsworthy may become so because news editors are desperate for something to report, and the tapes of the Sunday interviews make a convenient source of material.

News stories are selected, and sustained, 'that would once have faded away. One result is that whenever a politician is in trouble, he tends to stay in trouble for much longer. The political interview, still something of a rarity in 1968, is now so commonplace that one feeds off another, renewing the sense of crisis.'[15]

'Crises' develop as throwaway remarks made by politicians under questioning in a Sunday interview become the target for detailed inspection by other news media, attracted as they are to narratives of disunity and difference within the parties. In 1995 John Birt, criticising the interviewing practice of his own organisation, observed that 'in the era of the soundbite and the tabloid, a strong remark, a poorly judged phrase on a Sunday morning programme – a repeated evasion, a careful nuance, a finely drawn distinction – can build by Tuesday into a cacophony of disputation and a political crisis.'[16] Sometimes, of course, this is precisely the intention of the interviewee, who seeks to use the media exposure as a platform for what is in effect a powerful form of proactive public relations, bypassing the formal channels and rules of internal party debate and communicating directly with other party members, or with the wider public.

The manufacture and inflation of crisis : a case – Clare Short and 'the people who live in the dark'

As a generality, statements made or extracted in the course of interviews are more likely to be newsworthy if they contain a significant piece of new information (a policy announcement, for example); if they provide further development of a story already on the news agenda (when, for example, Prime Minister Tony Blair appeared on John Humphry's *On The Record* to apologise for his presentational failures in the context of the Formula One funding controversy);[17] if they are the occasion for a serious error or 'gaffe' (Kinnock's 1987 statement on defence to David Frost); or if they occur during a quiet period in the political cycle, such as the summer holiday months of July and August. This latter is the most likely explanation for the fact that an interview given by Clare Short MP to the *New Statesman* periodical in August 1996[18] set the agenda in the rest of the political media for the best part of a week (and indeed contributed much to the subsequent formation of a narrative framework for making journalistic sense of New Labour, up to and including the resignation of Peter Mandelson in December 1998).

In 1996 Short was already a well-known and outspoken Labour figure, who in previous interviews had made controversial and widely reported statements (contradicting Labour's official policy) about the decriminalisation of cannabis and the desirability of raising income tax. This allowed her *New Statesman* interview to be perceived by journalists in the mainstream media as further development of a story which we might

102

summarise as 'Labour's troublesome left-wingers upset the New Labour bandwagon'. Coming as it did in the journalistic 'silly season', in a highly news-managed environment where bad-news stories about Labour were thin on the ground, her remarks to a relatively obscure left-of-centre periodical became a major story in the days following their publication, not least because they were leaked in advance. In the national press over the four-day period August 8–11 there were no less than fifty-seven news items, columns, feature articles and cartoons on the Short interview, including front-page leads in the *Express* and the *Guardian*. The story led political coverage on all the sampled broadcast media on August 8, and dominated the following Sunday's interview programmes.

The key element which established the extraordinary newsworthiness of the story and defined its shape was her use of the phrase 'the people who live in the dark' to describe the communications advisors around Blair, who though himself 'a principled and decent man' was alleged by Short to be in danger of being led astray by his spin doctors. These comments, noted her *New Statesman* interviewer, put Short 'in the vanguard of those who have felt dispossessed by the Blair revolution'. Reports, columns and even editorials followed publication of the interview, which was characterised by the *Financial Times* (thus justifying the prominence given to the story by its political editor) as 'the fiercest criticism [of Blair] yet from within the shadow cabinet'.[19] An editorial in the next day's edition of the same paper declared gravely that, 'It is no longer possible to assume that nothing can stop Labour from winning next time.'[20]

The *Telegraph*, *Express* and other pro-Tory newspapers seized on her remarks as proof of their collective view that New Labour was a propagandistic slogan, without policy substance, while the less pro-Tory *Times* criticised her 'self-indulgence'. The *Herald* in Scotland called the interview 'a notably silly piece of prose' and 'arrant and damaging nonsense', while Robert Harris rather ungraciously conceded in the *Sunday Times* that 'in her ghastly, inchoate, whining, muddle-headed way, Clare Short does sum up what a lot of Labour supporters feel about Blair's new party'.[21] The media as a whole took the story as an opportunity to engage in an extended discourse on the evils or otherwise of 'spin' (for a more detailed analysis of 'the demonology of spin' see Chapter 7), this being at the time the aspect of New Labour's identity or policy then perceived as being most vulnerable to journalistic criticism. In the event, Clare Short's remarks about 'the people who live in the dark' did not keep her out of the first Blair government, where she was given the opportunity to prove herself as overseas development minister.

Conclusion

The Short case is a good example of how political interviews can set agendas, particularly at 'quiet' moments in the news cycle, and particularly when given by (self) promotionally adept political actors. As Birt says, statements made in interviews can be built by a news-hungry media into 'a cacophony of disputation' which may damage the interests of some politicians, and advance others. They are powerful forms of political communication, on which careers can be built and destroyed, and some politicians are very good at exploiting them for public relations purposes. They are unpredictable, however, and an increasingly important forum, in an era of hyperactive news management, where political actors can be confronted with questions and issues which they might rather see left alone. Occasional examples of Paxmanesque hyperadversarialism do not negate their value as instruments of critical scrutiny.

6

THE SOUND OF THE CROWD
Access and the political media

Thus far I have discussed the political media in terms of their functions of *reportage*, *interpretation* and *interrogation*. In each of these contexts, journalists in a liberal democracy are called upon to stand between political actors and the public, mediating between the two groups in ways which are, overall, intended to be beneficial for the political process. Throughout this mediation of the political process the public is present only as an abstract, imagined audience, receiving information about and analysis and interpretation of events in the political sphere as a support for attitude-forming and decision-making. Through political interviews, as we have seen, citizens are able to evaluate politicians' performances under interrogatory pressure.

All these forms of mediation, if the system is working as it should, have value as mechanisms for the circulation of political information in the public sphere. In none of them, however, is the citizen an active participant in the process (other than as a member of the 'active audience', of course). In none is she more than a recipient of information gathered, filtered, processed and packaged in various ways before it reaches her. And by itself (regardless of the quality of the political journalism under consideration) the receipt of information is inadequate to the realisation of a fully democratic political culture, and a public sphere which is more than an intellectual abstraction. A properly functioning public sphere requires *mass access*, not just to the consumption of political information through journalistic media of quality (however one defines that term) but to its production.

If one is to apply normative standards, then the public in a democracy should have opportunities not just to read about, or to watch and listen to the development of political debates as spectators, but to participate directly *in* them, through channels of access. This quality of the properly functioning public sphere can be defined as the ability of citizens, through the media apparatus furnished by a society's given state of technology, to contribute to and participate in politics: communicating vertically, via the institutions of the media to those of the government and the state, as well as horizontally to other members of the media audience. For those citizens who are not actually members of political organisations this is, apart from voting itself, the most practical and likely mode of political participation.

If this is true as a general statement of the ideal it is obvious, despite the positive value of that ideal as a goal to be reached, that there can be no real *universality* of public access. The entire adult population of a state, which may number many millions, cannot possibly be physically present in the public sphere (in its mediated form, that is) as contributors. But there can be *selective* access, to a greater or lesser degree representative of the public, which allows a sample of the population to express its opinions, both to the public as a whole (or that portion of the public which comprises the audience), and to the political class nominally making decisions on their behalf. Access of this kind may be viewed, if not as a condition for democracy in general, then as an essential element of the public sphere in a *mass*, people's democracy. Prior to the act of voting itself, public access is the moment in the cycle of political communication when 'public opinions' are articulated, exchanged and contested. Access is also, and increasingly in recent years, a context within which ordinary citizens can join with journalists in the interrogation of political rhetoric – an extension to the public as a whole of the 'interrogative moment' examined in the previous chapter.

The validity of the access principle has always been recognised by the political media, which from their earliest incarnations have allocated space for the publication of readers' letters. Readers' letters remain an important forum for the expression of public opinion, though they are limited – by constraints on space, obviously, and also by the fact that, with some exceptions, the opinions expressed in them are addressed to the readers of the particular publications in which they appear, and do not usually circulate beyond that readership. Any given newspaper represents and addresses only a sub-region of the public sphere. With the coming of electronic media, however, new forms of granting citizens' participatory access to public debate have become available which give at least the appearance of greater representativeness and universality than readers' letters have ever achieved. These new forms include talk and debate shows (debates, that is, involving ordinary members of the public as opposed to panels of experts brought together in studios), phone-ins, and simulated 'people's parliaments' in which debate not only takes place, but the participants are invited to 'vote' on the issues.

For some observers of these developments, appearances are deceptive. The proliferation of public access media which address contemporary politics, it is argued, has not qualitatively enhanced the public sphere, but has in fact degraded it. Livingstone and Lunt note that for Habermas and others of a similarly pessimistic outlook, 'the mediated public sphere is an illusion which masks the hegemonic domination of the masses by the bourgeoisie' (1994, p. 24). The preceding discussion of political journalism has already rejected this conception of the ideological, 'masking' function of the contemporary public sphere, on the grounds that it understates the profound changes forced on capitalistic culture by the mutually reinforcing processes of democratisation and marketisation. Without at least some mass access, however, charges that the public sphere remains an elitist, bourgeois conspiracy clothed in an illusory 'massness' would be much harder to refute. Access formats are important because through them, to a greater extent than elsewhere in the public sphere, 'the media may play a potentially emancipatory role, albeit unintended, if we see appearing on television [or on radio for that matter] as cutting across the exclusivity of traditional forms of representation' (ibid., p. 26). Blumler and Gurevitch, in their generally pessimistic account of the crisis of British political culture, identify the rise of 'talk show democracy' as one of the few positive trends (1995).

The questions for this chapter, then, are the following: are the vast media audiences of contemporary capitalism enabled, through forms of direct (albeit sampled) physical access to the public sphere, to participate as empowered citizens in a genuine exchange of information, which enhances their ability to act, individually or collectively, in a rational way? Or are they, as Bourdieu, Habermas and others would have it, participating merely as puppets in the illusion of access necessary to the legitimation of democracy; invited to be spectators of, but never players in, a game to which they have no significant input, and the outcome of which is of little importance to the exercise of political power? Has the principle of access implied by the ideal model of the public sphere been hollowed out under the pressure of commodification and the market, until only a shallow imitation – a sham of democratic participation – remains? Or do contemporary forms of public access to the political media represent a qualitative enhancement of our democratic system, a significant extension to the participatory possibilities available to previous generations?

These questions require us to consider how the various institutional elements of the public sphere constitute their 'publics'; how they encourage (or discourage) popular participation in the debates which they stage; how access to the public sphere – universal or otherwise – is managed. Previous chapters have demonstrated how that key principle of the ideal public sphere – 'critical publicity' directed towards the powerful – is expressed in the journalistic work of reportage, interpretation and interrogation. In this chapter we consider what relationship the public, as audience, are permitted to have to this criticism.

The three ages of access

The evolution of public access to the political media has been characterised by three parallel trends, or movements:

- from elite to mass (reflecting the development of the media and political culture generally);
- from self-selection to relatively random access (though media professionals always retain the right to draw up the rules which govern access);
- and from journalistic control of the content of the contributions made in access spaces, to relative lack of control, verging at times on the chaotic.

These trends have corresponded to the evolution of media from print to electronic, from recorded to live, and from uni-directional to interactive forms.

The reader's letter

The earliest form of public access to the political media, and one which is still a prominent feature in the pages of newspapers today, was the unsolicited reader's letter, submitted in response to a political statement or event, or to media coverage of that statement or event. The reader's letter was and remains an important medium for accessing the views of those members of the public who are motivated and literate enough to compose and submit a few paragraphs in the required style. In so doing it has fulfilled three related functions. Firstly, it permits direct, relatively unmediated representation within the public sphere *of* the public, or at least that section of the public which reads the newspaper or periodical in which the letter appears. Secondly, premissed on the first, it provides a space in which debate can take place *between* citizens, in full view of the readership as a whole, in exchanges of opinion which may continue over a period of days or even weeks. To cite an example (which I quote unedited, because of its particular relevance to this book), the *Sunday Times* of February 8 1998 published a letter by the Chief Executive of BBC News, responding to a column written one week earlier in which accusations of dumbing down had been made.

No 'dumbing down'

Last week Ferdinand Mount[1] wrote that I intend to reduce the number of television and radio interviews with politicians because the public finds them boring. I have not and would not say any such thing.

The last thing the BBC will do is 'dumb down' its news. We have a public service responsibility to cover politics and we are committed to engaging our viewers and listeners in the significant political issues of the day. Interviews with our elected representatives will always be a central feature of what we broadcast. It is true that we have been talking to viewers and listeners as well as politicians about how to invigorate political coverage and those discussions have been fruitful and constructive.

The same commitment to quality extends across the range of the BBC's output. Strong contemporary drama, regular programmes on books, actuality coverage from parliament are all there.

Tony Hall
Chief Executive, News

This example, while illustrating the value of the letter form as a vehicle for the kind of debate characteristic of the ideal-type public sphere, also points to one of its limitations. Gaining access to the letters' page is often the product of the status enjoyed by those already in elite positions, who are also more likely to have the skill and confidence in writing letters of this kind. This is not a criticism since, as noted in Chapter 2, elite newspapers like the *Sunday Times* will tend to have elite readerships, and to pursue in their readers' letters as much as in their reportage and commentary a particular style and register. But this mode of public access, now as in the past, assumes a facility and ease with formal letter-writing conventions which relatively few citizens have. It *presupposes* the kind of civically minded, politically involved, knowledgeable citizen which the institutions of the public sphere theoretically exist to assist in bringing into being.

Thirdly, readers' letters have functioned historically as a means for the communication of public opinion *to* politicians. Letters are read by politicians and others as an index of the state of those particular readers' opinions. Although only a small proportion of letters can be published, and those which are are subject to editing, they ideally comprise a representative sample of that title's readers' opinions. To the extent that the ideal is realised, letters to the editor are a form of bottom-up political communication, with messages flowing from citizen to politician.

For the editors and journalists themselves, the letters' page is an important means of giving expression to the title's public voice, and of establishing a bond with a community of readers which is essential to its identity in the market place. It is the principal means, though imperfect, of representing the opinions of this community of readers to themselves, as well as to others whom the newspaper may wish to influence or impress. An important function of the reader's letter is thus to act as a lobbying device. In so far as print media are institutional political actors, seeking to influence the decision-making processes of government, they may mobilise readers' opinions, as expressed in letters, to back up their appeals. In so doing they seek to create the appearance of 'public opinion', although it is always a limited form (limited to the 'public' opinions of that newspaper's readers), and always subordinate to the political objectives of the media concerned.

To demonstrate an application of these principles in action consider the example of the Soviet Union, where 'proletarian dictatorship' and the absence of a democratic polity required surrogate forms of expressing the 'popular will' to be found. In the pre-*glasnost* USSR, readers' letters in newspapers were held up by party propagandists as an authentic expression of public opinion. As one Soviet-era journalist put it, readers' letters 'constitute a channel of two-sided communication. Establishing a return link from people to party they serve as a platform for the expression of popular opinion and assist in the formation of that opinion' (quoted in McNair, 1991, p. 25). Both the formation and expression of popular opinion, as contained in readers' letters to party-controlled newspapers like *Pravda* and *Izvestia*, were of course highly selective, and free from any form of independent scrutiny or public accountability.

Like party-controlled newspapers of the Soviet era, newspapers in liberal capitalist societies such as Britain are free to manipulate and select readers' opinions in whatever ways their editors and proprietors see fit. In most circumstances, one can extend the benefit of the doubt and suppose that the editors of letters' pages do their best to represent their readers' opinions fairly, but they are under no obligation to do so. Letters pages may be a platform for honest representation of readers' opinions, or they may be a cynical device for persuading readers to follow editorial policy, on the grounds that this is what the public (i.e., that section of the public represented in the letters pages) thinks. There are inevitably biases amongst the readers of particular newspapers, and these will inevitably be reflected in the content of letters. There will be a temptation, however, particularly for 'red top' newspapers of the popular-demagogic type, to turn this means of demonstrating public opinion to the advantage of a favoured cause. The application of modern market research techniques has enhanced the scope of this usage by allowing readers' polls and other forms of apparently spontaneous and 'authentic' public opinion to be mobilised. In late 1996 the *Sun*, at the end of a week of hostile coverage of European monetary union, presented the results of a readers' telephone poll showing the remarkable figure of 94 per cent opposition to EMU and only 6 per cent in favour. This apparently overwhelming degree of popular euroscepticism was not, curiously enough, reflected in the general election which followed just six months later, nor in the results of other opinion polls conducted around the same time. In this case, it is reasonable to assume, readers' access to their newspaper was manipulated so as to produce the desired propagandist outcome, then used as a device by which the *Sun* and its anti-EMU proprietor could seek to influence the policy of both the Tory and Labour parties as they approached the forthcoming election. In what is a particularly good example of the limitations of public (readers') access to the press, we see the collective readership dragooned into the proprietor's private army, thence to be used as a battering ram on the doors of party and government policy.

Whether professional politicians take any notice of such tactics depends, of course, on their perception of how large and representative the readership accessed in this manner actually is (and, as Labour's courtship of News International since 1994 has more than once demonstrated, the *Sun*'s multi-million readership *is* perceived to carry weight), and how closely its views correspond to other measures of public and elite opinion.

In the past, before the era of mass print media, citizens accessed in this manner were, like the users of media generally in that period, an unrepresentative elite – a privileged bourgeois public, addressing in their letters a political class whose members had little reason to take seriously the views of the non-literate, non-enfranchised majority of men and women. As mass audience newspapers developed, however, they incorporated the reader's letter as a means both of accessing readers' opinions, and of confronting the politicians with them. With circulations of millions, professional politicians came to respect the opinions expressed in the tabloids' letters, perhaps even to fear them as, in keeping with the characteristics of popular political journalism examined in previous chapters, they have become steadily more irreverent and declamatory in tone. Typically, the *Sun*'s letters page invites readers to 'Have a Go' at the politicians, and recent history may be interpreted as a warning that doomed is the politician, Labour or Tory, who ignores or discounts the views of the *Sun* reader.

Valuable mechanism for non-elite participation in the political communication process though it can still be, then, the reader's letter is necessarily limited in its ability to deliver mass access to the public sphere. By the nature of the print medium, the debates and feedback which it allows are not live and immediate. Editors edit the letters, and politicians can choose to ignore or evade the criticisms they contain. They can take time to consider their responses carefully. This is not always a bad thing, of course, but it means that letters, and the debates which they engender, lack spontaneity and are more likely to be calculated, manufactured assemblages of opinion. Politicians are not confronted by their constitutents face to face. Moreover, letter-writers tend to be self-selected individuals of a particular, relatively rare type, often stereotyped as obsessive and meddling. If the stereotype is inaccurate and unfair, it is undeniable that letter-writers *are* unrepresentative of the public as a whole, few of whom ever get round to expressing their anger or concern about politics in print.

Access and broadcasting

Some of the limitations of public access to print media are present also in the broadcast sector. There is, for example, a high degree of self-selection in the procedures by which broadcast access is organised. Those who put themselves forward are, inevitably, those who believe themselves to have something of value to say; who probably keep in touch with, and know about current political debates, to a greater extent than the average citizen; who have a greater awareness of, and sense of identification with, the notion of civic responsibility. They are not, in short, representative of the population as a whole, and may never be. They are nevertheless a more effective means of extending critical publicity – from public to politicians – than is available through print.

The foremost examples of the broadcast access programme in Britain are *Question Time* (BBC1) and *Any Questions* (Radio 4). Both confront panels of politicians and other relevant authorities with an audience of members of the public, who put questions, listen to the panellists' responses, and follow up with further questions and comments of their own. Their questions reflect issues in the news at the time of the broadcast, and are agreed in advance of transmission, so that the chairman knows what is coming, and when. After the initial question is put and answers given from the panel, the chair invites and manages interventions from the rest of the audience. These are less predictable in content and tone, from the point of view of the chair, but in the vast majority of programmes politeness and order are maintained. Although audience members are rarely stopped from saying what they want to say, broadcasts are rarely transmitted live, just in case some judicious editing of libellous, blasphemous or offensive remarks is required.

An important feature of broadcast access in Britain (as of all political broadcasting) is its impartiality. The audience/reader manipulation displayed by the popular tabloids in pursuit of political goals is not permissible in British broadcasting. Instead, TV and radio producers must find ways of constructing 'neutral' platforms from which impartial access, leading to impartial debate, can be organised. The oldest model of such access seeks to reproduce in the studio a recognisable simulation of the adversarial, representative style of politics which characterises British democracy. Thus, *Any Questions* on radio and *Question Time* on television assemble what audiences are asked to accept is a balanced cross-section of citizens (balanced as between gender, ethnicity, political alignment and so on), who are then invited to question a panel of experts – usually, two or three politicians drawn from the right, left and centre of the spectrum, complemented by a fourth or fifth figure of authority from the worlds of business, media, art or some comparable sphere of achievement. (A 1997 edition of *Question Time* included, in a rather uneasy

112

break with tradition, surrealist transvestite comedian Eddie Izzard amongst its panel; a 1998 edition featured *The Beautiful South*'s singer-songwriter Paul Heaton.) Between these two groups sits the journalist-chairman, mediating in the asking and answering of questions and ensuring that none – in the audience or on the panel – breaks the rules of engagement, for example by speaking out of turn, taking too much time, or behaving inappropriately.

The rule-governed nature of these set-ups results in relatively ordered, polite debates, which operate largely within the parliamentary consensus obtaining at any given time. The presumed authority and expertise of the panellists is rarely challenged by an audience whose members, with very few exceptions, appear to understand and accept the terms within which access is granted. For that reason, the question–answer–debate format has been criticised as tokenistic, boring, an illusory form of access which symbolically reasserts the status divisions and power disparities which exist between leaders and led, elite and mass: 'debates', to use Bourdieu's phrase, 'that seem genuine, but falsely so' (1998, p. 31). Bourdieu refers here to French television debates, which are different in format, and exist in a very different cultural context than do British programmes like *Question Time* and *Any Questions*. But his point is not without applicability to the UK context. Such programmes constitute a highly *controlled* access, subject to elite-defined rules and conventions, and which function, on the meta-discursive level, as an extended ideological lesson about the nature of democracy itself. Jonathan Freedland's book-length attack on the limitations of British democracy criticises the format of *Any Questions* and *Question Time*, and the elitist phrasing of their titles, 'implicitly inviting the public to put questions to those in authority rather than voice their own opinions' (1998, p. 25).

An alternative, less dismissive reading is possible, however, since, in fact, members of the studio audience *do* voice their own opinions, subject to the broad rules of verbal exchange which are necessary in any debating context. Although access formats of this type are quite carefully policed, they do permit politicians to be probed before the mass audience, in conditions over which they do not have complete control. They allow a limited form of public interrogation of politicians, and at the same time signal to the public as a whole that they are, indeed, present in the public sphere; that their voices are heard and taken seriously. To this extent they offer a symbolic demonstration of how British democracy works. They may not be perfect expressions of citizen–politician dialogue, but they *are* valuable as a means of direct public access-by-proxy to politicians who are otherwise largely free of any obligation to confront their public. Nick Clarke (who has frequently presented *Any Questions* in the absence of Jonathan Dimbleby) argues that:

> In an era where political meetings have gone ... any direct meeting between real people and politicians is probably a good thing. I don't think you should overstate what *Any Questions* does, because it is so structured. It is not open access, it is not free-for-all, but it is a format which works very well. Sometimes it is very sterile. If politicians just mouth what they have been told to mouth by their party bosses, it isn't very interesting. What it does mean is that people get to look in the eyes of the people speaking the words. I think that's very helpful to them, and the more we do it, the better it is.

Writing of political journalism in the United States, Daniel Hallin observes that with the rise of 'sound–bite news' – the trend towards the use by journalists of shorter and shorter quotes from politicians in news bulletins[2] – 'the public never has a chance to hear a candidate – or anyone else – speak for more than twenty seconds' (1997, p. 65). 'Sound–bite culture' may not be so far advanced in Britain as in the USA, but on our prime-time news bulletins too the trend is evident. In that context, public access programmes, structured or not, are an important counter to the sound-bite, requiring politicians to address voters directly, and at length, in circumstances which, if the programme is unedited (and many are), is unpredictable and thus potentially useful as a moment of voter evaluation of political rhetoric. In the 1997 general election all the main party leaders agreed to participate in special editions of *Question Time* which pitted them, on their own, against the audience for an hour (the leaders of the Scottish and Welsh nationalist parties shared a programme). While it is not possible to say with any precision what viewers concluded about the respective political leaders on the basis of these exchanges, the fact that they permitted the leaders' performances and rhetorical statements of policy to be publicly interrogated can in itself be regarded as nothing less than a significant contribution to the construction of an informed, knowledgeable electorate.

Experiments in access

Broadcasters are, like their counterparts in print, effective gatekeepers of public access, able (and indeed required by regulatory guidelines) to edit those whose views are deemed to be unacceptable. While this capacity is never likely to be given up completely, the broadcaster's ability to edit has been steadily eroded as time has passed and the impact of declining social deference, intensified competition and programme-making technologies which enhance the liveness and immediacy of broadcast output has been felt. The *Question Time/Any Questions* model is the exemplar of the polite, rule-governed, still somewhat deferential tradition of public access programming in British broadcasting, and it remains a prominent feature of the political coverage provided by the BBC. But as declining deference and increased journalistic irreverence make their impact on the access genre, that model is being replaced by more adversarial, relatively *uncontrolled* forms of putting politicians and their publics together.

The increasingly common form of the radio or television phone-in, for example, allows for a greater degree of unpredictability, and a certain roughness and spontaneity in the contributions made. Although the producers of phone-in shows have the protection of a short delay with which to cut off an obscene or otherwise offensive caller, the immediacy of contributions is what gives the form its distinctiveness. On Adam Boulton's *Tonight* show for Sky News, expert witnesses speak first on the issue of the day before viewers are invited to call in with their views. Boulton greets 'Dave from Shrewsbury' or 'Mary from Bracknell', and encourages them to come quickly to their point. If they have no point, or are unable to express it very well, he cuts them off without hesitation. After the callers have spoken, the expert witnesses get another chance to comment, and to reassert their status as authoritative definers of the issues – but not before 'the people' have spoken, in a relatively unconstrained and opinionated way. Have they said anything of value? Very often not, but that is the inevitable result of a selection process in which not only the polished, practised speakers get on. An experienced professional politician remarks:

> Part of the power of the phone-in is that you are getting the questions direct from the public across a range of issues ... It's much tougher than an interview with a supposedly tough interviewer.

In 1997 the BBC launched *You Decide*, another attempt to develop the access format in a more spontaneous direction. In this programme, chairman Jeremy Paxman brought to the production his reputation as a fiercely adversarial interviewer (see previous chapter), and guided his audience through a currently newsworthy issue (topics covered during the first season of programmes included, in the aftermath of the Dunblane massacre, firearms restrictions; the future of the monarchy; and the legalisation of cannabis). Setting up the debates, on which the studio audience were able to vote (followed by the television audience in a telephone poll – hence the programme's title) opposing panels of authoritative experts presented short films arguing for or against the motion of the week. These films, and the panels, would then be interrogated by Paxman, by members of the opposing panel, and by the studio audience itself. At the end of this cross-examination and debate a vote would take place.

This high-profile, big-budget production was a further expression of the broadcasters' contemporary desire to be seen to be accessing the people and giving them a voice on the important public issues of the day, creating a truly 'public' sphere in which non-elite views can be heard. An enhanced measure of drama and unpredictability was ensured by the liveness of the programme. During the firearms discussion, for example, a member of the studio audience took exception to something said, stood up, walked theatrically across the studio floor and out of the debate, to the futile protestations of Mr Paxman. It was good television, if contributing little of substance to the firearms debate as it was being pursued at that time. Commenting on the growth of access programmes on television, and their increasingly dramatic formats, Anthony Sampson observes that:

> Debates on television have increasingly taken over in public interest from Westminster. At best they can be much sharper than parliament's, with fiercer questions, sometimes backed up by filmed interviews and evidence. They can sometimes detect groundswells of public concern and revolt before they reach MPs, attention. Yet televised debates provide no real answers, no solutions, no follow-up to legislation.
>
> (1996, p. 47)

That may be so, although Sampson assumes that 'real answers' can be found anywhere in the public sphere. Neither debates in the House of Commons, nor the musings of elite pundits, nor the inquisitorial grillings of the star interviewers, nor the 'discos' involving opposing politicians on current affairs programmes of the utmost seriousness, deliver 'real answers' to anything beyond the least contentious of facts (and even those, in the form of statistics, are usually constructed and contested). Phone-ins and structured debates like those presented on *You Decide* are no more likely to resolve complex political issues than are debates in the houses of parliament. What they *can* do, uniquely, is signify the existence of a politically aware public and give it some degree of access to the means of expression of political opinion. The opinions accessed in such programmes can be primitive and reactionary, or profound and articulate, reflecting the varying competences and diverse views of real people. This is both their strength and their weakness, and it is the uncertainty and tension arising from their dual character which must be presumed to give them much of their audience drawing-power, as well as prompting much of the criticism of the form which has accompanied its recent evolution.

The potential for boundary-stretching, taboo-breaking television provided by public access programmes unsettles many observers, and warnings as to the dangers posed for the British political system by their growth appear in many variants of the dumbing-down thesis. Others welcome the shift towards less controlled access formats as democratically progressive. David Goodhart observes that 'the recent changes to the format of the BBC television programme *Question Time* encapsulate the new tone. Formerly the politicians spoke from the podium and the public were allowed to ask questions and to respond, very briefly. Now the studio audiences are central to the programme – they speak more and even vote on the issues.'[3]

A case: the monarchy debate

Nowhere have these debates been more loudly heard than in the context of Carlton TV's *Monarchy: The Nation Decides*, broadcast at peak time on ITV in early January 1997. This programme (referred to from now on simply as the monarchy debate) represented an important moment in the evolution of public access programming in the directions discussed in this chapter. It may also turn out to be a defining moment in the crisis of mass representation referred to in the introduction to this book: a point at which, due to the sensitivity of the subject matter (the performance and future constitutional role of the British royal family), and the unprecedentedly open and irreverential nature of the debate which it inspired, shocked and alarmed those observers most pessimistic about the unfolding cultural implications of mass democracy. For David Starkey, constitutional expert and regularly accessed broadcast pundit, the monarchy debate 'put a question mark over the future of studio audiences'.[4] For Starkey, though himself no stranger to rudeness, arrogance and aggressive point-scoring in his capacity as a panellist on the BBC's *The Moral Maze*,[5] the monarchy debate represented no less than the ascendancy of mass-mediated mob rule to heights which were incompatible with British democracy.

The programme was of course made possible only by the preceding sixteen years of steady demystification of the British royal family which had been taking place first in the popular tabloids and then in more elite-oriented outlets like the *Sunday Times*, with its 1992 serialisation of the Andrew Morton biography of Princess Diana, and *Panorama*, in its epochal Diana interview. Broadcast interviews with Prince Charles, in which he confessed to adultery, combined with shock-horror exposés of various forms of royal deviance from the minor (Sarah Ferguson having her toes sucked by an American playboy) to the more sinister (the Duke and Duchess of Windsor's sympathy for the Nazis in the Second World War), created the conditions in which something like the monarchy debate could be produced as peak-time current affairs television. The post-war decline of deference, and the commercially driven journalistic irreverence of the tabloids in particular, had by 1997 created a climate in which, for the first time in recent British history, the current and future roles of the monarchy were perceived as legitimate topics of debate, not only by traditional republicans but by the mainstream public. Carlton's monarchy debate was an attempt to acknowledge this change and, no doubt, to reap the ratings rewards of being the first journalistic organisation to dare to do so in prime-time.

The programme was introduced to viewers as 'the biggest live debate ever in the history of television, on the most contentious issue of the decade', and involved 3,000 people – 'the biggest cross-section of the public ever, handpicked to represent everyone from housewives to national heroes, from accountants to Olympic athletes, from world-cup winning footballers to window cleaners'. These, along with the media audience as canvassed in opinion and telephone polls, would be taking part in 'a unique royal referendum as we ask – do you want a monarchy?'

Leading off the debate – setting the agenda and defining the issues – was a panel of authoritative royal experts and cultural commentators, including authors of royal biographies and exposés, constitutional experts, friends and noble defenders of royalty like Frederick Forsyth, and the republican agony aunt Claire Rayner. These 'primary definers' were asked to respond to a series of filmed contributions putting forward arguments for and against the monarchy. The exchanges were chaired by renowned TV door-stepper Roger Cook (of *The Cook Report*), famous for his tough, no-nonsense-tolerating approach to dodgy second-hand car dealers and other small-time rogues.

The iconoclasm of the debate, and the manner in which it would be conducted, were established early on when, following a short attack on the current 'respectability' of the royal family by leading court correspondent James Whittaker, Professor Stephen Haseler, billed as 'Chairman of the Republican Movement', was asked if he was 'about to lead the storming of the ramparts?' Haseler resisted this invitation to assert his revolutionary aspirations and replied instead that 'republicanism is now on the agenda of British politics – really for the first time – since the nineteenth century. This show is an example of that.' For Haseler, this turn of events was a consequence of the royals' own misbehaviours over an extended period. However, the issue was not simply 'the scandals of the royal family'.

HASELER: The real issue, I think, is that the British public are increasingly wanting to choose their next head of state.
COOK: That they may well do, and that they may get a chance to indicate this evening.

As applause rippled around the huge auditorium, decked out in red and blue banners and flags, Cook brought in Frederick Forsyth to answer the question, 'Is the monarchy in terminal decline?' Forsyth sought to put the debate in historical context.

No, I don't think it is. It's going through an extremely troubled period. That actually has happened twenty, thirty, forty, fifty times in the monarchic history of this country, which goes back nearly a thousand years.

Following this quite pertinent and interesting point, Forsyth then turned on Professor Haseler and inspired the first cheers of the evening from the studio audience.

> If we are talking about the monarchy as the monarch (and not the thirty-five members of the royal family as a group) then let's do that. Let's talk about our magnificent queen who has been forty-four years our monarch and never put a foot wrong. You, sir [wags finger at Haseler, as the crowd begins to cheer, clap and stamp their feet] are a muck-raker, because every family in this country, with thirty-five members in it, has got a couple that they really would prefer not to have.

From this exchange – initiated not by the audience but by the expert panel – began the programme's descent into the undoubted rowdiness and rollicking, reminiscent of a drunken university students' union debate, which followed. The audience, which until then had responded politely to contributions from pro- and anti-monarchists alike, now took its cue on how to conduct the debate, and how to respond to panel members' increasingly dogmatic and extremist positions, from the experts. At the same time, Roger Cook as chair used his position to accuse exposé-writers like Allan Starkie of being 'out to destroy the monarchy', prompting boos from an audience who were clearly by this time thoroughly enjoying themselves.

After these early skirmishes members of the studio audience were themselves invited to participate by voting on the question, 'Have royal scandals damaged the country's reputation?' (red card 'No'; blue card 'Yes'). After voting (a majority thought 'Yes') a selection of audience members were permitted to speak. Here, and throughout the programme, the views expressed were refreshingly forthright and unambiguous, whether for or against the monarchy. Obsessive royalists, radical republicans, socialists and cynics were all accessed, allowing what can reasonably be described as a balanced, uncensored and penetrating debate, albeit one lacking in the traditional deference towards royalty shown by British broadcasters. The following anti-monarchy comment was representative of the tone of the audience contributions.

> The Queen is the head of the Church of England. She's the richest woman in the world. She is the head of a rotten, class-ridden, corrupt political and social establishment [some of the crowd cheer and clap, others boo] which is directly responsible for this nation's terrible decline.

The cultivated outrageousness of the debate was thus established at the outset, setting up an atmosphere which could easily and soon did turn rather more rowdy and difficult to control than the programme's producers may have intended. One pro-monarchist in the audience condemned its 'trivialisation'. A republican declared of the Queen simply that 'the sooner we get rid of her the better'. Forsyth then fuelled the increasingly raucous tone of the debate by inviting audience members with whom he disagreed to 'Shut up and listen.' Thirty minutes into the broadcast, however, the audience were firmly in control, refusing to 'shut up and listen' to the experts, as the tradition of British TV debates suggested they should have. One hour in, and the chanting began.

Despite the irreverence and unruliness of the debate as it progressed (expert panellists and audience members goading each other on all the while) many substantial points were made, and the attentive viewer would have learnt much from the various opinions and perspectives represented. Andrew Morton, the author of the Princess Diana biography which thrust the debate on the British monarchy into a new era, observed from his position on the experts' podium how polarised the debate was, but welcomed its significance as an index of changing social and political attitudes.

> The very fact that tonight we can have a debate about the monarchy, even in this fetid atmosphere, shows that we've come a long way from the 1950s, when three out of ten people believed that the queen was descended from god.

For most observers, however, the fact of the debate's taking place was insufficient recompense for the alleged debasement of the public sphere which it represented. Columnist Linda Grant, in a piece inspired both by the monarchy debate and her own appearance on BBC radio's *The Moral Maze*, typified the response of the liberal critics when she argued that 'our current, so-called debate' had become 'childish and infantile', the audience alienated by 'gladiatorial battles'.[6] Others welcomed the event as a healthy injection of popular feeling into a debate traditionally conducted (in public at least) in oppressively polite and deferential terms. Many observers criticised the British broadcast media's coverage of the death and funeral of Princess Diana later that year for its sickening sycophancy, and its structuring assumption that deference towards the royal family was a universal attribute of the British people (Merck, 1998).[7] The monarchy debate was structured around no such assumption, breaking decisively with more than forty years of media-relayed 'consensus' about the virtues of the royal family. The tabloid-led criticism of the Windsors in the wake of Diana's death was foreshadowed in this event.

Conclusion

The phenomenon of 'talk-show democracy' as realised through public access programming is, like political interviewing, an element of the modern public sphere which divides critics and analysts. Where some, like Blumler and Gurevitch, see the form as one area of improvement in a generally deteriorating public sphere, others, such as Bourdieu, assess the access/debate form as artificial and lacking in democratic authenticity: an entertaining diversion from the 'real' issues ('real' being defined by Bourdieu and his fellow intellectuals, of course). This chapter has rejected that view, at least in the British context, arguing that the formal evolution of the genre as described above is a significant manifestation of the emergence of a democratically empowered mass public, able and willing to participate – as viewers and listeners, and as studio audience members – in meaningful discussions of current issues. Actual, eye-to-eye debate between members of the public and political elites remains limited, as it must always be given the physical laws of the known universe, to samples of the public, but better this than nothing. In some cases, such as the monarchy debate, competitive pressures to heighten the dramatic and confontational aspects of the form – pressures we have seen at work also in relation to political columns and interviews – may result in unscripted, unanticipated moments of noise and undisciplined anger, which make good television but are not necessarily helpful to the progression of a debate.

Then again, that is precisely how people conduct political debates in their own lives. Occasional examples of excessive spontaneity or politeness breakdown are a small price to pay for the wider democratic impact which the witnessing of public access programmes might be presumed to have on the citizenry as a whole. In this category of political media, as in others, the identification of a crisis, the accusation of dumbing down, is best understood as an elite response to the admittedly rather noisy spectacle of mass representation in the public sphere. It has little to do with the defence or improvement of the democratic process, within which the public access broadcast is now an essential element. The sound of the crowd isn't always music to the ears, but no democracy worthy of the name ought to exclude it.

7

'SPIN, WHORES, SPIN'[1]

The demonisation of political public relations

No contemporary study of the relationship between political journalism and democracy can ignore the role of public relations, either as a factor in the production of political journalism, or as a subject of intense journalistic interest in itself. In the first of these contexts the public relations industry has been extensively and critically analysed[2] and I will focus here principally on the second, less frequently discussed set of issues. Specifically, what is it about 'spin' which so preoccupies the political journalists? What is the substance of their complaint about this sub-species of professional communicator, and do the critics have any valid grounds for concern? Is spin a qualitatively new factor in the construction of British political journalism, or merely the application of a fashionable Americanism to a communicative practice which has a long-established and legitimate place within the public sphere?

On spin, and the causes of spin

Columnist and former political editor Julia Langdon observes that 'it is only in the second half of the twentieth century that news management has been developed as a professional art',[3] and she is at least partly right, since this period does indeed mark the emergence of public relations as a *visible* element of the political communication process, reflected by its appearance on the political news agenda, and its integration into popular culture through fiction, cinema and TV.[4] MacKendrick's *The Sweet Smell of Success* (1953), referred to in Chapter 4's discussion of columnists, is the first Hollywood film production in which political public relations (as practised through the sinister figure of J.J. Hunsecker) is centre stage. *Bob Roberts* (Robbins, 1992), *Wag the Dog* (Levinson, 1997) and *Bulworth* (Beatty, 1998) are more recent examples of mainstream cinema's attempts to acknowledge and exploit the role of spin and image management in the political process.

Spin before spin

However, the communicative practices which are today associated with 'spin' long predate WWII. At the turn of the twentieth century, the American pioneers of public relations as a marketable skill were selling their expertise to corporate actors engaged in the lobbying of politicians, and to businessmen and politicians concerned with the management of public opinion. Political news management was an important contributor to the 'red scares' of the 1920s in Britain and the United States (McNair, 1999b), and was used before then in the governments of Disraeli, Palmerston and Lloyd George.[5] Even Samuel Pepys (as arch-spinner Peter Mandelson pointed out when trying to cast himself as the heir to a long and distinguished tradition of news management) can be viewed with hindsight as a kind of spin doctor in so far as he was Charles II's 'press handler'.[6]

In the seventeenth century, of course, as described in Chapter 1, the media or public sphere to be 'handled' was a restricted, exclusive space, inaccessible to and detached from the great majority of the non-enfranchised population. The work of opinion management focused on small groups of the powerful and influential, undertaken mainly through informal, face-to-face channels. These privileged few were the only 'public' whose opinions mattered to the political elites of late feudal, early capitalist Europe, for whom well-resourced armies and god-fearing populations were much more valuable in the maintenance of popular support than sophisticated political communication. In so far as opinion management did matter, however, there were even then those who strove to understand and shape it, by whatever means available. One might justifiably say that political public relations, defined as purposeful political communication targeted at those (one's public) whose opinions one wishes to influence, is as old as human communication and language itself.

The rise of a recognisably modern form of political public relations, and the gradual professionalisation of the activities to which that term refers, was organically entwined with the evolution of liberal democracy and the corresponding growth in the weight and importance of public opinion which that process produced. Alongside the gradual democratisation of the political system which took place after the English revolution, as both an essential element of and accompaniment to it, came the development of communicative techniques and infrastructure which brought truly *mass* media into being for the first time, supporting an expanded public sphere. From the late eighteenth century on, as voting rights were extended to larger and larger sections of the population (culminating with the introduction of universal suffrage to Britain in 1918) the process of democratisation, underpinned by an expanding media system, gave a political role to effective opinion management which had not existed before.[37]

This unleashed what Jay Blumler calls a 'competitive struggle to influence and control popular perceptions of key political events and issues through the major mass media' (1989, p. 103). As the twentieth century progressed, competition between politicians, business leaders and others with political agendas to pursue for 'access to limited news holes' (ibid.) funded the emergence of various kinds of communication professional (organised into the distinct fields of public relations, marketing, and advertising) who developed and could apply technical expertise to communicative practices which, if they had always been present in political activity, had not hitherto been pursued with such scientific precision. As democratic rights were extended, and the role of publicly available information in supporting the exercise of those rights increased, the nature of the political environment was transformed from one characterised by secrecy and ruling-class 'clubbiness' to one of widening accessibility, openness and non-deference.

These changes were gradual, and took the best part of a century to culminate in such spectacles as Monicagate in the United States, or coverage of the tangled love lives of Piers Merchant and Robin Cook in Britain. Most observers cite the Kennedy presidency as a key moment in the emergence of professional public relations as an essential tool of political communication: the moment when a photogenic, inspirational politician and his advisers, employing the still new medium of TV, began to manipulate images and sound-bites with an intensity and professionalism never previously witnessed in a liberal democracy. John F. Kennedy had many skeletons in his political cupboard, and his private life was a sordid mess of betrayals and deceptions (Hersh, 1997), but image-management (in which journalists at the time colluded) ensured that he was perceived as presiding over a squeaky clean 'Camelot'. So powerful was this image that after his death he was subject to secular canonisation, and is still regarded by many Americans – despite the revelations which have subsequently appeared about his political and personal conduct – as a saint-like symbol of all that was good in American politics. Richard Nixon, on the other hand, Kennedy's narrowly defeated opponent in the 1960 campaign, suffered from poor image management, most notoriously in the live TV debate where he appeared pale and tired next to Kennedy's sun-tanned vitality and good looks. Nixon never forgave the 'liberal' media this experience, and his own presidency when it finally came was dominated by the public relations disasters of the Vietnam War and the Watergate scandal.

The 1960s taught politicians important lessons about the conduct of war-fighting, whether military or political, at home or abroad, in the media age. They also persuaded politicians, all over the liberal democratic world, that 'the success of their careers and their causes depends upon a steady flow of media publicity' (Tunstall, 1996, p. 230). This should be qualified, of course, by the proviso that only *positive* publicity was desired.

When that was not possible, much of what public relations professionals did and still do is concerned with stemming the flow of negative publicity, sealing off those proliferating 'news holes' through which images of scandal, corruption or incompetence can seep into public awareness and, beyond that, shape political behaviour. The rise of spin reflects the fact that in an expanded information market, the hunger for stories, and the competitive requirement for journalists to find an original angle on a story, renders any event, no matter how insignificant it may first appear, potentially newsworthy, and thus damaging in publicity terms. Andy McSmith puts it well when he observes that:

> Spin doctors are a product of the age of instant communication, operating in the tiny space between when a political event takes place and when it is first reported to the wider public.[8]

For that brief moment, an event has the potential of being read and interpreted in many different ways. Spin seeks to close down all meanings which are not in the perceived interests of the client, and to make the client's preferred reading the dominant one in media terms. As Simon Heffer puts it:

> The press officer, even if he was a party rather than a government employee, would mainly concern himself with the provision of facts and background information ... The spin doctor is concerned mainly with spin. His role goes beyond the facts; it is to outline to journalists exactly what he feels the thrust of their story should be; it is to persuade them to accentuate the positive or at least play down the negative.
>
> (1995, p. 8)[9]

Politicians have always had to persuade, of course, but now they have to persuade in an environment of rapid and chaotic information flow, where something as innocent as a White House blow job or a £10 cannabis bust can be whipped into a major political crisis within hours, and to do so, if possible, without being seen to. Spin doctors, in this sense, are the 'providers of invisible footnotes to speeches and policy'.[10] Their increased visibility is a reflection of the late twentieth century's partial loss of faith in facts, or at least the recognition (we are all relativists now) that the potential for multiple interpretation of the 'facts' is the starting point for all political communication.

If it is a response principally to the impact of popular political struggle (more democracy) and the evolution of communication technology (more media), the professional management of opinion is also one element in the growth of promotional culture – the introduction into politics of quasi-

125

commercial sales techniques, in which politicians' policy positions are combined with symbolic meanings and articulations of style. The late twentieth century in particular, and the decline of party ideology which has accompanied the end of the cold war – expressed in Britain by the concept of the radical centre and the 'third way', and in America by that of triangulation – has encouraged politicians and their communication advisers to seek 'buyers' by indulging in what some observers view as a form of product marketing. As the *Financial Times'* Joe Rogaly sees it:

> The media has become more dominant since the disappearance of ideology. Parties that existed to implement a vision scorned publications that opposed them. Now, most factions offer the same broad economic and social policies. Those who seek space on our crowded media shelves come as supplicants who must differentiate themselves from one another.[11]

What spin doctors do

If professional public relations is a phenomenon of the late twentieth century, because that is when the combination of mass democracy and mass media made it both possible *and* necessary, the use of the term 'spin doctor' to describe a particular kind of political public relations professional can be dated more precisely to the 1980s. The American journalist William Safire is said to have coined the term in 1984, and a Russian spy to have used it even earlier to describe the disinformation/propaganda activity of the American Central Intelligence Agency. Etymology aside, the term has emerged as shorthand for an especially manipulative, sinister and threatening form of political public relations which goes far beyond the older, more respectable and accepted (by journalists) work of the press or publicity officer.

Traditionally, a press officer was someone who performed the politically neutral function of supplying information to the media in an 'undoctored' manner. As a professional public relations practitioner of this type might put it, the goal of such work was to facilitate the effective communication of information about government departments, as well as more overtly ideological clients like political parties, candidates, or any other political actor with communicative goals to pursue. The Whitehall information apparatus, for example, has functioned for most of its history in this relatively non-controversial manner, only on occasion attracting criticism from those who believe it to be excessively 'politicised' (Cockett, 1989). A favourite defensive tactic of the more infamous spin doctors of today is to assert that the accurate and efficient dissemination of information, pure and simple, remains their principal professional task. They claim to be, like their predecessors, mere functionaries of political masters, albeit operating in a media environment radically different from that in which their predecessors worked. Alistair Campbell, for example, in defending his role at a time of intense journalistic interest in spin, wrote in his own defence that 'much of the work involves ensuring all [media] outlets are spoken to, a consistent line is taken, and our central points communicated'.[12] None of which, he insisted in defiance of his critics, 'stifles debate'. But if effective communication of the client's central points were all that political public relations professionals did, it is unlikely that the demonisation of spin described below would have occurred. So what is the key difference between spin and its more respectable parent, and the source of its demonisation?

In essence, the concept of spin connotes aggressive advocacy, where the role of the spin doctor is 'to extract the best possible outcome of any given situation for your client'.[13] If the traditional press officer was a paid functionary, a technician blind to the client's ideological bent and able to move between parties with ease, the spin doctor is part of the senior management team, in an era when presentation is perceived to be just as important to the achievement of organisational goals as the substance of policy. Spin is characterised, therefore, by a degree of politicisation which is unsettling to career civil service press and publicity officers. In the United States, it is true, some spin doctors, such as Dick Morris, have transferred their loyalties from Republican to Democratic employers with relative ease, albeit in the context of President Clinton's 'triangulation'. The same thing could certainly happen in Britain, as the right–centre–left spectrum loses definition. Crucially, however, the spin doctor must 'believe' in his or her client – in the 'project', whatever it is – and not rest with providing only a professional service.

Peter Mandelson exemplified this quality in his pursuit of the Labour Party's re-establishment as a credible electoral force. As 'Bobby' he engineered Tony Blair's successful 1994 campaign for the Labour leadership, and was the principal designer of New Labour's news management style. He has been described as, in the British context at least, a qualitatively new breed of source professional: not only 'the first significant British example of a "spin doctor"'[14] but 'the first spin doctor with a policy agenda which he is pushing through successive Labour leaders'.[15] By standing for election as MP for Hartlepool in 1987, Mandelson signalled his desire to play a role in policy formulation as well as presentation. This he subsequently did, earning himself the reputation in some quarters of being a sinister, Goebbels-type figure (a deployment of imagery which exemplifies the demonology of spin described below).[16]

The demonisation of spin

One of the first British journalists to use the term 'spin doctor' in a main-stream newspaper article was Mark Lawson in the *Independent* of March 24 1992. Then, and for sometime afterwards, 'spin' was the subject of occasional journalistic interest only. Lawson returned to the subject in late 1994, writing – rather prematurely, perhaps – of 'spin doctors heading for a dizzying demise',[17] echoing the point made in a 1993 piece by leading PR 'guru' Sir Tim Bell. Anticipating the demonology of later years (though rather wide of the mark in predicting the technology-driven demise of spin), Bell wrote then that the profession of political public relations

> faces extinction over the next twenty years because the media will begin to fragment. Technology will mean you can pick your stories, even print your newspaper off a screen. The great, satis-fying bundles of dailies and Sundays will lose control over the big mood-making stories of the day. Everybody will be into niche news and the monstrous fixers will be out of a job.

In the same article, *Sunday Times* culture critic Bryan Appleyard agreed with Bell in predicting that the extinction of public relations would take place within twenty years.[18]

As late as 1995 coverage of spin, and of political public relations more widely, was still relatively sparse, although Simon Heffer wrote a lengthy piece on the subject for the *British Journalism Review* (Heffer, 1995). By 1996, however, journalists were becoming alert to this new danger in their midst. In a survey of national print media conducted for this book, 992 articles about various aspects of spin were found in a twelve-month sample period (comprising March 1996–February 1997).

At the centre of this upsurge in journalistic interest were the spin doctors of New Labour. Just as the successful introduction of political marketing to Britain is generally perceived as the achievement of the Thatcher-era Conservatives (Scammell, 1995; Kavanagh, 1995, 1996), the emergence of spin in the British context is closely associated with – or blamed on, depending on how damaging one feels spin to be to the demo-cratic process – the Blair-era Labour Party. 'Labour pioneered the introduction of these black arts into Britain'[19] writes one observer, although the Thatcher government and its chief press secretary Bernard Ingham were hardly naive innocents in the techniques of media manage-ment. It is true, nonetheless, that if the Thatcher-era Tories were prolific users (some would say abusers) of such political PR staples as leaking, disinformation and aggressive media lobbying, they were never accused of spin doctoring, if only because the term was not in common usage during their administration. As late as 1995, when journalists were beginning to register Labour's adoption of a much more business- and 'middle-England'-friendly political strategy, and the movement of New Labour insiders into City PR companies,[20] this was not reported within a narrative framework of 'spin'.

The election of Tony Blair as Labour leader in 1994, and his subsequent reforms of the party's identity, policy programmes and communicative structures, changed things, however. Under the pseudonym of 'Bobby', Peter Mandelson was brought in from the exile imposed on him by John Smith's leadership to advise Tony Blair's campaign. Success in that campaign, followed by the transformation of 'old' Labour to New, and the mounting of a much more effective opposition to the Tories in the final years of the Major government, encouraged the emergence of a narrative framework for making sense of Labour's advance which emphasised the role of political communication. David Michie typifies the application of this framework when he wrote in 1998 that 'the success of New Labour, indeed its very creation, is the product of spin-doctoring, practised with relentlessness and virtuosity'.[21] Communicative professionalism did not bring approval, however, even from Labour's own supporters, and the application of something called 'spin' to the business of left-of-centre electoral politics produced a wave of critical coverage – a demonology, as it were.

A prominent element of this demonology was the alleged arrogance of the spin doctors. This argument contrasted a past when press officers dealt neutrally in information, from a position of subordination vis à vis the journalist, with the present-day environment of uppitty spin doctors who dared to question the dominance of the journalistic profession as the 'fourth estate'. The spin doctors became in this account a 'fifth estate'. One commentator, for example, evoked an era of communicative innocence when he wrote that :

> Once upon a time the political parties' employed press officers to answer factual questions about policy and distribute the speeches of politicians. Now they have spin-doctors who refuse to give out information until they are ready to release it and peddle the hidden message behind the most anodyne remarks.[22]

Columnist Iain MacWhirter also resented the new breed of communication professional.

> Labour media minders cruise the lobbies these days like celebrities. No longer are they the servants of the press, whose function is to get the party message across as clearly and as widely as possible. They now regard themselves as players in their own right.[23]

Spin doctors contribute to the dumbing down of politics, it was argued by Bryan Appleyard when he wrote that 'whatever they [the spin doctors] may, with sporadic coherence, say, they are all about triviality, about reducing everything – politics, culture and life – to present action. They exploit our radical ignorance of and impotence before the complex and baffling systems of the world.'[24] In the United States, complained another commentator, as a result of public relations:

> It has come to be held that the sort of people politicians are and what they actually do is not really important. What is important is the perceived image of what they are and do. Politics is not about objective reality, but virtual reality. What happens in the political world is divorced from the real world. It exists for only the fleeting historical moment, in a magical movie of sorts, a never-ending and infinitely revisable docu-drama.[25]

Spin doctors were also said to be responsible for a perceived increase in the incidence of lazy journalism. Articulating this view in 1993, Bryan Appleyard suggested that:

> They [PR professionals] establish their position as powerful middle-men, brokers of stories. What they tell the journalist may not be true or it may be so tendentious as to be untrue in effect and, either way, it will be known to be serving a cause. Yet it will probably not be checked because of the strange authority of the source – an authority that arises not from truth but from his known centrality within the system.[26]

The case of the Clare Short interview in the *New Statesman* was discussed in Chapter 5. That story, and the response it generated from politicians and others, focused a growing concern amongst journalists about how news agendas are set and, in particular, the extent of journalistic dependence on political sources for material. The Short interview, as we saw earlier, received such intensive coverage largely because of its timing – the journalistic 'silly season' of high summer, when hard news is relatively hard to come by. But the impact of this and other political stories raised questions about the journalists' readiness to be led by their sources into initiating artificial controversies, hyping relatively trivial events into allegedly major stories, and setting in motion futile cycles of news which reveal little of value to the audience. Part of this debate concerned the role of party communication specialists – the spin doctors – in pressurising journalists to promote or suppress particular stories. On September 30, the first day of Labour's 1996 annual conference, BBC's *Panorama* devoted an entire edition to the issue of spin doctoring and its impact on political journalism. Tony Blair's press secretary, Alistair Campbell, pre-empted the broadcast with an article in the *Sunday Times*[27] which defended the role of the professional communications advisor. He turned the dumbing-down argument against the journalists by complaining, among other things, that the media's growing interest in spin doctoring was itself evidence of the media's tendency to trivialise politics and avoid coverage of serious policy matters.

Campbell might have found some support for his argument on September 29 1996 when the *Sunday Times* interviewed Labour's shadow foreign secretary, Robin Cook. The interview, conducted on the eve of the Labour Conference, was interpreted by *The Sunday Times* in its lead news item under the headline 'Cook rounds on Blair'. Cook was reported to have attacked Blair in his comments, which were then put in the context of ongoing leadership splits over the direction in which Blair was taking the party. In fact, careful reading of the interview revealed no such attack. Cook made no obvious criticisms of Blair in his comments, which bore little apparent relation to the newspaper's interpretation of them. This was an attempt, clearly, to set in motion a 'Labour split' story, on the eve of a conference which seemed likely to portray Labour as united and disciplined. Although the *Sunday Times* story then became the starting point for a television interview with Cook by Jonathan Dimbleby, it quickly 'died' as Cook and Labour's spin doctors successfully demonstrated how exaggerated it in fact was. On this occasion, the *Sunday Times* failed to establish its preferred news agenda in any other media.

On other occasions, however, the politicians have been less successful in containing such stories. In December 1996 the *Daily Telegraph* published a story suggesting a split between John Major and Kenneth Clarke on the issue of Europe. The story developed into a serious political crisis for the Tories, and contributed to the symbolically important loss of the party's overall majority in the House of Commons. Although the Conservatives *were* split over Europe, this story attracted the criticism (and not just from the politicians who suffered by it) that journalists were driving the news agenda in inappropriate ways. In the *Guardian* Roy Greenslade called the story, and the crisis which it generated, 'the consequence of the media's love-hate relationship with spin-doctoring'.[28]

> Stuck within a lobby culture of anonymous leaks, the press has allowed itself to be dragged into a round of briefing and counter-briefing which makes story-telling more convoluted than necessary.

Similar points were made by many observers of Labour's first government in eighteen years.

The people who live in the dark, in the light: the spin doctors in power

Labour in office has been accused of 'spinning out of control', finding in their efforts to manage and manipulate the journalistic agenda a compliant press corps which 'appears to be wholly caught up in the frenzy of the spinners, desperate to stay in favour, craven to their political masters'.[29] Iain McWhirter argues that 'political journalism should be about breaking stories, revealing the workings of government and charting the evolution of policy'.[30] Since May 1997, however, 'journalists are finding themselves breaking stories that the government wants revealed, and on occasion protecting sources who are actually part of the government machine.' And it was not, reported the media, only journalists who found the activities of the Labour government's spin doctors disturbing. A poll of backbench Labour MPs conducted by the *Sunday Times* in June 1998 found that some 30 per cent found the party's leadership too authoritarian and centralised. Seventy per cent did not, however – an interpretation of the evidence which did not prevent the *Sunday Times* from turning this entirely predictable bottom-up criticism of the boss into the suggestion that 'an increasing number of Tony Blair's backbench MPs believe parliamentary democracy is under threat from spin doctors'.[31] and providing thereby an excellent example of the 'demonology of spin'.[32]

Spin: the case for the defence

What's new?

When BBC Scotland gave what Alistair Campbell regarded as undue prominence to the story of the *Sun*'s June 1998 denunciation of Tony Blair as 'the most dangerous man in Britain'[33] (the story was second in the offending bulletin's running order), he personally called the producer to register his complaint. While this and other similar incidents have been interpreted by the majority of political journalists as unacceptable intimidation of the media, Campbell's defenders argue that in an era of chaotic and unpredictable information flow, bullying the media (who can, of course, bully right back, as Peter Mandelson and Charlie Whelan discovered to their cost in December 1998) is an inevitable part of the press secretary's function. A former Conservative Party Director of Communication writes in a letter to the *Sunday Times* that:

> In truth, the most effective prime ministerial press secretaries down the years have also been the most combative with the media and have indulged in aggressive advocacy whether or not they have been appointed from party ranks. They have also sought to

control the government's announcements and activities simply because any organisation's presentation has to be managed sensibly.[34]

One journalistic observer places Campbell and Mandelson in a tradition of 'aggressively loyal' media minders stretching back to Joe Haines and Bernard Ingham.[35] The latter, as is well known and was much written about long before New Labour's 'people who live in the dark' became the demons they are, 'was encouraged to establish a dominance of government media relations which had not previously been attempted in peacetime' (Tunstall, 1996, p. 273). In this respect Campbell, presumably under the direction of the prime minister, was merely following a precedent set by Margaret Thatcher in the 1980s, who was in turn doing little that Harold Wilson had not done in the 1960s and 1970s. As such, argues Hugh Colver, 'to suggest that democracy is under some kind of threat ... seems to be hogwash'.[36] Alistair Campbell's approach to news management in Number 10 Downing Street has been described as 'centralised, picture-driven and presentational, rather than concerned to dot the i's of policy details. Its instincts are tabloid in tone.'[37] If this is true, and it probably is, then Campbell is doing what may be new in terms of the post-Thatcher era Labour Party, but which Ingham, Haines and others did with equal fervour for previous prime ministers.

In terms of recent British political history Campbell is a new kind of press secretary in one other respect – the fact that he was not recruited from the ranks of the Whitehall civil service, as was Bernard Ingham, but instead moved from the media to join the Labour spin operation in opposition, and then went with it into government. Where Ingham was by his own account a neutral public servant to begin with, only becoming politicised *after* his appointment by Margaret Thatcher and her subsequent enthralment of him (Harris, 1991; Ingham, 1991), Campbell was Blair's man from the outset. If, however, one discounts the fiction that effective chief press secretaries can ever be really neutral in respect of their prime ministers, the transparency of Campbell's position may seem to be more honest and accountable than that of, say, Bernard Ingham who, though forever declaring his political neutrality, was clearly an aggressive and extremely loyal advocate of Margaret Thatcher in her dealings with the media, as with dissidents in her own party and government. New Labour's politicisation of governmental public relations, far from being a danger to democracy, might just as easily be interpreted as refreshing pragmatism, an acknowledgement by the new governing elite of what was always true but hitherto denied. In which case, better the devil one knows ...

Demonology notwithstanding, New Labour's communication professionals have presided over several positive changes to British governmental public relations. Campbell, for example, broke in November 1997 with the long and oft-criticised tradition of non-attributable lobby briefings, moving to a system in which journalists could identify him (and thus the prime minister) as a source. The lobby may still be viewed by some commentators as 'a cosy conspiracy to manage the news',[38] but it is now a considerably more transparent conspiracy, and one in which journalists know that 'Campbell's quotes, true or false, express exactly the Labour leader's position on everything. There is no separation between them.'[39] The piece from which this extract is taken contained a lengthy profile of Campbell, characterised only half-jokingly as 'the enforcer'. Through it, and in similar pieces which have appeared in recent years,[40] Campbell and the governmental information management operation which he heads can justifiably claim to be the most talked about and best understood in British political history.

Mandelson, meanwhile, permitted in the first year of Labour government an unprecedented run of TV documentaries about himself and his colleagues in government, in which the activities of the spin doctors were exposed with disarming frankness. In one of these,[41] the chancellor's main news manager, Charlie Whelan, was filmed in the midst of an intense spin operation of the type, possibly, which forced his own resignation in late 1998. This remarkably honest and open film helped establish a journalistic framework for making sense of Whelan's relationship with the media which eventually brought him down. In *Blair's Year*, a review of the Labour government's first year in office,[42] Peter Mandelson indulged in some self-criticism, conceding that he had perhaps been overly zealous in the presentational dimension of his work. In another 'fly-on-the-wall' documentary, development minister Clare Short criticised the spin doctors and image managers of her own party (now her colleagues in government), in terms reminiscent of her 'people who live in the dark' interview.

The significant and at the time of their broadcast generally unacknowledged feature of these programmes is that, while they were themselves clearly part of a sustained propaganda campaign to portray Labour in office as open and accessible, the propaganda was at least partly true – through them we *did* see and hear more of Labour's spin operation, and not all that we saw and heard was complimentary – than we have seen of any previous government's. And having witnessed it, one might suppose, we are – journalists and citizens alike – less vulnerable to manipulation by it.

The myth of the all-powerful spin doctor

At the very end of 1998 the real, as opposed to the mythical power of the spin doctors was revealed by the forced resignations of both Peter Mandelson (no longer a spin doctor, but trade secretary in Blair's cabinet), and Charlie Whelan, Gordon Brown's press secretary. Whether they deserved to lose their posts or not, it should be reassuring for those who fear the 'high priests' of spin that Mandelson, despite the aura of Machiavellian manipulativeness which surrounded him on election day 1997, received some of the worst press of the Labour government's first year, and was finally hounded out of office by a gleeful political media (he returned to government as Northern Ireland Secretary in October 1999). Neither he nor Whelan were able to prevent negative media coverage of their activities, to the point that both found their positions had become untenable, and that they had become victims of the demonology of spin.

If the fortunes of Mandelson and Whelan in December 1998 are not enough to substantiate the view that the power of spin doctors is over-stated by journalists with an interest in doing so, consider the September 1996 edition of *Panorama* devoted to spin referred to earlier, widely viewed at the time as a response to consistent bullying of the BBC's jour-nalists by both Labour and Tory spin doctors (although the BBC publicly denied this).[43] Whatever was intended by BBC managers in broadcasting such a programme so close to a general election (the official campaign began six months later) it functioned as both a retaliation for the sins of spin doctors already committed, and a pre-emptive shot across the pre-electoral bows of the parties, by then in heavy BBC-intimidation mode. The programme prompted responses in article form from the main Labour demons, Campbell and Mandelson, and contributed to a wave of meta-discursive, reflexive journalism on radio, TV and in the press which, if nothing else, added to the stock of useful political information available to the public. This and other examples of how spin impacts on the public sphere show that as spin has become more intense in the management of politician–media relations, it has also become more visible to the citizen, through critical and deconstructive media coverage – the journalism of process discussed in Chapter 3.

Journalists need spin

Fortunately for political communication professionals, competition for media space – the work of maximising positive and minimising negative publicity – is not conducted entirely in opposition to, or isolation from, the professional interests of the journalists (although the demonology of spin may often suggest otherwise). On the contrary, as noted in Chapter 3, the latter *need* politicians as primary sources of information in the construc-tion of political news. Before becoming the prime minister's press secretary, Alistair Campbell defended his professional role by noting that 'we live in the media age. There are more newspapers, magazines, television and radio stations than ever before. They all have space to fill, and they look to politics to fill a good deal of it. The political party that does not under-stand the needs of the media is doomed.'[44] If the politician needs publicity, from the journalistic viewpoint public relations is a convenient way of sorting and sifting through the accelerating flows of information circulating in the public sphere. Perhaps too convenient, it is argued by the critics of spin.

Peter Mandelson, before his own demise at the hands of treacherous leakers of unwelcome facts, blamed the demands of a news-hungry media for some of the worst features of contemporary political PR, suggesting that 'much of the packaging of politics is dictated by the media, and in particular the broadcasters. It's the pressure from the broadcasters on the politicians to get their sound-bites in forty seconds, because that's what fits into their one minute thirty seconds package for their evening bulletins.'[45] There is much truth in his argument, as anyone who has participated in a broadcast interview or debate knows. The communicative limitations of broadcast media (as opposed to print, which as literary media have the facility to communicate rather more complex ideas), and the formal conventions and technical constraints within which they work, impose a presentational logic on contributors – or those who know that their words are likely to be used in a news package – which inevitably simplifies and sloganises content, sometimes beyond the point where any useful information can be gleaned. (Although the content of a sound-bite like 'the lady's not for turning', or 'the people's princess', may itself constitute a powerful political message.)

For better or worse, however, the journalists' need for the raw materials of news-making, alongside political actors' desire for positive coverage (which may mean no coverage of potentially damaging stories) structures a relationship of mutual dependence, and at the same time gives the demonology of spin some of the character of a 'phoney war'. Both sides need each other, it is clear, but neither can be seen to need the other too much. Managing the delicate balance between dependence on, and distance from the media, is an important element in the legitimation of both categories of communication professional It is in this context that the demonisation of spin is explicable as the defensive reaction of one profession, engaged in the interpretation of political events for a wider public, to the emergence of another, similarly engaged but working on behalf of private interests. The journalists see themselves as independent reporters and sense-makers, building their very professionalism on that independence, and the public's perception that it is real. Furthermore, as has been noted, the commercialisation of the media has established independence as an important brand factor in a market of many news providers. One can thus understand how journalists must resent public relations – a profession whose very existence threatens that independent image, and the status (and profits) built upon it.

Conclusion

The demonisation of spin, for all its hyperbole and lack of historical context, can be understood as the adoption in a competitive journalistic environment (meaning competition between journalists, and between journalists and public relations professionals) of a new narrative framework for making sense of political developments in an era of declining ideological differentiation between parties: one which first became available with the Thatcher–Ingham partnership of the 1980s (but did not become established due to the intense ideological polarisation of the Thatcher years), flourished after the election of Tony Blair as Labour leader in 1994, and became the dominant framework applied by journalists to the coverage of New Labour in power.

It is attractive to political journalists not just because it gives them something to write about, but because it positions them as victims rather than villains. It erects crucial, and commercially valuable ethical distance between two mutually dependent professional groups, in the interests of preserving journalistic legitimacy in the wider public sphere. If it also leads to the avoidance of engagement with ideological questions, as has been noted by some critics, this may be attributable less to the influence of spin than to the fluidity of post-Cold War politics and the realignment of left, right and centre which is now underway throughout the advanced capitalist world, and which New Labour spearheads in the British context.

Chapter 3 argued that process journalism, within which coverage of spin is a major sub-category, can be defended as a rational response to, and product of, a political culture in which performance and promotion (executed through a variety of forms of public relations activity) are recognised as central to the communication of political ideas and symbols. The demonisation of political public relations described in this chapter, if intelligible in terms of professional rivalry, is the point at which process journalism tips into a kind of moral panic, as one elite group, one species of professional communicator, long established and respected in its fourth estate role, becomes defensive and paranoid about the activities of another, newer breed; and where the pack-like instincts of the journalistic community are asserted in the labelling of 'spin doctors' as the folk devils of the media age. As is the case with all moral panics, the media analyst should be cautious in endorsing the journalists' terms and referential frames.

Academic analysts and political scientists for their part, following Jurgen Habermas, have condemned the rise of public relations as part of the twentieth century's 'refeudalisation' of democracy. But there is no logical reason, beyond nostalgia for an era of pure, disinterested publicity that never existed, why the professionalisation of political communication (which is all that political public relations is) should be seen as more evil or menacing than the technological advances which have allowed the expansion of the journalistic industry. Public relations is by now embedded in the supporting infrastructure of mass-mediated democracy, no more a 'bad thing' in itself than the cables, computers, digital editors and other communicative tools which allow political messages, and journalism about politics, to be disseminated with ever-increasing speed and efficiency to the mass audience. From this perspective, indeed, public relations is a valuable element of the modern democratic process. Just as citizens in today's information-dense environment have an enhanced need for the sifting, sense-making journalism of interpretation and meaning, so journalists, as the producers of political news, need reliable suppliers of their main raw material – data about the political world. Ideally – as the ethical bodies of the public relations industry remind us in their proliferating codes of practice – this data is uncontaminated with lies and distortions, the work of the source professional a service provided by one branch of the communication industry to another. In so far as the ideal is achieved, and ethical codes followed (they are not always, of course), there is nothing which can be said to be inherently 'undemocratic' about the PR function in itself.

The public relations professional used to bang at the journalist's door, desperate for access, through news, to the public. My earlier discussion of columnists noted the inferior, 'dogsbody' status of the 'press publicist' portrayed by Tony Curtis in *The Sweet Smell of Success*. Now, the relationship is much less one-sided. Spin doctors find themselves the much-sought-after suppliers of a precious raw material – one might call it *news-potential*, or *desired knowledge* – which, with the added value of processing and refinement by the journalist, becomes the saleable commodity form of news. As a key input in this production process, public relations has become a powerful sub-sector of the wider culture industry. This shift in the balance of power between the media and public relations industries need not mean the death of democracy. To repeat what was forcefully argued in Chapter 3: the gradual increase seen in the proportion of political journalism devoted to process (and the process of spin in particular) constantly checks the power of politicians and their media managers.

The rise of spin, then, is not the cause of a deterioration in the quality of the public sphere, but a response to its technologically driven expansion, on the one hand, and its democratisation on the other. Both processes have combined to create a need for political actors to influence public opinion, and a profession geared to delivering that service. The demonology which depicts these professionals as sinister manipulators feeding propaganda to defenceless journalists and gullible audiences is not credible, if only because journalists have shown themselves to be perfectly capable of responding to spin with retaliatory measures of their own, devoting more and more time to uncovering and critiquing the activities of their 'evil twins'. Political journalism and political public relations have evolved together, responding to each other's adaptations and innovations. Aggressive interviewing, as we have seen, is defended by its practitioners largely on the grounds that it helps to penetrate the 'gloss' of political public relations and news management. And just as one cannot 'disinvent' the adversarial political interview (nor should one wish to), spin and spin doctors are here to stay, an integral element of a communicative system which they have both helped to create, and been created by. As one observer puts it, 'there have always been spin doctors. The difference today is that the media is [sic] in the driver's seat.'[46]

8

THE MEDIA AND POLITICS, 1992–97

We end with a review of the performance and role of the media in what was arguably the most important party political event in Britain since the victory of Margaret Thatcher in 1979 – the 1997 general election, which brought eighteen years of Conservative government to an end and replaced it with Tony Blair's New Labour administration. Then, as in all British election campaigns since at least 1959, practitioners of journalism and political communication combined to construct a 'media election'.

The 1997 campaign is especially significant for the student of political communication, since it saw the historic transformation of the hitherto 'Tory press' into something altogether more unpredictable and interesting. It was also a campaign defined, to a greater extent than its predecessor in 1992, by an agenda set by journalists rather than politicians.[1]

The press and politics, 1992–97 – from cheerleaders to bystanders

The 'anatomy' of the political public sphere presented in Chapter 2 grouped the media in relation to the socio-demographic characteristics of their audiences. Also important, for the press in particular, is the political position from which they contribute their information, analyses and interpretations of political events. The public service broadcasters, as already noted, are obliged to maintain 'due impartiality' in respect of public policy matters (and Sky News, as noted earlier, adopts a similar stance, notwithstanding its position as part of the News Corporation empire),[2] but the partisanship of the press has always been allowed within the British system, and is an important element in the positioning of a title in the media marketplace. Newspapers, as Jeremy Tunstall puts it, 'exercise a continuing prerogative both to bias the news and to slant the comment' (1996, p. 1). Historically, for most of the century and a half or more since the emergence of a mass commercial press in Britain, the majority of newspapers and periodicals have been overtly right-of-centre in their political orientation, with a minority either left-of-centre or independent. So rare is press neutrality, indeed, that the founding editor of the *Independent*, on the tenth anniversary of its launch, defined its unique selling proposition as one of 'no commitment to causes other than the paper's own ... A refusal to place the newspaper on the left or right of the political spectrum.'[3]

The historical fact of right-wing press bias has produced much justified criticism of the public sphere, on the grounds that grossly unbalanced partisanship undermines the normative principles of pluralism and free debate (Miliband, 1973; Franklin, 1997). The arguments are well known, and need not detain us here. If the right-wing bias of the press was once a taken-for-granted fact of British political life, however, the situation in recent years has been transformed. The 'Tory press', such as it was, became considerably less Tory in the period between 1992 and 1997 to the extent that for most of the 1990s, and during the period of New Labour's ascendancy covered by this book, only four of the nineteen national newspapers (the *Telegraph* and *Express* titles), and one of the three political periodicals (*The Spectator*), could be described as wholeheartedly pro-Tory, with four others (the *Times* and *Mail* titles) best described as agnostic. In so far as the degree of editorial diversity in the print media is one measure of the quality of the public sphere, therefore, there has been an improvement rather than a deterioration in recent years, as the political affiliations of the press have become unprecedentedly volatile. The limits of editorial diversity continue to be shaped, as they have always been, by a conservative (with a small 'c'), pro-systemic consensus, since newspapers are businesses and remain pro-business in their editorial policy. But within the conventional constraints of parliamentary party politics there was, in the run-up to the 1997 general election, more support for the left in the British press than most citizens would be able to remember. Indeed, by the onset of the election campaign itself, the traditional pro-Tory, right-wing bias of the British press had been reversed.

Between 1945 and 1994 or thereabouts the British press were both unmistakably partisan and biased in favour of the Conservatives, although Labour enjoyed what Jeremy Tunstall describes as a 'reasonable' share of editorial support until around 1979 (1996). Table 8.1 shows that the Tories consistently led Labour in press support throughout this period, with advantages (or press 'surpluses') of between 10 per cent (1950) and 18 per cent (1974). During the Thatcher years, however, and especially from 1979, pronounced pro-Conservative partisanship was the editorial norm for most newspapers. The Tories' 'lead' over Labour during this period ranged from 38 per cent in 1979 to 53 per cent in 1983, principally because the traditionally pro-Tory *Mail*, *Express* and *Telegraph* titles were joined by the massed ranks of Rupert Murdoch's News International empire. By February 1992, shortly before the general election of that year, seven national dailies, with combined sales of ten million copies, supported the Conservatives, as against only two titles – the broadsheet

141

Guardian, and the tabloid *Mirror/Record* (combined circulations: three and a half million) – for Labour, giving the Tories a 43 per cent lead in circulation share. Political columnist Robert Harris observed at the time that 'the imbalance is even more pronounced than that, for the figures fail to measure the seething, partisan mendacity of papers such as the *Mail* and the *Express* which, on their day, can make the equally partisan *Mirror* look like the *Christian Science Monitor*'.[4] Brian MacArthur, a former News International editor, acknowledged that 'newspapers have never been fair, and the best have always been partisan, particularly during elections', but added that 'the popular press have never been quite so biased as they are today, nor so potent a threat to standards of political debate'.[5]

MacArthur's linking of press bias to the conduct of the democratic process was a restatement of a familar theme in British public debate about the political media: that newspapers have the power to influence their readers in ways significant for the outcome of election campaigns,

Table 8.1 Editorial allegiances in the 1997 general election

	Conservative	Labour	Lib Dem	None	Circulation*
Dailies					
Sun		*			3,819,908
Mirror**		*			3,052,362
Star		*			740,568
Mail	*				2,153,868
Express	*				1,220,439
Telegraph	*				1,132,789
Times				*	756,535
Guardian		*			429,101
Independent		*			263,707
Financial Times		*			319,400
Total share (%)	32.5	62			
Sundays					
News of the World		*			4,429,387
Sunday Mirror		*			2,211,527
People		*			1,908,363
Mail on Sunday	*				2,129,376
Sunday Express	*				1,153,873
Sunday Times	*				1,331,656
Sunday Telegraph	*				910,803
Observer		*			480,426
Independent on Sunday		*			278,465
Total share (%)	37.25	62.75			

Source: Audit Bureau of Circulation

* Average figures for May 1997
** Incorporates figures for *Daily Record* in Scotland

and that a newspaper market which leans editorially toward one party or another can unfairly stack the odds in favour of that party, in violation of the normative principles of democratic politics. In the run-up to the 1992 election the Labour Party shared that concern, accusing the *Sunday Times* and other titles of conspiring with the Conservatives to manufacture anti-Labour stories. In the *Sunday Times'* case Labour pointed to the example of a story linking then Labour leader Neil Kinnock to the Soviet KGB, a classic 'red scare' tactic of pro-Conservative newspapers ever since the 'Zinoviev letter' of 1924. The story, which appeared in February 1992, just two months before the election, sought to cast the routine and entirely proper diplomatic activities of a British Opposition leader visiting abroad in a sinister pro-Soviet light, in an era when collective memories of the cold war were still fresh enough for such accusations to inflict domestic political damage.

So concerned by pro-Conservative press bias had the Labour Party become by the early 1990s that it promised to weaken the influence of the big, mainly right-wing proprietors when in government, by reforming the law on ownership and control of media. In the event, of course, Labour lost in 1992 and the reform policy was never implemented. But Labour fears about the partisan performance of the press were fully realised in the course of a campaign which produced the famous *Sun* headlines 'Nightmare on Kinnock Street' and 'If Kinnock wins today, will the last person to leave Britain please turn out the lights',[6] around a plethora of stories ranging from the bizarre (a psychic confirmed for the *Sun* that, were they still alive Stalin, Mao and Robert Maxwell would all be voting for Labour) to the dishonest (a *Daily Mail* report on 'Labour's tax plans', based without acknowledgement of its source on nothing more reliable than a Conservative Party briefing).[7] Such stories represent what David McKie has termed 'the cheerleader tendency' (1995) typical of much of the pro-Tory press at this time: a press not merely partisan (partisanship is a historically well established and wholly proper characteristic of newspapers, as distinct from broadcast journalism's legally determined adoption of an impartial stance) but deliberately and knowingly unfair and deceitful with it. This he contrasted unfavourably with a 'bystander' approach, where partisanship is combined with a sincere attempt at objectivity and fairness.

In these circumstances it was perhaps predictable that the unexpected (by most pollsters, pundits and Labour supporters alike) Conservative victory of April 9 1992 would be attributed, at least in part, to the pro-Tory press. Neil Kinnock certainly held this view, as did Margaret Thatcher and, notoriously, at least one of the pro-Tory editors involved. The *Sun*'s 'It Was The *Sun* Wot Won It' editorial of April 11 made the point honestly and with pride. In the *Sunday Telegraph* of April 13 former Conservative fundraiser Lord McAlpine opined that the editors of the pro-Tory press were 'the heroes of this campaign'.[8]

If, indeed, this *is* how the 1992 election was won, British democracy was in serious trouble. A fragile creature at best, for it to be so easily manipulated by ideological warfare conducted through the privately owned press would confirm the most vulgar of marxist analyses. Fortunately, the evidence on this point is rather more contentious than some commentators allowed, and has to be set against the fact that many had good reasons to blame the newspapers for the 1992 outcome. For the defeated Labour Party, and leader Neil Kinnock in particular, the pro-Tory press were convenient scapegoats for a campaign later acknowledged to have been complacent and misjudged. For Margaret Thatcher and Lord McAlpine, on the other hand (no friends of John Major in 1992), highlighting the role of the press made more explicable the latter's victory, and avoided the need for the eating of too much humble pie by those who warned that her downfall would mean the end of Tory government. For the *Sun's* editor (if not its proprietor, who angrily 'bollocked' editor Kelvin MacKenzie the day after the 'We Won It' editorial appeared) the suggestion of a pivotal role in the Conservatives' re-election reflected a familiar tabloid bravado, and an air of self-importance about the paper's preeminence in the British media market. When politicians began to wake up to the potential regulatory implications of the *Sun's* claim being true, the paper back-tracked, fearful of provoking restrictive legislation.

What, then, *was* the role of the press in 1992? For Labour MP and former *Guardian* journalist Martin Linton, the author of a detailed report on the press and the 1992 campaign,[9] it was not necessary to look hard for a strong pro-Conservative effect. Citing research which suggested that Silvio Berlusconi's ownership of three television channels had swung three million voters to his Forza Italia movement in the Italian general election of 1994, he argued that the pro-Tory press had played a similar role in Britain. According to ICM/MORI opinion poll data cited by Linton, an 8 per cent swing from Labour to Conservative occurred amongst readers of the aggressively pro-Tory *Sun* in the three months prior to the 1992 election. Readers of the *Guardian* showed no such swing. Swings of a similar size were also recorded amongst readers of other pro-Conservative titles, leading Linton to conclude that 'the widely held assumption that traditionally Conservative newspapers have no influence in elections turns out to be quite wrong.'[10]

Bill Miller's research on the 1987 election (1991) had found support for a milder version of this 'strong effects' thesis, arguing that pro-Conservative press bias had provided the Tories with a measurable advantage over Labour, manifest by the 'Basildon effect'. In 1987 this Tory-held marginal, with the highest density of *Sun* readers in the country, showed a smaller than average swing from the Conservatives to Labour, a pattern repeated in other marginal constituencies with a high density of *Sun* readership.

Less convinced of the claims made for the pro-Tory press in this respect were Margaret Scammell and Martin Harrop, whose analysis of the 1992 campaign suggested a minimal impact, if any, on its outcome, given that Labour did much better in 1992 than it had in 1987, when press bias was a less obvious feature of the campaign (1992). Similarly, David McKie explained the deviant swing amongst *Sun* readers detected by the 1987 polls with the survey finding that they tend in general to be less politically committed than *Mirror* readers, and are thus more likely to shift allegiance from one party to another. However, McKie accepted the evidence that 'Conservative voters are more likely to stay loyal if they read a Conservative newspaper, while uncommitted voters are more likely to choose the Conservatives if they read a Conservative newspaper' (1995, p. 132).

Evaluating the evidence for and against media impacts in any category of output (the debate around images of sex and violence is similarly unre-solved) is a notoriously complex exercise. In the context of political campaigns, comparisons of like with like are extremely difficult to make. If, for example, we can agree that the Labour Party won more parliamen-tary seats in 1992 than in 1987, despite an equally, perhaps more hostile press than five years before and a poor campaign performance by the leader Neil Kinnock, this might suggest that pro-Conservative newspaper bias had little influence on the electorate's voting behaviour. On the other hand, offsetting features such as an improved Labour image and campaign organisation, or the change of Conservative leadership from Thatcher to Major, have also to be taken into account. When one does so, the specific contribution of the press to voting patterns becomes obscured in a complex web of political, economic and social calculations. Newspaper coverage of politics undoubtedly has effects, but precisely what they are, and their expression in electoral outcomes, cannot be straightforwardly disentangled from the many other causal factors involved in influencing voters' decisions. In a rare public statement of his views on this subject, Rupert Murdoch has denied that his newspapers, or those of any other proprietor, can have a decisive impact on campaigns. 'It's not true,' he argues.

> It's very exaggerated. You give a little momentum, a bit of help to a party ... if you're relevant and intelligent and know how to popularise an issue, you're going to help set the agenda.[11]

Notwithstanding the opacity of the causal connections between media coverage and political behaviour, two significant effects-related points *can* be made. Firstly, as already observed, the 1979–92 period was one of unprecedented pro-Conservative partisanship in the British press, with Labour enjoying in the 1992 campaign only 26.6 per cent of daily support including the *Financial Times*, which came out for Labour at the end of the campaign) and 31.2 per cent of Sundays. Linton notes that 'Labour has never won an election when it was more than eighteen per cent behind the Tories in press share',[12] a stark fact that remains as true after the 1997 campaign as it did before.

Secondly, and regardless of whether Linton's analysis of the importance of the press in determining election outcomes is right or wrong, it was shared by the Labour Party. After 1992 Labour media managers embarked on a sustained public relations campaign to reduce the party's 'press deficit' (i.e., the gap between its popular support as measured by opinion polls and its share of editorial support as measured by circulation). Partly as a result of this campaign, and for other reasons explored below, that deficit had shrunk, indeed disappeared, to the point where in the years and months preceding the 1997 election the concept of a 'Tory press' had become a misnomer. As early as the election of Tony Blair as Labour leader in the summer of 1994 most if not all of the Tory 'cheerleaders' amongst the British press had become 'bystanders' whose editorial stances, if not quite 'anti-Conservative' or 'pro-Labour' were, by the standards of the 1979–92 period, uniquely open to harsh criticism of the Conservative government, and to favourable reporting of the Labour alternative. What they subsequently became is unprecedented in post-WWII British press history.

Shifting allegiances

The beginnings of a shift in the allegiances of the pro-Tory press can be traced back to the late summer of 1992, a few months after the election of a fourth Conservative government, when early examples of 'tentative and symbolic criticism'[13] were reinforced by the government's humiliating exit from the exchange rate mechanism. By the summer of 1993 criticism of the government from newspapers hitherto noted for their pro-Tory bias had become so vociferous as to be the subject of a growing number of press commentaries. In the *Guardian* of June 28 1993 Henry Porter observed that only the *Express* titles remained loyal to the government.[14] In the *Sunday Times* a month later, Martin Jacques noted that 'over the past year traditionally pro-Conservative newspapers have become bitter critics of the government'.[15] In *The Times* that September, Roy Greenslade described how 'encouraged by editors and proprietors – who have moved from scepticism to hostility – Tory political journalists are enjoying their new, central role as crisis-makers'.[16] How had this transformation in the partisanship of the British press come about? What had brought an end to the many years of 'cheerleading' on behalf of the Tories that had passed for political journalism in the majority of British newspapers?

The Major factor

Of prime importance was the growing perception of incompetence in the Conservative government, centred on the complex and contradictory figure of John Major. While Major's election to the leadership was largely the product of Margaret Thatcher's indications that he was her preferred choice as successor, she also made it plain that she would rather not have been forced to resign, and a number of editors and proprietors shared her regrets. British newspapers of the 1979–92 era were not just pro-Tory: they were pro-Thatcher, and when she was rejected by her own party in 1990 her successors were unable to command the same loyalty, whether from backbench MPs, cabinet ministers, or media barons and editors. The post-92 trend of anti-government political journalism was at least in part the result of a personal vendetta against John Major and his allies in government, as revenge for their role in Thatcher's downfall. Revenge, then, combined with genuine dissatisfaction following the ERM debacle (not to mention the succession of sex and corruption scandals which dogged the government in the early 1990s), meant that the perceived incompetence of the government, focused on John Major's hesitant performance as leader, became a recurring theme in the now-becoming-rapidly-less-Tory press. By early 1994 relations between the Conservative Party and the newspapers 'had never been so bad'.[17]

The press as surrogate opposition

Several explanations – other than revenge – for the post-92 break with British press tradition have been advanced. Some commentators suggested that the readiness of traditionally pro-Conservative journalists to attack the Major government in such terms as became commonplace from 1993 onwards was the perverse consequence of the ineffectiveness of Labour in opposition. According to this line of reasoning the press were encouraged, out of honourable commitment to their traditional 'fourth estate' role, to form a surrogate opposition. But if this was the *effect* of the shift in editorial allegiances it seems unlikely, following more than a decade of loyalty to Thatcher, in conditions of equally if not more ineffectual Labour opposition, that the British press would suddenly have developed a political conscience.[18]

The post-Cold War dealignment thesis

A more sociologically sophisticated explanation was suggested in a *Sunday Times* column by former *Marxism Today* editor Martin Jacques (whose employment as a columnist by News International at this time was itself an illustration of his thesis that boundaries between left and right, Tory and Labour, were being blurred in the post-Thatcher, post-Cold War era). Jacques identified a broad trend of political dealignment taking place in post-Cold War Europe, eroding the organisational principles which had structured British politics before 1991, and prompting newspapers to loosen their ties to the Tories. In his view, class-based allegiances had 'declined in importance and the old left/right division no longer enjoys the same pervasive influence'.[19] British society and its newspapers were becoming less polarised, as reflected in a reduction of the blind loyalty displayed by so many traditionally right-of-centre titles towards the Conservatives.

Labour's long march

Jacques' thesis is only partly right, in so far as it attributes shifts in press allegiance to the 'de-ideologisation' of British society as a whole (and indeed of the entire European continent), rather than the Labour Party in particular. After the election of 1992 the Tories remained a party of the right, and the newspapers in question continued to be owned by the same constellation of right-wing proprietors as before: Rupert Murdoch, Lord Rothermere, Conrad Black and others did not suddenly encourage their journalists to criticise John Major and the Conservatives merely because the Soviet bloc ceased to exist, or because of some more generalised 'end of ideology'. They did so because, after the defeat of 1992, the Labour Party under the leadership of John Smith continued and accelerated the process of modernisation begun by Neil Kinnock in the mid-1980s, and which happened to coincide with the tail end of the Cold War.

This process amounted, in part, to a 'declassing' of the party's political identity and the marginalisation of, on the one hand, the unions, and on the other, of the 'hard left' which had made significant policy-making advances after the 1979 defeat. While Neil Kinnock began the process, however, it had not advanced sufficiently by the election of 1992, and Kinnock was carrying too many personal 'negatives' to make a dent in the pro-Tory press consensus. Kinnock's successor John Smith, on the other hand, complemented Labour's continuing policy development with a political persona which emphasised his moderation and economic competence. With Smith as leader, Labour did indeed begin to disassociate or 'dealign' itself – in the public imagination – from what some had characterised as the 'hard left' interpretation of its ideological roots established in the early 1980s. As a direct result of this process, Labour became from the right-of-centre newspapers' point of view a much more palatable alternative to the increasingly unpopular Conservatives of John Major.

The Blair factor

By the spring of 1994, then, internal reform of the Labour Party had already produced a considerably improved press environment. It is far from certain, however, that this trend would have continued until a general election had it not been for a decisive, if tragic and totally unexpected further development. In May 1994 Labour leader John Smith died suddenly of a heart attack. To replace him, in July 1994 the Labour Party elected Tony Blair, one of its rising front bench stars. Blair immediately took forward the modernisation of Labour's policies and identity, and did so in the context of a youthful and dynamic personal image which proved irresistible to many in the print media. Bastions of Thatcherism in the press, such as the London *Evening Standard*, waxed enthusiastic about the new Labour leader from the start. Not only was he recognised by the hitherto pro-Tory press as an exceptionally talented politician who might be able to end Labour's long exclusion from power; to the shock of many (this writer included), after fifteen years of unremitting pro-Tory cheerleading, the possibility was welcomed and applauded. After July 1994 simmering press dissatisfaction with, and criticism of, the Conservative government existed alongside a 'love affair' with the new Labour leader. Henceforth, hostile press attitudes to John Major and the Tories formed against the background of an increasingly viable alternative government.

Political public relations and the courting of the tabloids

Blair's media-friendliness was not merely because he was young and (by the standards of politicians) relatively good-looking. Blair's successful campaign as leader, and his subsequent drive to reform party policies and organisational structures, were greatly assisted by the highly professional media management apparatus featured in Chapter 7. In July 1994 Blair appointed Alistair Campbell to be his press secretary. Campbell, a well-respected former journalist who had worked for tabloids of varying political affiliations, proactively sought press support for Blair, and was largely successful in gaining it. The journalistic disposition to like 'nice' Tony Blair was reinforced by skilful public relations from the leader's office as both Campbell and Peter Mandelson, the party's director of communication, lobbied and spun on their leader's behalf. Since 1985 Mandelson had been pursuing this strategy on behalf of successive Labour leaders (although John Smith chose not to use his services). With Blair he had found an especially able client.

The key target in Labour's post-Smith era of enhanced public relations professionalism was News International. Signalling the new approach, in 1995 Blair travelled to Australia as the guest of Rupert Murdoch to brief News Corporation executives on future Labour policy on media and to lobby for support. Coming as it did not long after a period during which – in protest at Murdoch's handling of the Wapping dispute – Labour politicians would not even speak to News International journalists, this excursion further reinforced perceptions of a warming of relations between British Labour and News Corporation. For media analyst Michael Leapman, these clear signs of a shift in the political affiliations of Murdoch's UK titles stemmed, 'like all his political shifts and pronouncements, from a realistic calculation of where his business interests lie'.[20] Murdoch's support for Thatcher had been rewarded with important commercial favours, as had his support for Labour in Australia. 'In the United States', noted Leapman, 'his links with local and national politicians allowed him to build a major press and television empire with the minimum of regulatory interference.' In this context, News International's strong pre-election hints of support for Blair were interpreted by many as an attempt to forestall a future Labour government's anti-monopoly legislation. As if to confirm this reading of events, in 1996 Labour announced a markedly more liberal policy on media ownership than even the Conservatives had up until then dared to propose.

The new approach continued up to the election campaign itself, with a focusing of effort on the popular tabloids. The political editor of the *Daily Star* during this period describes it thus:

> Labour had a far slicker operation in terms of spin-doctoring. They were absolutely brilliant. A tiny example: we were planning an auction of celebrity clothes to raise money for charity. We got in touch with Alistair Campbell, just wrote to him and said, any chance of getting an item of Tony Blair's clothing. I didn't expect him to do it, but almost by return post Blair's tie turned up, with a photograph of him wearing it, and a letter – which I didn't ask for – confirming that it was his. It's that kind of thing which the Tories weren't so good at, that actually made you warm to these people. During the election campaign the Tories tended to treat the *Daily Star* rather sniffily, as a bit below their level. Labour didn't. Labour came to us with stories, with some very good stuff, that recognised what we are.[21]

Shifting public opinion

This PR offensive encouraged proprietors to respond pragmatically to opinion poll and market research signals of a movement in popular support away from the Conservatives towards Labour. Newspapers, in this sense, were responding to commercial imperatives in following the market. As early as 1994, Robin McKie interpreted News International's by then already significant support for the new Labour leader as being caused by 'a combination of the group's commercial interests, a broader political assessment, and a judgement on the mood of the readers'.[22] For the *Sun* in particular, moving closer to Blair's Labour Party was not inconsistent with its long-standing aspiration to 'stand for' popular opinion. In the election of 1992, 45 per cent of its readers had voted Conservative, as against 36 per cent who voted Labour.[23] As British public opinion moved left between 1992 and 1997 the *Sun* moved with it, not only to improve its relations with a possible future government, but to maintain its readership and reputation for backing winners. Murdoch's astuteness in doing so was confirmed when in the 1997 election 52 per cent of *Sun* readers voted Labour, compared to 29 per cent for the Conservatives. Of course, the precise nature of the connection between this fact and the *Sun*'s editorial policy during the 1994–97 period remains unclear. Did the *Sun*'s coming out for New Labour reflect its reader's shifting opinions, or did readers' shifting opinions reflect the title's less hostile stance? In all probability it was a bit of both, in what became a spiral of gradually increasing support for one party, and a decline in support for another.

The proprietors of the *Daily Star*, which had supported the Tories in 1992, made a similarly pragmatic calculation, not least to ensure that it would not be outdone by its larger circulation rival. The paper's political editor suggests that

> For the *Daily Star*, it was a recognition that the Tories were so unpopular, particularly in our circulation area; that although we supported the Tories in the 92 election, it would have been madness not to take notice of what our readers felt. If we'd come out and said 'vote John Major' – a lot of the readers don't actually care – the *Sun* would have said, 'the *Daily Star* is so out of touch with what you think' that they might have cancelled it. So it was partly a commercial decision as much as anything, a feeling that this was what our readers expect us to do. It wasn't very difficult, because the Tories were making such a cock-up of so many things.

The end of the Tory press

After Blair's election as leader, the combination of factors discussed above ensured that Labour had an unprecedentedly favourable coverage in the British press. His skilful party management – as shown in his successful attempt to revise Clause Four of Labour's constitution – and his ability to project a positive public image through the media, produced positive reviews from the most unlikely sources. At the same time, John Major continued to receive a battering from the Tories' traditional press allies, to the extent that when he was forced to stand for re-election as Conservative leader in July 1995, only the *Express* newspapers considered him worthy of their editorial support. In the *Sunday Times* Peter Cole observed that, after the 1994 Conservative Party conference, a 'Tory press' had effectively ceased to exist. 'Never', wrote Cole, 'in the field of political conflict has so much generosity been expended on a Labour leader.'[24]

There were, however, moments when it seemed that the familiar pattern of pro-Tory, anti-Labour bias might be reasserting itself. As the election approached, criticism of Blair and his party increased. This never amounted to a return to the blatant pro-Tory partisanship of the 1979–92 period, but reflected the emergence of the spin-centred narrative framework for interpreting Labour's activities identified in the previous chapter. This, as we saw, produced unease about the allegedly manipulative, cynical character of the party's news management and public relations apparatus, and a growing readiness to expose it. In late 1995 controversy flared up around shadow health spokeswoman Harriet Harman's decision to send her child to a grammar school, in preference to her local comprehensive and in contradiction to Labour policy. This event, most commentators agreed, was badly handled by Blair, and marked the beginning of a phase in which his leadership style came under closer critical scrutiny. On the BBC's debate show *The Midnight Hour*, broadcast on February 18 1996, pundit Roy Greenslade declared that it was a return to business as usual in Labour Party–press relations, with the Harriet Harman affair the decisive moment. In the event, this analysis was wrong, and the Harman story proved to be a mere blip in the otherwise vigorously pro-Labour press coverage which lasted up to and beyond the 1997 election.

Indeed, most of the raw material for press criticism of Labour during this period came not from the pro-Tory right, but from within the party itself, as 'old' Labour stalwarts took their opportunities to attack what was now being called 'New Labour' and its key figures, especially the media managers. The summers of both 1995 and 1996 – traditionally quiet periods for the media, and thus opportune moments for generating journalistic interest in relatively trivial stories – saw Labour dissidents like Roy Hattersley, Ken Livingstone, Brian Sedgemore and Clare Short initiate public debate about Blair's style, and about the policy direction in which he was taking the party, leading to much media coverage of internal divisions, personal feuds and other 'negatives' which Blair and his communication advisors would have preferred to remain private. The more critical coverage of Labour seen from the end of 1995 was in no sense akin to the anti-Labour propaganda of the British press witnessed between 1979 and 1992, therefore, but was a predictable journalistic response to the need for some negative stories about the party, a need fulfilled by tales of internal conflict. The press did not initiate or invent the critical coverage of this phase, but simply reported what the Labour Party was saying about itself (some titles with more glee than others, of course).

As the 1997 election came closer, and the Conservative government continued to lag behind in the polls, the broadly pro-Labour/pro-Blair pattern of press coverage persisted, despite occasional hiccups and frequent predictions that the 'honeymoon' would shortly end. Far from stepping up their criticism of Blair and his party as the Tories' nemesis approached, several right-wing proprietors and editors let it be known by late 1996 that they would consider endorsing Labour in the election, if they felt it to be in the 'national interest' to do so. Commenting on Tony Blair's speech at the 1996 Labour Party conference, the *Sun* declared that 'this was more than just a brilliant conference speech with something for everyone. It was a powerful manifesto delivered with conviction by a man of decency and courage.'[25] In the following day's *Sun*, columnist George Pascoe Watson praised Blair for turning Labour into a 'lean, mean, vote-winning machine'.[26]

The 1997 election

In the event, the first and most dramatic 'defection' from the Tories following John Major's announcement of a May 1 election was indeed that of the *Sun* which, on March 18 1997, announced that it was 'backing Blair' and, with some misgivings, the Labour Party which he led. If recent history had contained clear signs that Rupert Murdoch was preparing to abandon his long-standing editorial policy of virtually unquestioning support for the Tories, the timing of the decision nevertheless surprised most observers. Ex-News International executive Andrew Neil, from his vantage point as editor-in-chief of the *Scotsman* titles in Edinburgh, declared that the *Sun*'s endorsement was 'the product of hard-headed, commercial consideration rather than political affinity',[27] and that it came with strings attached. Neil confirmed what had been widely rumoured.

> Blair privately made it clear to Murdoch that how a future Labour government would treat his multifarious media interests in Britain depended on how Murdoch's papers treated Blair and the Labour Party during the campaign.

Guardian columnist Hugo Young, like many on the left, found it unsettling that such a relationship could be struck between Labour and the proprietor who, more than any other in his view, symbolised all that was wrong with the British newspaper industry. In a column penned one week before the election, Young attacked Labour for seeking the *Sun*'s support and aligning itself to 'one of the most odious cultural enemies of a better, more decent, more communitarian Britain'.[28] He also attacked the *Sun*, curiously (could it have been expected to do anything else?), for 'selling its soul to the most commercial bidder'.

> All papers have some kind of core identity, and breaking with it
> can be a counter-productive gesture, confusing to readers and
> liable to take the guts out of the journalism.

Whether backing Blair was the outcome of a considered decision to ditch
the tired Tories, or of economic pragmatism in the face of shifting public
opinion, the *Sun* led the way in finally ending the press deficit which had
accompanied (if not necessarily caused) Labour's near twenty-year exclusion from power. If, as Martin Linton suggests, history has shown it to be
difficult, perhaps impossible for the Labour Party to win power with less
than 50 per cent of the national press support, 1997 was the first election
in more than twenty years when support of more than 50 per cent was
forthcoming. By polling day on May 1 only three daily and four Sunday
newspapers remained in the Conservative camp (see Table 8.1). Even these
titles qualified their support with frank admissions of the inadequacies of
the Major government, and acknowledgements of the successes of Tony
Blair and New Labour. Their readers were urged to support the Tories
with reluctance only. As the *Sunday Times* half-heartedly put it, in its eve-
of-poll editorial, 'only the Tories, warts and all, offer the prospect of
lasting improvement'. The rest of the press supported Labour with varying
degrees of enthusiasm, while the *Times* cast a plague on both houses and
stood alone in urging its readers to vote for the 'Eurosceptic' candidate,
whether s/he be of the Labour left or the Conservative right.

May 1997 thus reversed the pattern of the four previous elections, with
Labour getting more (quantitatively) and better (qualitatively) coverage
than the Conservatives (Figure 8.1). A study of 5,500 press articles by
CARMA International (Computer-Aided Research and Media Analysis)
found that 43 per cent had been negative towards the Tories, as compared
with only 32 per cent for Labour.[29] Similar results emerged from the monitoring activities of Test Research and other organisations.[30]

As to the impact of this coverage on the outcome of the election, the
evidence was (as always) ambivalent. Swings to Labour were *larger*
amongst readers of the remaining pro-Conservative titles (the *Express* and
the *Mail*) than amongst readers of the Labour-supporting *Guardian* and
Mirror, suggesting that the direction of a particular title's bias was relatively unimportant in determining its readers' voting behaviour. The
highest recorded swings to Labour were registered amongst readers of the
Sun (15.5 per cent) which actively backed Blair, and readers of *The Times*
(17.5 per cent), which did not.[31] There was, in short, no obvious correla-
tion between the fact of a title's support for, or hostility to, Labour, and
the size of the pro-Labour swing amongst its readers. The 1997 result did
not answer the age-old question of which comes first – the backing of the
press, or the winning of public opinion and then elections? That said, the
1997 outcome did nothing to undermine Linton's thesis that no party can

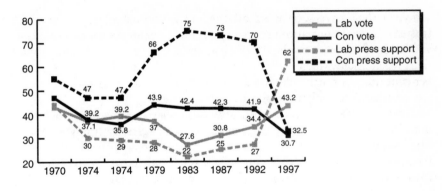

Figure 8.1 The Conservative press surplus, 1970 –97

win a British general election in today's media environment with a press deficit of more than 20 per cent.

Broadcast journalism, 1992–97

While the biases of the press are traditional, and the subject of criticism only if it is perceived that they swing so heavily in one party's favour as to threaten the democratic process, broadcast journalism has always been regarded in Britain as the most neutral, impartial medium of political communication. This has not dissuaded successive governments from seeking to challenge or subvert that tradition because, as one writer observes, 'ever since politicians came to realise that television was the key medium of mass communication, there has been tension and sporadic open warfare'.[32] The best-known skirmishes have been associated with governments' managing conflict, internal or external, and finding the broadcasters, and the BBC in particular, unwilling to toe a propaganda line: during the Suez crisis, for example; the 1982 Falklands war; the bombing of Libya in 1986; and the thirty-year conflict in Northern Ireland. In each case, the right of the broadcasters to be impartial has had to be defended against attempts by politicians – usually those politicians, left or right, who happen to be in government at the time – to redefine and neuter its impact on the content of coverage.

In political competition between the parties, too, and particularly at election time, the broadcasters have frequently come under pressure from the representatives of one side or another, concerned that their views are not being reported fairly or adequately. It is tempting for independent analysts to dismiss such criticisms as crude attempts to intimidate the broadcasters, but this *is* an important issue for politicians, who must take seriously the evidence that of all the media, broadcasting is the most trusted as an information source, and the most regularly accessed by voters. At the outset of the 1997 election campaign a Harris poll found that, when asked which medium could be trusted in political reportage, 63 per cent of respondents identified television, compared to only 37 per cent who trusted their daily newspaper.

The merest suggestion of political bias on television or radio, therefore, immediately produces angry denunciations and aggressive lobbying by the offended party. The BBC is most often the target of such attacks because it remains the national broadcaster of choice, enjoying a greater share of trust and status than ITN or Sky News. While commercial television has attracted criticism from politicians in the past – *Death On The Rock* being the best-known example – the output of the BBC is, as a matter of routine, more closely scrutinised, and more sensitively received than that of any other broadcaster. As far as the politicians are concerned, it is the performance of the BBC which matters most.

The 1992 election

Unsurprisingly, then, the run-up to the 1992 election was a difficult period for the BBC, though arguably not as difficult as the 1983 and 1987 elections had been. On those earlier occasions Margaret Thatcher, Norman Tebbitt and others in the Conservative leadership appeared to be irredeemably hostile to the very concept of the BBC as a public service broadcaster. By the early 1990s, with Thatcher gone and John Major in control of the party, a ceasefire had been called, although the BBC had yet to receive any guarantees on the future of its Royal Charter, due for renewal in 1996. The government consequently had some useful leverage as the 1992 campaign began, and exercised it. In October 1991, just after the Conservative Party conference, John Major and other senior Tories began accusing the BBC of 'biased' conference coverage.[33] Party chairman Chris Patten announced at the same time that 'subtle pressure' would be applied to the BBC – particularly the *Today* and *Nine O'Clock News* programmes, as the election approached.[34] A few days later News and Current Affairs chief Tony Hall defended the corporation in the following terms:

> Political correspondents and programme producers make hundreds of editorial decisions a day under pressure. Some decisions are bound to cause public comment. But on those rare occasions when we make mistakes, we admit them.[35]

On this occasion errors *were* admitted and the row blew over, to the extent that several BBC staff received honours in the prime minister's New Year list. The suspicion that governmental arm-twisting had made some lasting impact on BBC editorial policy was strengthened, however, when an edition of *Panorama* devoted to the failures of UK economic policy, and thus inevitably critical of the government which had by then been managing the economy for thirteen years, was cancelled at the last moment. Few believed the public version of events – that the programme was of poor quality – since it was written and presented by John Birt's close friend Peter Jay, preferring to think that it was simply judged by management to be too sensitive, and too close to the election of what would probably be another Conservative government, to be worth the risk.

The run-up to 1997

Such episodes were common in the 1980s and 1990s, with all the parties subjecting broadcast political journalism to close monitoring, both of the 'stopwatch' variety, in which the proportion of time devoted to a party is correlated with its sense of its own importance, and qualitative evaluations of how policy is reported. The Conservatives were especially vociferous in this regard after 1979, because they were in government throughout that time, but Labour and the Liberal Democrats also put the boot in on a regular basis. Key events in the period between the elections of 1992 and 1997 included the Scottish Labour Party's successful attempt to prevent the broadcasting of a *Panorama* interview with John Major on the eve of local elections in April 1995. On this occasion, a Scottish court accepted the view that to give the prime minister such prominent and 'unbalanced' coverage in Scotland at such a politically sensitive time was a breach of the BBC's impartiality obligations.[36]

In March 1995 the chief secretary to the treasury Jonathan Aitken accused the BBC's *Today* programme of 'bias' and 'open partisanship' against his party and in favour of Labour. The BBC was dubbed by some Tories 'the Blair Broadcasting Corporation' (some improvement, perhaps, on the preferred 1980s' term of abuse, the 'Bolshevik Broadcasting Corporation'), and accused by home secretary Michael Howard of 'giving prominence' to Labour policy on crime, in preference to his own. In May 1995 defence secretary Malcolm Rifkind claimed on the *Today* programme that 'the BBC are becoming a real menace' and were guilty of 'shabby journalism'. For Tony Hall, all this was clear evidence of an impending election.

> As election fever mounts ... as the politicians' survival instincts take over, all parties begin to apply pressure on the broadcasters – through public statements and off-the-record briefings, through monitoring and totting up of our output, and through the well-

tried mechanism of 'heavy duty' phone calls from the party publicity machines.[37]

Although the election was still two years away, no party undertook this lobbying more enthusiastically than Labour, whose new, Mandelson-led communications professionalism was directed at the broadcasters in a manner hitherto monopolised by the Conservatives. Notoriously, when the verdict of the O.J. Simpson murder trial threatened to overtake coverage of Tony Blair's 1995 conference speech in the BBC's running order of news, his press secretary Alistair Campbell dispatched a fax making the case for the speech to be the lead story. The fax was leaked, and the weight of political pressure on the broadcasters became a news story in itself.

The increasing frequency of such interventions, emanating from both main parties, produced an angry response from the BBC, which instituted a system of internal monitoring of party political attempts to influence its news and journalistic output.[38] It also generated a counter-attack in the form of a *Panorama* documentary on political news management, much of which focused on the Labour Party (see Chapter 7).

Many of the 'bias' accusations of this period, such as Jonathan Aitken's in March 1995, focused on the style of broadcast political interviews, and the conduct of interviewers who, as we have already discussed, were alleged to be excessively confrontational, aggressive, and even disrespectful. Although, as noted, such criticisms came mostly from the Conservatives, in government for more than a decade and thus most frequently the target of confrontational interviewing styles, Labour was not excluded. In November 1996, with the last possible date for an election clearly in sight, Labour's head of 'rapid rebuttal', Brian Wilson, attacked John Humphrys in the *Daily Telegraph*, accusing him of abandoning 'even-handedness' and 'common courtesy' in his interviews with Labour politicians.[39] Contrasting interviews conducted by Humphrys with John Major and John Prescott, Wilson alleged that the latter had been subjected to 'rudeness and constant interruption', and that the interviewer had been guilty of egotism, hectoring and generally failing to uphold the BBC's proclaimed standards of impartiality.

Criticism of adversarial interviewing was given added force in early 1995 by the Director General of the BBC himself. In a speech given in Dublin, John Birt addressed the subject of the media's 'complex interplay' with the political system, and acknowledged concern about the potentially negative impact of this interplay on the quality of public debate.[40] Observing that the media had moved to the centre of the political process since the 1970s, and that the expanding role of communication in politics had had many positive, pro-democratic consequences – 'politicians have to account for their policies, actions and decisions as never before. They must rely on their arguments, not their status' – Birt also accepted the view that 'there may be too much disputation and too little reflection in our public life', at the expense of 'analytical discussion, and the painstaking development of policy'.

Birt began the speech by addressing his comments to the media in general, but soon made clear his concern for the responsibility of the broadcasters in particular, who had permitted an unhealthy growth of 'studio argy-bargy' in their news and current affairs programmes, allowing confrontational styles to crowd out policy exposition and analysis. In a passage widely interpreted as a criticism of the Radio 4 *Today* team, and leading presenter/interviewer John Humphrys above all, Birt attacked 'overbearing interviewers who sneer disdainfully at their interviewees'. He suggested that 'politicians have a higher claim to speak for the people than journalists', who should adopt a more 'humble, dispassionate and rational' stance in their interviews with the former. More broadly, he urged broadcasters to avoid the 'ritualistic encounter which is little more, normally, than a brief opportunity to bicker, to exchange insults and to assign blame. Such encounters add little of substance to general understanding, and irritate our audiences'. As an example of how complex issues suffered from the overly confrontational, 'disputational' approach, Birt cited coverage of the debate on European union. The broadcasters, he suggested, were failing to provide a 'substantial and informed national debate', focusing instead on 'the political positioning and posturing on all sides of it'. High-level management intervention of this kind inevitably transformed what might have been viewed as predictably partisan attacks on the BBC into a wider public debate about the role of broadcast journalism in the political process (see Chapter 5). Birt's comments also provided ammunition for such as Jonathan Aitken[41] and Malcolm Rifkind to intensify *their* attacks on the BBC.[42]

This debate continued to surface in the run-up to the 1997 general election. In March 1996 Conservative Party chairman Brian Mawhinney became involved in a bad-tempered exchange with *Today*'s Sue Macgregor. In his capacity as chairman of the Conservative Party Mawhinney was being questioned about the Tories' continuing low place in the polls (local elections were imminent). As they discussed this issue, Macgregor drew a parallel between 1996 and an earlier period, when the Tories were similarly unpopular.

SM: In 1990 you did something dramatic. You got rid of the poll tax. You also got rid of Mrs Thatcher. Aren't you going to have to do something as dramatic as that not to lose a lot more seats?

BM: Oh come on, Sue, let's stay in the real world, can we?

SM: I'm talking about the real world.

BM: What you have just suggested to me and the nation is that we should dump the Prime Minister. Don't be ridiculous. That isn't even worthy of an answer.

SM: I wasn't suggesting you should get rid of the Prime Minister, I was saying ...

BM: Of course you were.

SM: ... dramatic gestures sometimes work.

BM: On the contrary, you drew the parallel with Thatcher, and that is a ludicrous and indefensible question, and if you think I'm annoyed with you, it is because it is that kind of sneering question by *Today* programme presenters which so annoys people who listen to this programme up and down the country.

SM: Dr Mawhinney, thank you.

On this occasion, however, Mawhinney found himself somewhat isolated from the mainstream of his own party, many of whom appeared to find his 'roughing up' of the BBC a questionable tactic in a pre-election period. Throughout the history of Conservative–BBC relations, the party has been divided into a patrician left, who view the anti-BBC campaign with distaste, and the right (at this time led by Aitken, Mawhinney and others) who openly sought to undermine the corporation's reputation and taint it with allegations of anti-Tory bias. Although Mawhinney's attack was not the last occasion when a senior Conservative would seek to challenge the BBC's approach to political journalism, the unease which it provoked did reveal a growing recognition amongst members of the Conservative Party as a whole that, as the election approached, more damage was done to the Tories' image than to the BBC's by such outbursts, especially when, as audience research indicated, nearly five times as many people perceived a pro-Conservative bias in the BBC as they did a pro-Labour.[43]

The style of political interviews nevertheless remained a sensitive issue for the broadcasters as they approached the 1997 election. In Britain as in America (Fallows, 1996) the increasing role of the broadcast media in politics was generating broad concern about the quality of the mediated political debate. Was an appropriate balance being struck between the aesthetics of confrontation and the requirements of rational discourse and exposition? Were politicians being shown the respect due them (at least in John Birt's publicly stated view), or were they being served up for ritual sacrifice by arrogant interviewers in pursuit of, at best, a misguided model of journalistic enquiry and, at worst, the inflation of egos and ratings? For the broadcasters, finding suitable answers to these questions (or dodging them) was a frequent task in the period under discussion, alongside the related but separate problem of how to resist behind-the-scenes party political lobbying of the type instanced above. Following the *New Statesman* interview with Clare Short in August 1996, the *Financial Times* reported that 'a senior Labour official yesterday wrote to BBC executives complaining about coverage of the latest row'.[44] While senior management, including the Director General himself, seemed at times to agree with the parties' criticisms of their own staff, on the issue of inappropriate party pressure the corporation held firm, with such efforts to shape and influence coverage being described as 'crass' or worse.

The broadcasters and the 1997 general election

Given the politicians' readiness to attack the broadcasters at any hint of 'bias', it is ironic that the main criticism of broadcast news coverage of the 1997 election campaign concerned its dullness and excessively 'balanced' style. Constrained, as in previous elections, by the rules on balance and access laid down in the Representation of the People Act, the BBC found the viewing figures for its flagship bulletins and current affairs programmes falling during the campaign. The audience for the extended *Nine O' Clock News* dropped to as low as 3.3 million (recorded on April 14) and only rarely during the campaign matched the pre-election average of 5.5 million. *Panorama*'s set-piece interviews with the leaders, chaired by David Dimbleby, were watched by a mere 2–3 million people. ITN's ratings also dropped, though not by such a large amount.

Explanations for the lack of audience interest in the televised campaign coverage included simple boredom – there was too much of it, over an unusually long (six-week) campaign period, with audiences stretched too thinly over a much greater quantity of political programming than they would normally be exposed to. Coverage was accused of irrelevance, in so far as some surveys found that around 50 per cent of the electorate had made their voting choices before the campaign started, and thus had little to gain from tuning in. Analysts also suggested – although there was no firm evidence to support this element of the 'demonology' described in the previous chapter – that audiences were reacting to the manipulation of the news by spin doctors.

The most influential criticism of coverage was made by future prime minister Tony Blair himself, when on April 13 he criticised the BBC by name for sticking too formulaically to the conventions on balance. On April 23 he accused the broadcasters of mounting a 'conspiracy against understanding' in their tit-for-tat balancing of one position against another. As Roy Greenslade reported, 'Blair does not believe this approach informs the public because it reduces complex arguments about policy to cat-calling soundbites.'[45]

The BBC responded, with justification, that they were bound by the requirements of the RPA, and that the complaints would have been both more numerous and more vociferous were they to deviate substantially from strict balance during elections. The BBC nevertheless embarked on a review of its election coverage shortly afterwards, with the expectation that any resulting modifications of past practice would be in place by the next election, due in 2001–2002. ITN, for its part, had already begun to break with convention in the 1992 election, abandoning the 'stopwatch' approach to allocating airtime in news coverage of the parties' campaigns. In 1997 too, ITN interpreted its public service obligations rather differently from the BBC, allowing 'newsvalues' a greater role in determining the balance of campaign coverage (as opposed to an arithmetical formula based on party strength). The 1997 election on TV was thus probably the last one to be conducted under the old rules of strictly observed balance. Neutrality and impartiality will not be cast aside in coverage of future campaigns, but the public service broadcasters are under pressure to interpret these terms more flexibly in the future. This pressure is heightened by the growing importance of Sky News in the political journalism marketplace, and the likelihood of other providers (such as BBC News 24) emerging with services which rival or supplant the traditional election coverage offered by the BBC and ITN.

The only aspect of broadcast election coverage which drew almost unanimous praise were the results programmes themselves. Here, by common consent, live coverage of the unfolding events matched the drama of Labour's landslide victory, with BBC1's programme being singled out by most commentators. Here, if not in the preceding six weeks of campaigning, the liveness and immediacy of television came into its own.

The debates that never were

One significant innovation desired by the broadcasters in 1997 but rejected by the politicians was the presentation of live debates between the leaders. Although such debates are commonplace in the United States, Canada, Australia, Germany and other comparable democracies, British incumbent prime ministers have always sought to preserve their elevated status (and the electoral advantage this is presumed to bestow upon them) by avoiding live debate with their opponents outside of the House of Commons (prime minister's question time allows leader-versus-leader debate to take place on a weekly basis, of course). In 1997 for the first time, however, the possibility of staging leaders' debates was seriously discussed by broadcasters and politicians, and media speculation about the impact of such confrontations on the election was a prominent feature of the first phase of the campaign. In the end the idea was dropped, following failure to secure cross-party agreement on terms and conditions, although it is likely to be revived for future campaigns.

The 1997 campaign: wot won it?

The final poll result of May 1 was, as it turned out, little different from that predicted by the opening opinion poll figures, suggesting that citizens had made their minds up before the campaign began, and were not strongly influenced to change their vote one way or the other by the media coverage. The general election of 1997 was, nevertheless, one in which, to a greater extent than was the case in 1992 (Butler and Kavanagh, 1992), the political media – especially the press – were at the centre of campaigning as agenda-setting actors in their own right. In 1992 the party news managers largely succeeded in keeping journalists on *their* agenda. Journalists in the main appeared to accept the argument that in a general election, if nowhere else on the political calendar, the journalist is subordinate to the politician, who must be Given adequate space to present and defend policy. The 'war of Jennifer's ear' in 1992 was the exception which proved the rule – a rare moment in the campaign when journalists hijacked the politicians' agenda and developed an alternative, subverting narrative which did neither of the main parties much good. In 1997, by contrast, journalists displayed an altogether more ambivalent relationship to the parties' issues management, refusing to be deflected from pursuing stories which were on no party's list of 'themes for the day', and more likely to challenge a party's preferred interpretation of an issue or event once it was put into the public domain.

This heightened journalistic pro-activity was partly the consequence of the changed environment as it has been described above, in which impatience with, and disloyalty to the Conservative government had become routine even amongst the most pro-Tory print media. It was also a result of the perception that journalists had allowed the 1992 campaign to be *too* controlled, and the coverage to be too predictable. In 1997, whatever else it was, the coverage was not dull. Indeed, the media were the source of many stories the absence of which would have led to a much less interesting and dramatic campaign.

The *Sun*'s declaration for Blair on March 18 established the pattern and set the tone. Here and throughout the campaign, a media story set the agenda and substantially defined the environment within which the parties had to present their policies, personalities and pitches. The 'We're backing Blair' editorial immediately threw the Conservative campaign onto the defensive, and became the main election story of that day and the next. On the evening of March 17, as all the broadcast news organisations were leading on John Major's earlier announcement of the election, *Channel 4 News* reported the *Sun*'s intentions for the following day, backed up by a view of the *Sun*'s front page and an interview with editor Stuart Higgins. BBC's *Nine O'Clock News* and ITN's *News At Ten* also covered the story, while *Newsnight* enlisted columnists Peter Riddell and Polly Toynbee to engage in a studio discussion. All the coverage focused on two themes: the view, right or wrong, that it was 'the *Sun* wot won it' for the Tories in 1992; and the explanation for its editorial shift in 1997.

For the parties on March 18, the first full day of campaigning, the economy was the preferred 'issue of the day', as expressed in news conferences. For the media, by contrast, it was the *Sun*'s pro-Labour declaration, for reasons which are not difficult to explain. In contrast to the predictable lines of the parties on the economy, here was an unpredictable (in its timing, if not the decision itself) and dramatic demonstration of how different 1997 was going to be from 1992. The head cheerleader of the Tory press for more than fifteen years had switched sides, and on the very first day of campaigning! The media environment had fundamentally changed. Both the *Financial Times* and the *Guardian* headlined with the story, as did the *Daily Mail*, reporting 'dismay at Conservative HQ as the *Sun* announcement spoiled what had been a strong first-day performance from the Prime Minister'.

By March 19 the broadcasters had moved on to other stories, but the press kept the *Sun* high on their news agenda. Both the *Guardian* and the *Daily Telegraph* ran editorials and commentary columns devoted to the motivations and morality of the *Sun*'s pro-Labour stance. Both were critical of the fickleness of the paper while acknowledging, as the *Guardian* put it, that this was 'an emblematic event of our times' and 'a symptom of the national swing to Labour', though 'not a cause of it'. All the media agreed that the *Sun*'s decision was an early psychological blow to the Conservatives, although most of the commentators accessed in coverage took a minimalist position on the question of effects: on Adam Boulton's *Tonight* (Sky News), Martin Linton presented his view (see above) that the *Sun* had made a marginal, but important difference in 1992, and could thus be expected to do the same again, particularly if it indulged in the kind of negative reportage against the Tories which had been directed against Labour in 1992. On the same programme Bernard Ingham argued that the editorial biases of the media had very little effect on voting behaviour.

Regardless of its effect on readers, however, the *Sun*'s defection had a major impact on defining the political environment within which the campaign was fought, putting the Conservatives onto the defensive from the outset, and directing attention away from Labour's policy programme. Every time John Major was reported denying the importance of the *Sun*'s stance on March 18 and 19, he merely confirmed that a turning point in post-Thatcher politics had been reached, and that Conservative hegemony over the British press was at an end. The impact of this 'meta-message' on public opinion and voting behaviour can only be guessed at, but inevitably reinforced Labour's campaign theme of 'Time for a Change'.

Sleaze

The second agenda-setting media intervention of the campaign was that of the *Guardian* and its coverage of the 'cash-for-questions' scandal, involving a number of (mainly) Tory MPs. This issue had been in the news long before the election was announced (see Chapter 3), but was given early prominence in the campaign by John Major's decision to dissolve – 'prorogue' – parliament early, and before the findings of the Downey Committee set up to investigate the 'cash-for-questions' affair, and the whole matter of parliamentary standards could be made public.

This story got off to a slow start, as if journalists were initially unaware of its significance. On *News At Ten* of March 18, a light-hearted item on prime minister's question time that day included reference to a question on the Downey Report by Liberal Democrat MP Simon Hughes, but the question itself was not broadcast, nor its subject reported. Martin Harrison observes that 'when Simon Hughes queried the fate of the Downey Report in the House, bulletins that evening focused more on the Speaker's rebuke than on the underlying issue' (1997, p. 137). In fact, Hughes had accused the prime minister of proroguing parliament earlier than necessary, in order to avoid the imminent publication of the Downey Report on parliamentary standards, which would inevitably contain much to embarrass the Conservative Party. Major denied that such was his intention, and the main evening news bulletins did not report the exchange as a 'sleaze' story.

Overnight however, and from these low-profile beginnings, the story began to build into the defining issue of the campaign – sleaze. On the morning of March 19, both the *Guardian* and the *Independent* headlined with the Hughes' allegations and reports of Gordon Downey's anger that his report was being sidelined until after the election. *The Times* ran an editorial on the subject, and the story was given some coverage (though only a paragraph) in the *Express*. Radio 4's *Today* programme featured the story, and it dominated that evening's TV news bulletins, at the expense of a governmental 'good news' story (falling unemployment figures). By March 20 sleaze, and the allegations of a governmental attempt to neutralise the Downey Report, were dominating broadcast and press news coverage. Then, on Friday 21 the *Guardian* published a full 15,000 words of evidence given to the Downey Committee by MPs Tim Smith and Neil Hamilton. As a result of this publicity Smith resigned one week later, generating another wave of sleaze allegations.

The *Guardian*, which along with the *Sunday Times* had led the cash-for-questions investigations, did not manufacture this eruption of the sleaze issue, which arose in the way it did because of the government's own decision to delay publication of the Downey Report until after the election. But the timing of its March 21 coverage, in an environment already thick with sleaze-related accusations and counter-accusations, ensured that the story – and the impression it made of a Conservative Party harbouring many corrupt MPs – remained dominant in the news agenda for a full three weeks. In CARMA's analysis of the election press, only the issue of Europe occupied more space in coverage of the Conservatives' campaign.[46] Regardless of why the story appeared when it did, therefore, the mere fact of its appearance gave the *Guardian* a key role in setting the election agenda.

Sleaze merchants

Sleaze quickly came to mean more than cash-for-questions, however. On Thursday March 27, the very day that the press were reporting the resignation of Tim Smith, the *Sun* led with the story of another Tory MP, Piers Merchant, and his adulterous dalliance with a young nightclub hostess. With photographic evidence to support its allegations, Piers Merchant became 'sleaze Merchant', and graphic images of Tory sexual misconduct were added to those of financial wrongdoing. On this issue again, there was a history and a narrative framework ready to be applied – the 1992–97 Conservative government had been plagued by several sex scandals. The Merchant story fitted the pattern, and the framework within which it had been made sense of for several years – Tory decadence and imminent demise – and would have been prominently reported with or without an election campaign to give it added urgency. In its timing, however (which the political editor stated in an interview with the author to have been entirely coincidental), the *Sun*'s story fed fuel to the flames of the growing bonfire of sleaze now consuming the Conservatives' campaign. In Scotland the Conservatives fed one of their own to the fire, as homophobic elements in the party 'outed' their own chairman Michael Hirst. His resignation dominated the news throughout the United Kingdom over the weekend of March 29–30.

In this manner the issue (or issues) of sleaze, which predated the 1997 election campaign, overwhelmed the campaign news agenda. Both the *Sun* and the *Guardian* were only doing what they had done many times before – the *Guardian*, exposing lapses in parliamentary standards; the *Sun*, exposing errant MPs sexual misbehaviour – but the timing of the stories, in a news environment already attuned to any hint of financial or moral corruption, bestowed upon them an agenda-setting influence rarely enjoyed by any media organisation in any previous election.

Newspapers contribute to the formation of public opinion in various ways, of course – by reporting and giving visibility to true stories which are negative for one side; by disseminating disinformation and propaganda disguised as news; by applying interpretative frameworks to the reportage of political affairs which close off a party's options – but only in conjunction with other environmental factors, such as citizens' lived experience of the economy, or the traditional class-based allegiances which still drive much voting behaviour. They are one cause of electoral outcomes amongst many, more likely to reinforce trends than to overturn or reverse them in the period of a campaign. The evidence of 1997 supports the view of many observers (and of Rupert Murdoch, quoted above) that if the editorial biases of newspapers do not *win* elections, with carefully timed and skilfully mounted interventions they *can* set agendas and thus contribute substantially to defining the environment within which campaigns are fought. Thus, in 1997, the prevalence of sleaze coverage created a highly unfavourable environment for the Conservatives, highlighting issues which were for them unambiguously damaging, and from which (largely due to their internal divisions) they were unable to shift journalistic attention, even that of their dwindling band of allies in the pro-Tory press.

Some of those allies tried to advance the debate by attacking their colleagues' emphasis on sleaze, asserting it to be an inappropriate usurpation of the politicians' rights to be heard in an election campaign. By departing so aggressively from the parties' carefully planned agenda the media were alleged to be undermining the democratic process. The *Telegraph*'s Stephen Glover argued, for example, that:

> It is not the proper role for journalists to set the agenda. We are not, after all, elected representatives. To determine what the election should be about is an abuse of power. We are the 'tribunes de la press', as is written on a ceiling in the French National assembly, and as such our job is first and foremost to report in an even-handed way, and then to explain, question and, if possible, to make the whole process as entertaining as possible.[48]

Such interventions were neither effective in changing the political environment, nor intellectually convincing, given the history of the pro-Tory press since 1979. From the normative perspective, indeed, it was a refreshing reassertion of the power of the 'tribunes de la press' that in 1997 they chose to override the efforts of politicians to downplay and hide their own misdemeanours, although any other approach would have been untenable. It had been the Tories, after all, who made 'back to basics' and 'family values' core elements of their political marketing after 1992, and who thus invited scrutiny of their performance on moral criteria. And few serious observers have ever denied that the cash-for-questions story was legitimate investigative journalism. If the media set the agenda to an inappropriate degree in 1997, it was an agenda only made possible by the hypocritical behaviour of politicians themselves during the preceding four years, and fed during the campaign by their own negligences, incompetencies and errors of judgment.

The broadcast agenda

Given their legal obligations for impartiality, it would be surprising to find broadcast journalists playing a proactive role in setting the election agenda comparable to that of the press. Apart from coverage of the leaders' debate, negotiations at the outset of the campaign (and which collapsed without success on March 27), and Tony Blair's comments on news style referred to above, there was no point at which broadcast news became a news story in itself, or where the broadcasters put a story on the main news agenda which was not first put there either by the press or the parties. On the other hand, as already noted, the broadcasters in 1997 showed a greater reluctance to be bound by the party news managers' daily agendas, and made a number of attempts to establish (usually through minority audience formats like *Newsnight* and *Channel 4 News*) debates on subjects which were, they suggested, being ignored or neglected elsewhere in the campaign.

One story which involved the BBC, reluctantly, in the campaign, and also served to crystallise the issue of the media's role in the election, was the decision by celebrity BBC correspondent Martin Bell to stand against Neil Hamilton in the Tatton constituency. He did so as an individual, and not as a BBC employee, and with the exception of one or two incidents his campaign was not widely reported (RPA guidelines prevented coverage which focused only on Bell and Hamilton, without giving coverage to the other candidates for the Hatton seat, most of whom were less than serious). Broadcast coverage of the Bell–Hamilton contest once it had begun was minimal, therefore, with the BBC in any case reluctant to be too closely identified with a particular side in a key election battle. Nevertheless, the mere fact of Bell's presence, and all the associations of 'BBC-ness' which he thereby brought to the election, and to the sleaze issue, enraged many commentators and provoked considerable media debate. Bell's Hatton intervention did not initiate the sleaze agenda which dominated the campaign but, like the coverage of the *Guardian* and the *Sun* discussed above, it contributed to the prominence of sleaze as an issue, and further locked the Conservatives into a debate which they could never win.

Postscript: the media and politics in post-Tory Britain

Since May 1997 the editorial realignment of the British press has continued, with the *Express* and *Mail* titles in particular continuing to steer a course away from traditional pro-Toryism (McNair, 1999c). The swing to Labour in the editorial realignments of the British press had, as this book went to press, remained intact, although the issue of European monetary union had provoked some criticism of the Blair government by the *Sun*, including references to the prime minister as 'the most dangerous man in Britain', and anti-EMU phone-in campaigns similar to those witnessed in the period before the 1997 election (see Chapter 6). This criticism was predictable, given the well-known views of Rupert Murdoch on EMU, and not in itself indicative of a return to the excesses of the Thatcher years. However, Britain has more than enough experience of what ideologically committed proprietors can do to the quality of political debate to suggest caution on the part of media analysts before declaring that the anti-Labour cheerleading days of the British press are over.

That the ideological repositioning of the Labour Party has temporarily removed the material basis for right-wing press propagandism in Britain does not mean that it has gone for ever. Big business and global capital can live with New Labour – may even be happy to embrace it – but it may not always be so, and the party can be sure that it will not always be in tune with the majority of voters in the country. The Tories, on the other hand, may justifiably feel that they were the victims of anti-Tory propagandism in the 1997 election, particularly from the *Sun* and the *Mirror*. If John Major never experienced the viciousness directed by the press towards Labour leaders in 1983, 1987 and 1992, he was nonetheless a victim of 'bias' in 1997. Parties of all political hues in Britain have an interest in not allowing future proprietorial abuse of the press for the pursuit of private interests, and the only way of doing that which is consistent with liberal democracy is to put meaningful limits on media ownership.

New Labour and the broadcasters

In February 1998 one journalistic observer noted that 'the BBC's future is entirely in the hands of the government of the day. There were many close shaves under the Tories, who did not like Auntie's in-built liberal bias. The barons were determined that the same would not happen with the Blairites. So ... they set about buying in some New Labour talent,' including Labour media advisers like Simon Buckby and Nigel Gardner.[48] The commercial channels, too, took steps to smooth relations with the new government. Jon Snow of *Channel 4 News* was one senior journalist who took the view that he and his colleagues in the political media should adopt a less adversarial interviewing style in the post-Tory era, and there was a noticeable softening by some interviewers in their approach to interrogating members of the new government. One pundit suggested that the 'great period' of the adversarial political interview was over, given the sheer size and unassailability of the Labour majority in parliament.[50]

Such proclamations of good will and best intentions did not prevent conflict, however. In June 1998 Alistair Campbell and Jeremy Paxman published pieces attacking each other in the *Times* and *Evening Standard* respectively. In February 1999 Campbell publicly attacked the broadcasters for following the press agenda too slavishly in their news output.

Such incidents revealed that, regardless of whether the government is Labour or Tory, the relationship between broadcasters and politicians will continue to be tense and difficult – an ever-present source of journalist–politician conflict, and thus of official interference in political coverage. In Chapter 7 the intensity of Labour news management in opposition was discussed and, despite the resignations of Peter Mandelson and Charlie Whelan at the end of 1998, it has hardly been a less formidable force in government. The main threat to the quality of the public sphere from this direction arises not from what the politicians and their advisers say to the media, but from the likelihood that the intimidatory efforts of the government's news managers will be frustrated by the demystificatory counter-tactics of the journalists, to the extent that administrative means of media management are adopted instead. The BBC and commercial companies remain economically vulnerable to governmental pressure around such issues as the level of the licence fee, franchising and business law. This is in the nature of our system, and will not change in the near future. Given that, and given that politicians, in and out of government, will continue to lobby and pressurise journalists with every means at their disposal, the least we can do is to support them in their continuing efforts to resist political intimidation.

9

POLITICAL JOURNALISM AND THE CRISIS OF MASS REPRESENTATION

The direction of the trends in British political journalism are not substantially in dispute. Political journalism has, as many point out, become more focused on the style of politics, and on the performance aspects of political communication. Politics has become, at least in part, spectacle and entertainment, and coverage of it is increasingly shaped by a sometimes uneasy blend of public service and commercial criteria, as the information marketplace has become steadily more competitive. Political journalism has acquired some of the character of a review medium, rating individual politicians as if they were opera singers or actors, and inviting citizens to do the same.

And political journalism is, as its critics argue, more focused than ever before on the mechanics of news management and public relations – on the game, the horse race, the 'who's in, who's out, who's hot, who's not' agenda. It has entered a *meta-discursive* phase, in which coverage of the *process* of political affairs (affairs governmental, sexual or financial) is inseparable from that of policy-substance.

Political journalism is, thirdly, more analytical and interpretative than it was in the past: less substantial and more speculative, presenting audiences with the more or less informed views of an expanding community of pontificating pundits and authorised definers of political reality.

While acknowledging these trends in this book, I have interpreted them not as evidence of dumbing down, tabloidisation, Americanisation or any of the related terms deployed in the various narratives of decline which characterise cultural pessimism, but as intelligible and in many respects welcome journalistic responses to changes in the technological, economic and political environments which shape political culture. The fact that contemporary political journalism nearly always contains a sub-text about news management, for example, I have characterised not as the journalistic flight from substance, but as the emergence of a demystificatory, potentially empowering commentary on the nature of the political process: an ongoing deconstruction of the relationship between journalism and the

171

powerful which adds to, rather than detracts from, the stock of useful information available to the average citizen.

The fact, too, that journalism has become steadily more adversarial in recent years, less deferential towards political actors, and that today's political media – even the most commercially driven and ideologically conservative of them – are often working against the abuse of privilege and the excesses of established power, I have argued to be consistent with the normative standards of the fourth estate against which political journalists are judged and so often found wanting.

The heightened adversarialism (if not 'hyperadversarialism') of the political public sphere is not the product of a sudden upsurge in the radical instincts or desire to subvert on the part of individual journalists, but because they are employed by institutions which in their evolving modes of operation tend inevitably to a kind of subversion of the powerful. The commercial imperatives of the media market, to cite just one source of the repeated journalistic destabilisation of political authority of recent years, made the exposure of elite deviance a highly saleable commodity in 1990s Britain. Both the monarchy and the Conservative Party – key institutions of the British establishment – were gravely injured by this fact. The post-Tory elite – the Labour Party in power – have proven to be just as vulnerable.

At the same time as the media can be accused (if accusation it is) of becoming ever more obsessive and meticulous in their critical dissection of the powerful and their ways of working, it can be argued that their commercial need for audiences, and for the raw material from which journalism can be fashioned, are creating new spaces for the accessing and meaningful representation of non-elite voices, as well as greater diversity in the styles and agendas employed by journalists. These trends are less a dilution or reduction of 'serious' journalistic content, a 'deficit of understanding', the ascendancy of irrational populism in the public sphere, or its contamination with infotainment, than a welcome reflection of the increased accessibility of contemporary political debate, and the heightened democratic accountability of political elites. To the extent that they signal a crisis, it is one caused not by the deteriorating quality of public communication but by the impact on elite and intellectual thinking of unprecedented levels of *mass participation* in politics and, through the expansion of access, of *mass representation* in the public sphere.

On occasion, such as ITN's 1997 monarchy debate, critics have been frank in expressing their unease about what they see as the negative political impact of these trends. Some fear the potential for reactionary populism of a relatively uneducated mass. Others simply resent the participation of the crowd in public debate, and its lack of deference for the hallowed institutions of the British establishment. Regardless of the intellectual content of the arguments, however, and their ideological underpinnings, most variants of the crisis thesis are at odds with the principles of democracy and accountability on which the British political system is founded. They are anti-democratic, in effect if not necessarily in intent. Broadcaster Sheena McDonald has complained of our (post) modern public sphere that

> Voters see wannabe prime ministers on chat-shows. Policy initiatives are floated on the thermal updraughts of interviews. Information seeps into our consciousness through leaked reports in favoured newspapers. The democratic process is a complex system of multimedia interaction, sponsored by big business, sampled with scepticism by an increasingly sophisticated citizenry.[1]

Taken as a whole, the article from which this passage is extracted expresses the sentiments of a cultural pessimist, but her comments as quoted here contain much that should give cheer. Complexity, interaction, scepticism, sophistication – these are precisely the characteristics of a mature, democratically empowered citizenry able to use, rather than being vulnerable to abuse by its media. Of course there are market-driven excesses in political culture, and the pro-systemic limitations of the media in a capitalist society are as evident now as they ever were.[2] Political journalism *is* increasingly market driven, even in its public service manifestations, and markets must create new demands as well as meet existing ones. Competitive pressures have encouraged media organisations to highlight and prioritise some political events and issues beyond what normative criteria of newsworthiness alone might predict. *Panorama*'s 1996 interview with Princess Diana was a legitimate reflection of the British people's 'human interest' in her views, at the same time as being an event of genuine politico-constitutional significance in itself. But it was also the product of an increasingly fierce struggle for ratings. The coverage of such events itself creates a public interest – people being what they are – that then becomes the justification for subsequent coverage of events which, though superficially similar in form, are of less obvious political importance. This may explain Channel 4's interview with Monica Lewinsky, broadcast in March 1999, at a cost to ITN of £400,000, by a highly respected journalist (Jon Snow) with a strong record of public opposition to coverage of sleaze. There were no constitutional implications for the UK in anything Lewinsky had to say, nor even by that stage for the United States, whose politicians had shortly before acquitted the president of impeachable offences.

Similarly, the sleaze agenda which dominated both broadsheet and tabloid political journalism in the 1992–97 period was an appropriate response to a particular party's, and government's, attempt to claim a monopoly on moral worth when they were clearly unfitted for that role. But the emergence of a narrative framework of sleaze was scant justification for the reporting of a junior and liberal Tory MP's alleged homosexuality, or for the exposure of Robin Cook's marital problems following his appointment as foreign secretary. Robin Cook never proclaimed the values of 'back to basics', and had the right to demand that he not be judged by them.

If these excesses provide evidence for the negative effects of commercialisation of the public sphere warned of by pessimistic commentators, this book has argued that they are not typical of British political journalism. Even in the tabloid newspapers, coverage of *issues*, rather than personalities – the issues of European union, taxation, constitutional reform – continued to dominate political news in the period under discussion. Apart from the outposts of tongue-in-cheek journalistic transgression occupied by such organisations as Live TV and the *Sport*, there is little hard evidence of the dumbing down of political journalism, unless by that is meant a public sphere which does not assume a university education on the part of every member of its audience. Citizens, in their capacity as consumers of media, clearly enjoy a measure of sensationalistic and salacious political news, particularly when it concerns the party they do not support, but that is not all they want. The progress of the Clinton–Lewinsky scandal in the United States showed that there are limits to the public's capacity for news about sexual sleaze, and that members of the mass audience are able to make their own judgements about the relevance to their lives and their politics of a particular sleaze story. In Britain, the 'outing' of Labour ministers in late 1998 produced comparably nonchalant responses from the media audience, despite the misjudged efforts of the *Sun* to establish a 'gay mafia' narrative framework for reporting the Labour government.

In the field of spin, the extension of universal suffrage and cultural consumerism in the twentieth century has led, as many critics have pointed out, to an increased emphasis on political promotion (Wernick, 1991). This has driven the professionalisation and rationalisation of the persuasive communication process through the practices of political public relations, marketing and advertising. Political news management, as we saw in Chapter 7, *has* become a key factor in the construction of political journalism, and the source of much critical commentary about the degeneration of the public sphere. At the same time, however, in the dialectical tradition of equal and opposite reaction, spin has become a central element in the journalistic narrative of politics. Journalistic scrutiny and critical publicity are now routinely extended not just to the public activities of politicians but to their media consultants and communications staff. Whatever is being done in the name of spin – and the core techniques signified by that term are not new to the late twentieth century, even if their intensity and professionalism are – it is being done in full view of media audiences.

The processes of spin and news management are dangerous to democracy in proportion to the secrecy which surrounds them. By exposing them to public view political journalists are not depriving citizens of rational information, so much as providing them with another set of criteria on which to make rational choices. Alongside policy rhetoric (the content of which remains a key factor in voter choice), we also judge presentation; alongside issues, we make judgements about image. Politicians throughout history have manipulated image and presentation, often with catastrophic consequences. In Britain, at the beginning of a new century, they must do so against the background of a vigilant and often ruthless media, and often in front of a live audience. Far from signalling a deterioration of the public sphere, this trend presents a rigorous test of ability and character for those who would wield political power. The presentational excesses of political public relations are increasingly undermined by a media which may at times appear to be obsessed with spin, but in being so stays alert to its abuse. It is, after all, because of the much demonstrated willingness of journalists to harry them and their advisers, to expose their secrets and probe their rhetoric without fear or favour, that politicians – and the Labour government in particular – now take seriously the notion of 'transparency' in such areas as governmental and official information. Governmental concessions to official openness (limited as they are) would not have been granted were it not for the fact that journalists had already forced a degree of openness on the political establishment.

In all these respects the political media have stayed truer, indeed moved closer to the normative ideal of the fourth estate and its role in the public sphere than their critics allow. When a self-avowed 'reactionary' like columnist Andrew Roberts can bemoan the negative impact on the monarchy of media coverage (and the Palace's adoption of public relations in the 1960s),[3] can there be any serious doubt that change in the political culture of the United Kingdom has been largely for the better? These voices locate the crisis of the public sphere precisely in the fact that the political media do indeed subvert and undermine established authority on a regular and sustained basis. Conservative commentators who understand that the survival of the capitalist system as an unequal, hierarchical one is closely related to the deference its people feel for their leaders (elected, appointed or hereditary), are alarmed by the political media's willingness to challenge that deference, and with good reason. If there is, as I have argued, no *real* deterioration in the content of political communication, there is undoubtedly an intensifying crisis of legitimation for the politicians, as a key basis of their authority – secrecy and the control of information (including information about image and personality) – is eroded by the subversive power of the journalistic media.

The question then arises: how much reportage and critical scrutiny of political elites is good for democracy? At what point, if any, does the expansion of a questioning, critical media begin to destabilise authority in *general*, and undermine the ability of *any* party to govern? Is there a point at which, as one writer has suggested, 'an untrammelled, populist media' can be 'too free for an intelligent democracy',[4] and have we reached that point in Britain?

To which questions I would answer respectively a tentative 'Yes' (some constraints on political journalism are clearly necessary, on both ethical and good government grounds), followed by a more confident 'No'. The modern public sphere is one to which 'the people' have unprecedented access and exposure; it is a popular public sphere in the best sense of that term, supporting a political culture which begins to hint at the democratic potential of advanced capitalism glimpsed by Marx in the mid-nineteenth century, but not viewed by him as a serious possibility because of the system's exploitative, pauperising tendencies. Marx was wrong about capitalism's inability to regenerate and reproduce itself, and marxist critics of contemporary capitalist culture (as well as their liberal co-critics) have been slow to acknowledge the extent to which the elements – economic, political, technological – shaping its evolution have produced an information apparatus of real value to the democratic process. 'Rational' discourses – policy-oriented, issue-led – are still fully, indeed disproportionately represented in the public sphere, as Chapters 2 and 3 showed, but so too are the discourses and concerns of those who, if they are not necessarily familiar or comfortable with elite definitions of 'worthwhile political debate', or indeed do not share them, still have the right to vote and be counted, and the need to be informed. There has been, not a degeneration of the public sphere, but its 'prodigious enlargement', as Frederick Jameson observes, and 'an enormous enlargement of the idea of rationality itself' (1991, p. 354). These trends should be welcomed by democrats, rather than dismissed as 'fashionable postmodernism'.[5]

Habermas writes of the 're-feudalisation' of the public sphere, meaning that it 'becomes the court *before* which public prestige can be displayed – rather than *in* which public critical debate is carried on' (1989, p. 201). This book has asserted, in effect, its *de*-feudalisation, meaning the *restoration*, through a competitive, market-driven media, of the critical publicity and scrutiny of elites which (for Habermas) characterised its early, ideal form; and the extension of access to the level of, if not the universal, then at least the masses, constituted as citizens irrespective of property or other qualifications.

Andrew Neil suggests that 'the new politics of the information age' are popular, anti-establishment, bottom-up, fuelled by the media. The people, he asserts, set the agenda, rather than vested interests.[6] This is going too far, since there is an obvious sense in which 'what the people want', or think, is itself a function of what political journalism says they should think about. But that the media are increasingly responsive to popular definitions of what is important is both self-evident and welcome.

There is a qualitative difference, of course, between a popular public sphere and one which is merely popul*ist*: between mediated democracy and what one might call *media-ocracy* – the latter being a state of affairs in which media professionals can push politicians, often by mobilising manufactured notions of 'what the people think', into unwise or rash decisions. There are, clearly, some politicians whose fear of unpopularity and electoral failure makes them vulnerable to the pressures exerted on them by the media-crats; governments whose members have taken decisions not because they believed them to be right (they may even have known them to be wrong), but because they felt obliged to by the weight of media pressure. One thinks, in this connection, of the Dangerous Dogs Act of 1991, and the anti-gun legislation of 1997, both of which, for better or worse, were examples of media-led law driven by media-generated assertions of 'popular will'. Politicians have always sought to please the crowd (or the crowd as the media present them to politicians) and these instances of the 'new plebiscitory democracy'[7] are probably not different in kind from previous examples of legislation being influenced by what governments perceived public opinion to be. There can, however, be little doubt that the proliferation of political media, and the acceleration of political information flows, has increased the pressure to please. There are today fewer politicians prepared to risk power by going against the grain of public opinion, even if that opinion is ill informed and artificially polarised by the media.

But the corrupting force of populism within the public sphere as a whole should not be overstated, nor cited as an argument for reining in a media which might appear at times to be indeed 'too free for an intelligent democracy'. Legislative instruments already exist to prevent political journalists from deliberately lying (and even, in more circumstances than is healthy for a democracy, from telling the truth). There is a case for, if not legislation, at least more effective regulation to discourage the violation of political actors' privacy, where private behaviour has no bearing on public life (McNair, 1998a). But attempting to impose further legal restrictions on political journalism, or to restrict its output to an elitist definition of 'the rational', even if it were possible, would be to go against the grain of four centuries of democratic progress, and to imply that, actually, democracy is alright but only if 'we' – the self-proclaimed arbiters of good taste in these matters – can control its consequences.

Final thoughts

Far from mounting a rational defence of normative standards of information in a democracy, then, assertions of dumbing down and the rise of infotainment *avoid* rational acceptance of contemporary capitalism's dramatically expanding democratic possibilities, deferring to essentially irrational judgements about taste. It is, I would suggest, the doom-mongers of dumbing down, rather than the audience, who are blinded by the glossy presentational aspects of contemporary political culture, and who fail to recognise that, notwithstanding the undoubted ascendancy of image and style as elements in contemporary political communication, both the quantity and the quality of useful political information now available to the average citizen far exceeds that to which past generations had access. They express *aesthetic* and thus essentially subjective objections to the style and tone of what is, undeniably, an increasingly raucous and irreverential public sphere, reviewing the political media according to the increasingly unstable and irrelevant categories of high and low culture.

The designer suits of today's politicians may be sharp, but so are the interviews, commentaries and editorials which so mercilessly debunk them. News management may be more intense than ever before, but so is the journalistic deconstruction of it. Politicians can rise on the back of expertly executed public relations and advertising campaigns, only to be brought back to earth (sometimes burning up in the process) by journalistic exposure of flaws in the packaging. There *is* populist excess in places, but that is how people are, and a democratic public sphere need not fear making some space for it. There *are* (and have always been) ethical lapses and resource constraints, usually caused by the demands of a competitive marketplace, which constantly threaten the quality of journalism. In Britain, however, the existence of a strong public service broadcasting sector, and the reluctance of many people to support the worst excesses of journalistic voyeurism (a trend evident before the death of Diana and reinforced after it) act as a significant counter to the media barons. Messrs Murdoch, Black, Rothermere and the rest may well own too much of our media, but they are not free to do with their properties entirely as they like.

The important issues for those concerned about the relationship between politics and the media in the new millenium will not be dumbing down, therefore, nor the many variants of the 'crisis of public communication' which have dominated the academy until now. Such concerns are as old as democracy itself, expressing the ongoing intellectual crisis caused by the arrival of the masses at the centre of advanced capitalism's culture and politics (Carey, 1992). The more urgent questions to be addressed in the years ahead, I would suggest, are these:

- now that the people have such unprecedented access to information about politics, what do they do with it?
- what *can* they, and what should they *want* to do with it, given what is politically possible in current conditions?
- and is there, from the point of view of the efficiency and integrity of the democratic process, an optimal upper limit, as well as a lower, on the quantity of information flowing in a society, and on the amount of critical scrutiny exercised by the media over elites and their rhetoric?

Those, however, are questions for another day.

NOTES

PREFACE AND ACKNOWLEDGEMENTS

1 Cohen, N., 'The death of news', *New Statesman*, May 22 1998.
2 From the BBC-supplied text of Birt's speech, delivered in Dublin on February 3 1995.
3 For recent work on the developing Scottish public sphere see Schlesinger, 1998.
4 The papers from this conference are published in Calabrese and Burgelman, 1999.

1 JOURNALISM AND DEMOCRACY: THE DEBATE

1 See Blumler 1997 for a more recent elaboration of the 'crisis', and the reasons for his assertion that 'the political communication process now goes against, rather than with, the grain of citizenship'.
2 Cohen, N., 'The death of news', *New Statesman*, May 22 1998.
3 Many examples of the rhetoric of dumbing down could be given, applied to the political media in general, or of particular outlets. In early 1998, for example, political columnist Ferdinand Mount attacked the deteriorating quality (as he perceived it) of the BBC's news and current affairs output. 'You often find more political news and analysis in the *Sun* or the *Mirror* than you do on the *Nine O'Clock News*', he complained (Mount, F., 'Television hits the dumber switch', *Sunday Times*, February 1 1998). I explore the differences in style and content of political coverage between various media in Chapter 3.
4 Walker, D., 'From our own 500 correspondents', *Independent*, October 1 1996.
5 Richards, S., 'In a one-sided election you can't please everyone', *New Statesman*, May 1997.
6 Walker, D., 'From our own 500 correspondents', *Independent*, October 1 1996.
7 Greenslade, R., 'Spin experts losing their balance', *Observer*, November 24 1996.
8 MacWhirter, I., 'When false prophecy usurps faulty politics', *Observer*, September 3 1995.
9 Richards, S., 'In a one-sided election you can't please everyone', *New Statesman*, May 1997; Greenslade, R., 'Conspiracy claim ignores reality', *Guardian*, April 23 1997.
10 For insider accounts of the role of political public relations in the Clinton presidency see Morris, 1997, Kurtz, 1998, and Stephanopoulos, 1999.

11 Snow, J., 'More bad news', *Guardian*, January 27 1997.
12 Goodhart, D., 'Who are the masters now?', *Prospect*, May 1997.
13 For a concise summary of the debate between pessimistic and optimistic assessments of the impact of the media on politics, see Corner, 1995, Ch. 2.
14 Rates of voter turn-out in British general elections have varied from 71% in 1945 to 70% in 1997.
15 This feature of the research shares Deborah Cameron's view that the characteristics of journalistic style do not represent 'purely functional or aesthetic judgements', but 'have a history and a politics. They play a role in constructing a relationship with a specific imagined audience, and also in sustaining a particular ideology of news reporting' (1996, p. 316).
16 Habermas writes that, from its origins in the coffee houses of early modern Europe, 'the public sphere of civil society stood or fell with the principle of universal access' (1989, p. 85).
17 Marr, A., 'Words and things', *Prospect*, April 1996.
18 I have grouped the output of political journalism into four types, defined by their distinctive communicative functions within the political media system as a whole. These are:

- *reportage*, defined here as the dissemination of new facts;
- *interpretation*, where journalists analyse, make sense of and comment on information contained in straight reportage;
- *interrogation*, where political actors are publicly questioned about their opinions and actions; and
- *access*, those spaces where the public are physically present in the political media, and have the opportunity to participate in mediated debates with each other, or with politicians themselves.

Any one outlet – be it a news bulletin, a broadcast magazine or a print periodical – will usually contain a mixture of these types of political journalism.

2 THE POLITICAL PUBLIC SPHERE

1 Here and elsewhere in this book, unless otherwise indicated, all quotes were obtained by the author in interviews.
2 I use the term 'underclass' to describe the 'non-working' classes: men, women and young people who exist permanently outwith the wage-labour economy, dependent on welfare, the black economy, and/or crime for their income. The Labour government which entered power in May 1997 pledged a significant reduction of this social group – one product of eighteen years of Conservative government – and the social problems which it both reflects and engenders.
3 See essays by David McKie and Colin Seymour-Ure in Crewe and Gosschalk, eds, 1995, for example.
4 The newspaper launched by pornographic magazine publisher David Sullivan in the 1980s, which imports the 'newsvalues' and agendas of pornographic publishing into the newspaper sector.
5 Robin Cook's marriage collapsed, with much embarrassing publicity for the New Labour, anti-sleaze government, in the summer of 1997. Many newspapers, including all the elite titles, reported that he had dumped his wife at the Heathrow departure lounge as they were about to go on holiday, in favour of his secretary.
6 Greenslade, R., 'Star that fell to earth', *Guardian*, October 19 1998.

7   1998 saw Murdoch's media interests provoke further controversy when, in February that year, his HarperCollins company announced that they would not, as agreed, publish a book by former Hong Kong governor Chris Patten. Most observers agreed that the clumsy treatment of the book was closely related to Murdoch's pursuit of his business interests in China.

8   See for example his essay 'A betrayal of purpose', in Pilger, 1994, pp.76–82.

9   Pilger, J., 'Gutted', *Guardian*, February 15 1997.

10 Greenslade, R., 'Return of the prodigal *Sun*', *Guardian*, January 19 1998.

11 Greenslade, R., 'Sulks, mischief and the triumph of ego', *Guardian*, January 11 1999. That same month the *Mirror* was threatened with take-over by Regional Independent Newspapers, a consortium led by former Conservative minister Sir Norman Fowler, with obvious potential consequences for its future editorial alignment. The bid was not successful.

12 For a discussion of the failure of the *New Statesman* to compete in circulation terms with *The Spectator*, see Harris, R., 'Why can't the left have a paper tiger?', *Sunday Times*, December 20 1998.

13 Lloyd, J., 'What's on after the news?', *New Statesman*, November 28 1997.

14 The BBC, it should be said, might reject my suggestion that it, like ITN, is mid-market in its mainstream news output. One senior BBC journalist states that 'they [ITN] are the *Daily Mail*, the *Daily Express*. We are *The Times*, the *Guardian*, the *Independent*, in terms of approach, in terms of where we would place our audience, and in terms of the agility with which we would leap on particular bandwagons.'

15 For more detailed discussion of trends in British factual broadcasting see Kilborn and Izod, 1997; Kilborn, 1998.

16 From an advertisement published in *Private Eye*, number 968.

17 Advertisements for the programme make this explicit by warning the potential listener that 'you won't like our programme if your idea of balance is a standard-issue BBC liberal presenter trying (and failing) to be impartial'.

18 'A farewell to breasts', *The Economist*, January 31 1998.

19 This fact, indeed, is a recurring element in the rhetoric of dumbing down of the political media, in so far as some observers clearly find it unsettling that elite and popular media – from the *Telegraph* to the *Star*, or from *Channel 4 News* to *News At Ten* – might share definitions of political newsworthiness, and that these shared definitions may include themes of human interest.

20 After Labour's election victory in May 1997 party sources let it be known that prime minister Blair preferred listening to, and appearing on the ITV breakfast programme, *GMTV*, rather than *Today*, since its audience was much larger and more representative. According to the source, 'the days when an ambitious minister went on the *Today* programme knowing the prime minister would be listening are gone', Prescott, M., 'Blair is not a *Today* person', *Sunday Times*, November 3 1997.

21 Harris, S., 'News nightmare', *Guardian*, February 16 1998.

22 Greenslade, R., 'No, they're not reading all about it', *Guardian*, July 7 1997.

23 Greenslade, R., 'Best of times, worst of times', *Guardian*, December 8 1997.

24 Greenslade, R., 'Red sales in the sunset', *Guardian*, November 17 1997.

25 For analysis of this trend see 'A farewell to breasts' in *The Economist*, January 31 1998.

26 Freedland, J., 'Dumbing down? Nonsense – the whole British nation is "braining up"', *Guardian*, March 11 1998.

27 Gott, R., 'The newspapers we deserve', *Prospect*, July 1996, pp. 28–33.

28 Freedland, J., 'Dumbing down? Nonsense – the whole British nation is "braining up"', *Guardian*, March 11 1998.

29 From the Parliamentary Channel's promotional material.

30 There is, in short, no lack of 'straight' political coverage. On the contrary, the quantity and quality of this coverage now available, albeit on electronic and not in print media platforms, is unprecedented.

31 Brown, M., 'The hour has come', *Guardian*, September 7 1998.

32 Hall, T., 'A prime-time balancing act', *Guardian*, September 7 1998.

33 Gibson, J., 'BBC to "tell us why news matters"', *Guardian*, October 7 1998.

34 Lloyd, J., 'What's on after the news?', *New Statesman*, November 28 1997.

35 Walker, D., 'From our own 500 correspondents', *Independent*, October 1 1996.

3 POLICY, PROCESS, PERFORMANCE AND SLEAZE

1 Figure for 1998.

2 For further details on changes to the system of governmental information management introduced by the Blair administration, see the 1997 Mountfield Report of the Working Group on the Governmental Information Service, and the June 1998 Report by the Head of Profession to the Head of the Home Civil Service.

3 Walker, D., 'From our own 500 correspondents', *Independent*, October 1 1996.

4 The source of this comment acknowledges that politicians, too, are to blame for this excess (if excess it is), in so far as 'they have a pavlovian reaction to microphones and television cameras. They love being on, and they have an opinion on everything. I have said to politicians in the past, "Why do you feel you have to have a view on everything? Wouldn't it be better sometimes to say 'I'm extremely busy, I'm running a department, I don't have time, I have no view on that at the moment, go away?'"'

5 Walker, D., 'From our own 500 correspondents', *Independent*, October 1 1996.

6 This section is based on a content analysis of *routine* (as routine as any can be, given that the political environment, and thus the priorities and concerns of political journalism, change all the time) political news over two two-week periods in late 1996 (September 1–14, and November 3–16). These periods comprised the two weeks shortly before the start of the annual party conference season, and another two weeks preceding the 1996 Budget speech (which turned out to be the last given by a Conservative chancellor). Although 'routine' in the sense I am using the term here, these were in other ways periods of heightened political activity, coming as they did in the 'long campaign' phase of the political cycle. All political actors in this environment were aware that a general election would have to be held no more than six months hence, by April 1997 at the latest (the 1997 campaign in fact began on March 17), and all parties were thus in unofficial campaigning mode. This may have inflated the presence of politics on the news agenda, by comparison with other points in the electoral cycle, such as the beginning of a government's five-year term of office, when the opposition parties are not likely to be so active. The four weeks of routine coverage examined here nevertheless provide an opportunity to study the structure of the political news agenda in the absence of major distorting events.

7   The political stories identified during these routine periods fell into three basic
    categories:

- coverage of political actors' and party activities, including statements of
  policy and philosophy, speeches by party figures, attacks on one party by
  other parties or by journalists, and campaigning activities of parties and
  lobby groups such as the anti-gun movement which was active in late
  1996, following the murders of schoolchildren and their teacher at
  Dunblane, Scotland. Table 3.1 shows their distribution as between particular parties and non-party organisations;
- coverage of government activities, such as the publication of Green
  Papers, and statements of policy and intention on such matters as
  European union;
- coverage of non-party specific political issues such as devolution and the
  health of the domestic economy.

As with all attempts to categorise news for analytical purposes, there are some
qualifications to be made on the particular approach to breaking down the
material adopted here. A number of stories could have fitted into more than
one category, and were placed according to the emphasis given by the journalist. Thus, a criticism of Labour policy by a trade union leader is counted
under 'Labour', while coverage of the TUC conference which took place in the
second week of September was given its own category, into which a substantial
number of stories fell. Many 'TUC' stories were actually about TUC–Labour
relations, however. Indeed, the tension of the relationship between the trade
union movement and New Labour was precisely what gave the TUC such
newsworthiness in this particular period. On September 12, for example, nineteen press items reported the post office workers' 'snubbing' of Blair's speech
to the TUC (the post office workers' union was then in dispute with the
employer, and resented Blair's reluctance to offer unqualified support).
Similarly, in the second week of November (week four of the sample) the
Confederation of British Industry conference took place. Coverage of this event
was also accorded a separate category, although many of the CBI stories were
actually reports of attacks by business leaders on either the Conservative
government or the Labour opposition. As with the TUC conference, this event
acquired enhanced newsworthiness for journalists because of what it might
reveal about relations between the business community (traditionally pro-
Conservative) and the ascendant new Labour Party in a pre-general election
period.

   The category of 'government' was of course, in late 1996, the location of
stories about the Conservative Party, still in power at this time (and also of the
opposition parties who, by the conventions of objectivity, are routinely
accessed in order to balance government statements). The British system maintains a distinction, however, between the administrative activities and
responsibilities of the government and the 'political' activities of the party from
which it is composed, a convention adhered to in Table 3.1, which separates
'government' from 'party' stories.

   Stories about Northern Ireland are excluded from this study, on the grounds
that this is (or was during the period under review) an area of bi-partisan
policy, exempt from the attack–defence rituals of routine party politics.
International stories are also excluded from what is a study of *domestic* political journalism, with the major exception of European union coverage. During

the period of the study European union was both a domestic and an international story, and featured heavily as an issue in both inter- and intra-party coverage.

8 Stories about 'issues' will also be read as stories about parties, of course, even when the latter are not mentioned directly. There are thus practically no stories about issues currently on the public agenda – whether social, economic or cultural – which do not have party political resonances. A commentary column warning of the dangers of devolution inevitably implies a criticism of pro-devolution parties, even if these are not mentioned directly in the text. Thus, the figures given for reportage of the parties in Table 3.1 can probably be said to understate their presence in the wider news agenda, and should not be taken as precise quantitative measures of the extent of party political coverage in routine news (which varies over time in any case with the development of the political environment). They do, however, serve to show the prominence of politics in the routine news agenda.

They show, too, broadly similar patterns of coverage across the two sampled periods, although these were separated in time by two months. Nor do the figures presented in Table 3.1 give any indication of the balance as between positive and negative coverage. Much coverage of government policy reports criticism, and may thus be considered 'negative', or as potentially damaging to the governing party's popularity and electoral aims. Likewise, the fact that the Labour Party received more coverage than the Tories during this period (if one excludes coverage of government statements) does not mean that the former received 'better' or more favourable coverage, since coverage may be critical or complimentary. Table 3.1 therefore tells us little about political news bias although, as it happens, 'negative' stories on such issues as political corruption (sleaze) were predominantly about the activities of Conservative Party politicians. Chapter 8 discusses the pattern of political news bias in the context of the 1997 general election.

9 The figures show broadly similar patterns of coverage across the two sampled periods, although these were separated in time by two months.

10 The statement was made in an interview given by Short to the *New Statesman* periodical, published on August 9 1996.

11 Nine items in total reported opinion polls, which are always a regular feature of political news in a pre-election period.

12 In addition to items in which political communication *was* the story, there were items not categorised as 'political communication' in which aspects of political communication were raised as a subsidiary part of a wider discussion, woven into its fabric as a taken for granted background element in the contemporary political environment. Table 3.1 thus does not do justice to the pervasiveness of political communication as a theme on the journalistic agenda.

13 Freedland, J., 'Clinton star to boost Labour', *Guardian*, November 7 1996.

14 And probably declining – at a conference in March 1997 the BBC's head of weekly current affairs programming, Mark Damazer, claimed that 'there has been an exponential increase in the amount of policy analysis and policy description on the BBC' (from comments made at the Soundbite Election conference, National Film Theatre, March 1997).

15 Massie, A., 'The blurring of Mr Blair', *Scotsman*, March 19 1997.

16 Kavanagh, T., 'Will gorgeous George end up tainting Tony?', *Sun*, November 8 1996.

17 Martinson, J., 'In the picture', *Financial Times*, November 7 1996. This article reported that, as the political parties were 'dominating the April order book'

for poster advertising space in Britain, a May 1 general election was likely. As it turned out, this was an accurate prediction.

18 During the sample period one commentary article noted of focus groups that 'everyone uses them. New Labour has practically been created in their image ... The Tories base their negative billboard campaigns on them' (Macwhirter, I., 'Power to the people', *Scotsman*, November 7 1996).

19 Rentoul, J., 'Blair brushes off explanation for gender gap', *Independent*, November 7 1996.

20 Johnson, B., 'No short cut to wooing women voters', *Daily Telegraph*, November 7 1996.

21 Johnson, B., 'No short cut to wooing women voters', *Daily Telegraph*, November 7 1996.

22 Gardam, T., 'Television news you can use', *New Statesman*, November 14 1997.

23 Kamal, A., 'News from the battle fronts', *Guardian*, November 6 1997.

24 Dugdale, J., 'Seeing and believing', *Guardian*, September 4 1995.

25 Norris, P. and Kalb, M., 'Editorial', *Press/Politics*, volume 2, number 4, pp. 1–3, 1997.

26 The majority of these stories concerned the Conservatives, although Labour and the Liberal Democrats also received some journalistic attention over their sources of funding.

27 Johnson, P. , 'The media candidate', *Daily Telegraph*, April 8 1997. Johnson's article linked sleaze journalism to coverage of the Royal family, condemning 'the shameless privacy invaders who have wantonly destroyed scores of valuable public figures, who have bought and published tapes of private phone calls by Prince Charles and Diana, Princess of Wales, and who have done everything in their power to damage our Royal Family and tarnish every traditional institution in the country'.

28 Norris, P. and Kalb, M., 'Editorial', *Press/Politics*, volume 2, number 4, pp. 1–3, 1997.

29 While some of the 'Labour sleaze' stories of the first months and years of the Labour government seemed like desperate attempts by pro-Tory journalists to get their own back and spoil the Blair 'honeymoon', it is probably just as well that a government with a 176 majority, and a certain degree of self-righteous zeal about it, is subjected to rigorous scrutiny of this kind from the media.

30 Snow, J., 'More bad news', *Guardian*, January 27 1997.

31 The interview with Monica Lewinsky was broadcast on Thursday, March 4 1999.

32 John Hartley observes that in early modern Europe 'sexual sensationalism [was used] above all in a tireless effort to prove that the old ruling classes were unfit to survive into the new age' (1996, p. 118). Sexually explicit images at this time were 'not only scandalous but also insurrectionary'. Such images were not, it is true, the product of a commercialised journalism, but an elite underground.

33 Sullivan, A., 'The American way of privacy is a public affair', *Sunday Times*, March 1 1998.

34 For a discussion of communicative ethics in journalism, politics and public relations, see McNair, 1998a.

35 Coote, A., 'Labour puts its neck on the line', *Sunday Times*, September 29 1996.

4 THE INTERPRETATIVE MOMENT

1 Martin Rosenbaum, for example, writes that 'twenty or thirty years ago, most political reporting was news. Now, especially in the broadsheets, there is much more analysis and commentary. In part this is due to the need for broadsheets to find a different role, given the new supremacy of TV, but latterly broadcasting too, notably on the BBC, has provided more analysis' (1997, p. 91).

2 For a recent example see *Observer* columnist Nick Cohen's argument that the rise of the columnist is a cheap alternative to 'real' news (Cohen, N., 'The death of news', *New Statesman*, May 22 1998).

3 The 'punditocracy', as it is termed by Nimmo and Combs in their excellent study of US punditry includes, in addition to journalists, academics, professional consultants of various kinds, present and past members of political, military and business elites, think-tank members and other intellectuals who collectively comprise the modern equivalent of what they call a 'priestly establishment' (1992, p. 24). My concern in this chapter is not with the punditocracy in that broad sense (see McNair, 1999b for further discussion of that wider group), but specifically with its journalistic elements.

4 The commentary industry also includes a number of 'guest' columnists – writers who are not professional journalists but who derive their authority from their political experience. When the former chancellor of the exchequer Denis Healey wrote a column for the *Sun* on 'the perils of a single currency' (part of that newspaper's on-going anti-European union campaign), he was introduced to readers who may not have recalled his years in office as someone with a distinguished WWII military record (thus qualifying him to criticise the single currency project without being branded 'anti-European') and as 'one of Labour's brightest Cabinet ministers'. These political and military credentials gave Healey's comments weight and credibility. Following Labour's 1997 election victory, new prime minister Blair made regular appearances as a guest columnist in a variety of newspapers, including the *Sun*, the *Daily Mail* and the *Daily Telegraph*. This was an extension of Labour's pre-election tactic of working with traditionally pro-Tory newspapers in order to communicate more directly and effectively with their readers. In contrast to the *Sun*'s appropriation of Healey's 'elder statesman' authority to bolster its anti-EU stance, Blair used the newspapers in which he 'wrote' (his staff would do the actual writing) to encourage a relationship comparable to that between the conventional columnist and his readership. In this way the 'guest' political column becomes a vehicle for political communication from elite to public. Political 'guest' columns also function as a means of intra-party campaigning. In the final years and months of the Major government, Tory Eurosceptics such as John Redwood frequently used columns as a platform from which to pursue politico-ideological warfare.

5 From his *Daily Mail* column of Friday, November 1 1996.

6 Heffer, S., 'The toadies who keep America in the dark', *Daily Mail*, November 2 1996. On the other hand, it is difficult to imagine the British media inflicting on a prime minister the public humiliations experienced by Bill Clinton following the Monica Lewinsky scandal.

7 Cash, W., 'Inspired by Britain', *Spectator*, February 7 1998.

8 Cash, W., 'Inspired by Britain', *Spectator*, February 7 1998.

9 Young, H., 'A quiet time in bed together', *Guardian*, November 19 1996.

10 The analytical-advisory column tends to have the following structure: i) the phenomenon to be interpreted is identified, and the necessary context and

background provided; ii) the debate is set up; iii) the columnist's insight (and any privileged information which he may have) are introduced to the discussion; iv) the column concludes with either a prediction of what will happen in the future, a warning to one or other of the parties about what will happen if the columnist's advice is ignored, or a call for action, often linked to the warning.

11 *Observer*, November 24 1996.

12 *Sunday Times*, March 11 1996.

13 Young, H., 'In Ireland, for once, politicians have taught the cynics a lesson', *Guardian*, April 14 1998.

14 In broadcasting, interpretation is inevitable, because there is no time for factual elaboration. In the press, interpretation is necessary because the facts are already known, through broadcasting.

15 Quoted in Mulholland, J., 'Labour's Mr Media', *Guardian*, February 17 1997.

16 From advertising copy, *Private Eye*, no. 968, 1998.

17 Comment by then-Conservative MP David Willetts at The Soundbite Election conference, National Film Theatre, March 3 1997.

18 Greenslade, R., 'Spin experts losing their balance', *Observer*, November 24 1996.

19 Quoted in Culf, A., 'BBC chief backs 'effective' Humphrys', *Guardian*, March 27 1997.

20 Unsigned editorial, 'Must the media decide?', *New Statesman*, May 20 1994.

21 'The cheaper sex: how women lose out in journalism', *Women In Journalism*, July 1998. Despite the gloomy title of this report, it actually presents a rather optimistic scenario, in which women journalists are advancing up the career ladder faster than men of the same age, and occupying more and more positions of editorial and management responsibility.

5 THE INTERROGATIVE MOMENT

1 *Mail On Sunday*, September 29 1996.

2 Mount, F., 'Television hits the dumber switch', *Sunday Times*, February 1 1998.

3 Marr, A., 'Words and things', *Prospect*, April 1996.

4 Humphrys, J., 'In the firing line', *Guardian*, May 24 1995.

5 Daniel Boorstin identifies this latter as the first 'proper' political interview (1962).

6 See the September 29 1996 editions of both titles.

7 Reported in Culf, A., 'ITN warned over Major interview', *Guardian*, August 1996. Culf also reported concerns that ITN's associate editor, Dame Sue Tinson, who had been involved in setting up the interview, was a close friend of John Major, and that his exclusive appearance on *News At Ten* was paid for with McDonald's over-friendly approach to questioning.

8 A Paxman puppet was a popular feature of the 1980s *Spitting Image* series, and impersonations of the interviewer have also been a speciality of Rory Bremner.

9 Cockerell, M., 'Whose finger on the mike?', *Guardian*, May 27 1995.

10 Mulholland, J., 'It's all nonsense', *Guardian*, December 15 1997.

11 Forrest, E., 'Why TV outrage is all the rage', *Guardian*, June 15 1998. In a press interview, Paxman insists that he is not a political animal, and considers himself to be an 'outsider' (*Guardian*, October 12 1998). Perhaps this is why he goes at politicians of all parties with such relish.

12 Rusbridger, A., 'The shrinking screen', *Guardian*, January 20 1997.

13 McDonald, S., 'Licence to grill', *Guardian*, January 25 1999.

14 Richards, S., 'The other sabbath ritual', *Guardian*, October 24 1994.

15 Richards, S., 'One brewed-up story, one headache', *Independent*, June 8 1994.

16 From the BBC-supplied text of a speech delivered by Birt in Dublin on February 5 1995.

17 This interview, broadcast on BBC1 on November 14 1997, also made the news because it was the first full-length interview given by Blair since his election as prime minister six months before, and because, uniquely for the executive arm of the British government, he admitted responsibility for his poor handling of the presentation of the tobacco advertising issue. Live and on the record, Blair declared that 'I take full responsibility ... I apologise'.

18 Interview with Steve Richards, *New Statesman*, August 9 1996, pp. 24–6.

19 Parker, G., 'Short in attack on Blair's leadership', *Financial Times*, August 8 1996.

20 'Labour's heels', *Financial Times*, August 9 1996.

21 Harris, R., 'Clare, the awkward squad made flesh', *Sunday Times*, August 11 1996.

6 THE SOUND OF THE CROWD

1 See Mount, F., 'Television hits the dumber switch', *Sunday Times*, February 1 1998.

2 See Hart, 1987 for a book-length discussion of the growth of the sound-bite in US political rhetoric.

3 Goodhart, D., 'Who are the masters now?', *Prospect*, May 1997. Nick Clarke of *Any Questions* doubts the value of this, however. 'I don't think the studio audiences help much. In order to clarify the issues we need people who have thought hard about it. You need to let the different points of view breathe.'

4 Quoted on *News At Ten*, ITV, January 8 1997.

5 Columnist Linda Grant is one of the 'victims' of *The Moral Maze* who has complained about Starkey's approach.

6 Grant, L., 'Maze that lost its way', *Guardian*, August 26 1997.

7 See for example Christopher Hitchen's film for Channel 4, *The Mourning After*, broadcast in September 1998 to mark the first anniversary of the Princess' death in Paris.

7 'SPIN, WHORES, SPIN'

1 I am indebted for the title of this chapter to Julia Langdon, whose article entitled 'Spin, whores, spin' appeared in the *Guardian* on August 9 1996.

2 See for example Shaw, 1994; Jones, 1996; Michie, 1998.

3 Langdon, J., 'Spin, whores, spin', *Guardian*, August 9, 1996.

4 See for example the US sitcom *Spin City*, starring Michael J. Fox as a vaguely George Stephanopoulous-type figure; the 1995 novel *Spin Doctor* by Michael Shea, former press secretary to the Queen; and late 1990s Hollywood movies such as *Primary Colours*, from the successful book of the same name (Anonymous, 1996). Non-fiction works by well-known spin doctors such as George Stephanopoulous (1999), Dick Morris (1997) and Howard Kurtz (1998) became best-sellers.

5 Andrew, A., 'Leaders who try to doctor the news', *Daily Mail*, October 4 1996.

6 Mandelson, P. , 'Out of the darkness', *Guardian*, September 28 1996.

7 For an account of the development of public elections in Britain, see L'Etang, 1998.

8 McSmith, A., 'In his own image', *Observer*, September 29 1996.

9 Heffer, S., 'Spinning for a living ... who cares?', *British Journalism Review*, volume 6, number 4, 1995, pp. 6–10.

10 Lawson, M., 'Spin doctors heading for a dizzy demise', *Independent*, October 18 1994.

11 Rogaly, J., 'The realities of life under media rule', *Financial Times*, January 18–19 1997.

12 Campbell, A., 'Auntie's spinners', *Sunday Times*, September 22 1996.

13 Langdon, J., 'Spin, whores, spin', *Guardian*, August 9 1996.

14 Lawson, M., 'Hartlepool gets spin doctor treatment', *Independent*, March 24 1992.

15 Nicholas Jones, quoted in Hencke, D., 'How high priests of spin keep order', *Guardian*, August 8 1996.

16 Spin doctors are also 'minders' acting as gate-keepers for their clients. Like Sir Bernard Ingham in his work for Margaret Thatcher, Alistair Campbell as Tony Blair's chief press secretary has sought to manipulate news coverage of the prime minister by controlling access to him.

17 Lawson, M., 'Spin doctors heading for a dizzy demise', *Independent*, October 18 1994.

18 Appleyard, B., 'John Major ate our monsters', *Independent*, February 11 1993.

19 Hibbs, J., 'Spin doctors who make the news fit to print', *Daily Telegraph*, September 30 1996.

20 Patrick Donovan, for example ('Coming up roses', Guardian, September 3 1995), reported that, for the first time in many years, big business was wanting to know what Labour was thinking, and to influence that thinking if possible. The Labour Industry Forum had been set up to act as a conduit in developing Labour's relationships with industry. A piece by Kirsty Milne in the June 23 1995 edition of the *New Statesman* contained a diagram of 'lobbyists for Labour', at that time still something of a rarity on the British PR scene.

21 Michie, D., 'Inside the secret world of the spin-doctors', *The Times*, April 10 1998. For a more detailed account of the public relations industry, see Michie, 1998.

22 Heffer, S., 'Spinning for a living ... who cares?', *British Journalism Review*, volume 6, number 4, 1995, pp. 6–10.

23 McWhirter, I., 'Running with the spin', *Independent*, October 21 1997.

24 McWhirter, I., 'Running with the spin', *Independent*, October 21 1997.

25 Kelly, M., 'The game and the show', *Guardian*, November 20 1993.

26 Appleyard, B., 'John Major ate our monsters', *Independent*, February 11 1993.

27 Campbell, A., 'Auntie's spinners', *Sunday Times*, September 22 1996.

28 Greenslade, R., 'Playing paper politics', *Guardian*, December 9 1996.

29 McGuire, S., 'A dance to the music of spin', *New Statesman*, October 17 1997.

30 McWhirter, I., 'Running with the spin', *Independent*, October 21 1997.

31 Norton, C. and Brennan, Z., 'I will not obey: Blair's Dalek MPs fight back', *Sunday Times*, June 15 1998.

32 See also reports of deputy prime minister John Prescott's reported views that the spin doctors 'are harming the government's standing with the public' (Grice, A., 'Prescott attacks spin-doctor reign', *Sunday Times*, June 21 1998), in the week when Alistair Campbell appeared before a parliamentary select committee to defend the government's alleged politicisation of the Whitehall information management system and the fact, for example, that under Labour

the number of 'special advisors' to government departments had increased from 38 to 70, and public spending on advisors doubled to £3.6 million.

33 The *Sun*, June 24 1998.
34 Colver, H., 'Storm ahead for top spin', *Sunday Times*, June 28 1998. Colver's letter was written shortly after Campbell appeared before a Commons select committee to defend his methods.
35 Hencke, D., 'How high priests of spin keep order', *Guardian*, August 8 1996.
36 Colver, H., 'Storm ahead for top spin', *Sunday Times*, June 28 1998.
37 White, M., 'In the frame', *Guardian*, July 7 1997.
38 MacWhirter, I., 'Running with the spin', *Independent*, October 23 1997.
39 Toolis, K., 'The enforcer', *Guardian*, April 4 1998.
40 See too White, M. and MacAskill, E., 'His master's voice', *Guardian*, February 2 1999.
41 *We are the Treasury*, Scottish Television, broadcast on ITV in two parts, during September and October, 1997.
42 Written and presented by columnist Andrew Rawnsley, *Blair's Year* was broadcast on Channel 4 on April 19 1998.
43 Grice, A., 'BBC "bias" is condemned by BBC aides', *Sunday Times*, September 22 1996.
44 Campbell, A., 'Auntie's spinners', *Sunday Times*, September 22 1996.
45 As quoted on Radio 4's *Today* programme, November 19 1996.
46 Crosland, S., 'One of us?', *Sunday Times*, September 29 1996.

8 THE MEDIA AND POLITICS, 1992–97

1 For detailed content analyses of press and broadcast coverage of the 1997 campaign see Harrison, 1997; Scammell and Harrop, 1997; Norris, 1998.
2 Sky News' journalistic impartiality is essentially market-driven, in so far as the organisation's managers know they are competing with the BBC, and that if they are to survive and prosper in a high-quality TV news market, they must occupy the same ground, editorially. Adam Boulton, Sky News' political editor at the time of this study, states that he was given assurances of the organisation's impartiality before accepting his position. There was, he says,

> a recognition by the head of news that [TV] is a different business, that, fundamentally, to cover news in the way the public expects, you need access to all sides... In crude terms, if we were in a position where we were taking a pro-government line, and if the Tory party said, 'we are just not going to talk to you, we are not going to put people up to appear on your programmes, we are not going to allow your cameras access to our party conferences', or whatever, we would be the losers. And therefore I think there is a strong pragmatic reason why, not just Sky, but broadcasting generally has stuck very closely to this politically impartial line.

3 Whittam Smith, A., 'The secret of this newspaper lies in its title', *Independent*, October 7 1996.
4 Quoted in MacArthur, B., 'Press-ganged all the way to the ballot box', *Sunday Times*, February 2 1992.
5 Quoted in MacArthur, B., 'Press-ganged all the way to the ballot box', *Sunday Times*, February 2 1992.
6 See the *Sun*, April 8 and April 9 1992.

7   For detailed analysis of the content of newspaper coverage of the 1992 campaign see McKie, 1995 and Seymour-Ure, 1995.
8   He went on to write that 'never in the past nine elections have they come out so strongly in favour of the Conservatives. Never has the attack on the Labour Party been so comprehensive. They exposed, ridiculed and humiliated that party, doing each day in their pages the job that the politicians failed to do from their bright new platforms. This is how the election was won.'
9   Linton, M., 'Was It the Sun Wot Won It?', seventh Guardian lecture, Nuffield College Oxford, October 30 1995.
10 Linton, M., 'Sun-powered politics', *Guardian*, October 30 1995.
11 From the text of an interview with Murdoch reported in Gibson, J., 'A man exposed', *Guardian*, November 11 1998. This article was in turn derived from a filmed interview shown on Channel 4 on November 21 1998.
12 Gibson, J., 'A man exposed', *Guardian*, November 11 1998.
13 Porter, H., 'Thunderer versus the blunderer', *Guardian*, June 28 1993.
14 Porter, H., 'Thunderer versus the blunderer', *Guardian*, June 28 1993.
15 Jacques, M., 'Traditional links grow weaker in the chains of British politics', *Sunday Times*, July 11 1993.
16 Greenslade, R., 'Gunning for Major's scalp', *The Times*, September 22 1993.
17 Porter, H., 'It's war', *Guardian*, January 17 1994.
18 It has also been suggested that the editors and journalists of the pro-Tory press simply became bored after thirteen years of unbroken Tory rule, and decided to liven things up a little when presented with the opportunity to do so. Such explanations are not wholly convincing, although boredom and restlessness may well have played a part in creating the conditions for the shift to take place. It is difficult to believe that proprietors such as Rupert Murdoch would have allowed such a radical break with the tradition of aggressive pro-Tory partisanship simply because their editorial staff felt like a change.
19 Jacques, M., 'Traditional links grow weaker in the chains of British politics', *Sunday Times*, July 11 1993.
20 Leapman, M., 'Who will bid highest for Murdoch's political allegiance?', *Independent*, August 10 1994.
21 This source gave the following example of Labour's PR adeptness:

> Right at the start of the election campaign I passed Alistair Campbell in the corridor and he said, 'Oh, I've got something you might like. Mick Hucknall, the pop singer, has been to interview Tony Blair for the Labour house magazine, and they haven't used a lot of it. We've got masses of material. We can hand it straight over to you – Mick Hucknall interviewing Tony Blair, for the *Daily Star*.' They were quite happy to do that. It's something which if we'd tried to arrange would have taken weeks, but there it was, on a plate, and they gave us all the words. We were able to do what we liked with them, we could change them round a bit, present it differently, and they had pictures as well, which they gave us. That to us was a godsend. Just up our readers' street. Rather than me, the political editor, interviewing Tony Blair about devolution, inflation, or whatever, which we think would have been a huge turn-off, we had a pop singer who our readers like, interviewing Tony Blair, and asking him the sort of questions that our readers are more likely to want to know answers to anyway. The Tories never did anything like that. They were perfectly friendly, but they never recognised us as a possible way of winning votes.

22 McKie, R., 'Five heads with a single mind', *Guardian*, August 15 1994.
23 Quoted by Sun editor Stuart Higgins in 'Nice one *Sun*, says Tony', *Guardian*, May 19 1997.
24 Cole, P. , 'Could it be that the press is not so Tory after all?', *Sunday Times*, October 16 1994.
25 *Sun* editorial, October 2 1996.
26 *Sun*, October 3 1996.
27 Neil, Andrew, 'Why Blair's honeymoon with Murdoch is going to end in tears', *Daily Mail*, March 19 1997.
28 Young, H., 'Murdoch chameleons look very unhappy', *Guardian*, April 24 1997.
29 From CARMA's Election Bulletin no. 6.
30 As reported in MacArthur, B., 'All's fair in tabloid politics', *The Times*, April 16 1997. MacArthur noted that 1997 had witnessed 'the fairest newspaper coverage of any election since 1955'.
31 Glover, S., 'Power of the press? No, power of the readers', *Spectator*, May 24 1997.
32 Ford, R. 'Major anger has long pedigree', *The Times*, October 15 1991.
33 Horsnall, M., 'Major has complained to the BBC', *Times*, October 12 1991.
34 Webster, P. and Wittstock, M., 'Tories to apply 'subtle pressure' over alleged bias', *The Times*, October 14 1991.
35 Hall, T., 'BBC bias? Not on your telly', *The Times*, October 16 1991.
36 For a defence of the BBC on this point see Hall, T., 'Panorama: the case for showing it', *Independent*, April 9 1995.
37 Hall, T., 'Panorama: the case for showing it', *Independent*, April 9 1995.
38 Culf, A., Wintour, P. and Smithers, R., 'Birt attacks "crass" pressure from Labour', *Guardian*, October 7 1995.
39 Wilson, B., 'This time he's gone too far', *Daily Telegraph*, November 1 1996.
40 Here and elsewhere quotations from the speech are taken from the BBC-supplied text.
41 Jonathan Aitken alleged that 'John Humphrys was conducting the interview not as an objective journalist seeking information but as a partisan pugilist trying to strike blows. There are too many examples of prominent broadcasters poisoning the well of political debate by this type of ego-trip interviewing.' Quoted in Culf, A., 'BBC Chief backs 'effective' Humphrys', *Guardian*, March 27 1995.
42 Politicians aside, the majority of the views expressed in this debate were 'for' the journalists. Richard Brooks and Anthony Bevins reported the findings of audience research that listeners and viewers preferred the confrontational style being attacked by Birt (Brooks, R. and Bevins, A., 'Listeners support Humphrys', *Observer*, April 2 1995.
43 Audience surveys in 1993 showed 23 per cent perceiving a pro-Tory bias on the part of the BBC, and only 5 per cent a pro-Labour bias (Culf, A., 'Eleven minutes that brought broadside', *Guardian*, March 29, 1995.
44 Kampfner, J., 'Short's attack dispelled as "silly season" story', *Financial Times*, August 9 1996.
45 Greenslade, R., 'Conspiracy claims ignore reality', *Guardian*, April 23 1997.
46 *The Power of the National Press*, CARMA International, May 1997.
47 Glover, S., 'The sleazy media', *Daily Telegraph*, April 4 1997.
48 Simon, S., 'BBC launches new Labour channels', *Spectator*, February 7 1998.
49 Lawson, M., 'Sewage and fluff', *Guardian*, July 4 1998.

9 POLITICAL JOURNALISM AND THE CRISIS OF MASS REPRESENTATION

1   McDonald, S., 'Westmonsters and the politics of TV', *Guardian*, March 2 1998.
2   The ideological limits of the media in a liberal democracy have been eloquently dissected by materialist sociologists from Marx to Miliband, and I do not argue here that they no longer matter. The autonomy of the journalistic media as power centres in a socially stratified, highly unequal society like that of the United Kingdom is still constrained by the exercise of economic and political self-interest. Their function as bearers of dominant ideas and values is still apparent in many spheres (though the question of what constitutes 'dominant values' now is much more open and contested – precisely because of the publicising effects of the media – than it used to be).
3   Roberts, A., 'The princess and the royal standard', *Spectator*, September 6 1997.
4   Goodhart, D., 'Who are the masters now?', *Prospect*, May 1997.
5   Cohen, N., 'The death of news', *New Statesman*, May 22 1998.
6   Neil, A., 'What really worries the voters is the underclass', *Sunday Times*, November 3 1996.
7   Neil, A., 'What really worries the voters is the underclass', *Sunday Times*, November 3 1996.

BIBLIOGRAPHY

Bardoel, J.: 'Beyond journalism: a profession between information society and civil society', *European Journal of Communication*, vol. 11, no. 3, 1996, pp. 283–302.

Baudrillard, J.: *In the Shadow of the Silent Majorities ... or the End of the Social*, New York, Semiotext, 1983.

Blumler, J.: 'Elections, the media and the modern publicity process', in Ferguson, ed., 1989, pp. 101–13.

—— 'Origins of the crisis of communication for citizenship', *Political Communication*, vol. 14, no. 1, Winter 1997, pp. 395–404.

Blumler, J. and Gurevitch, M.: *The Crisis of Public Communication*, London, Routledge, 1995.

Boorstin, D.: *The Image*, New York, Basic Books, 1962.

Boston, R.: *The Essential Fleet Street*, London, Blandford, 1990.

Bourdieu, P.: *On Television and Journalism*, London, Pluto, 1998.

Brants, K.: 'Who's afraid of infotainment?', *European Journal of Communication*, vol. 13, no. 3, 1998, pp. 315–35.

Burke, P.: *Popular Culture in Early Modern Europe*, Wildwood, Hants, 1988.

Butler, D. and Kavanagh, D., eds: *The British General Election of 1992*, London, Macmillan, 1992.

—— *The British General Election of 1997*, London, Macmillan, 1997.

Calabrese, A. and Burgelman, J-C., eds: *Communication, Citizenship, and Social Policy*, Oxford, Rowman and Littlefield, 1999.

Cameron, D.: 'Style policy and style politics: a neglected aspect of the language of news', *Media, Culture and Society*, vol. 18, no. 2, 1996.

Carey, J.: *The Intellectuals and the Masses*, London, Faber and Faber, 1992.

Cockerell, M., Hennessey, P. and Walker, D.: *Sources Close to the Prime Minister*, London, Macmillan, 1984.

Cockett, R.: *Twilight of Truth: Chamberlain, Appeasement and the Manipulation of the Press*, London, Weidenfeld and Nicholson, 1989.

Cole, J.: *As It Seems To Me*, London, Phoenix, 1996.

Coleman, S.: 'Interactive media and the 1997 UK general election', *Media, Culture and Society*, vol. 20, no.4, 1998, pp. 687–94.

Corner, J.: *Television Form and Public Address*, London, Arnold, 1995.

Crewe, I. and Gosschalk, B., eds: *Political Communication: The General Election Campaign of 1992*, Cambridge, Cambridge University Press, 1995.

Curran, J. and Seaton, J.: *Power Without Responsibility*, London, Routledge, 1997.

Dahlgren, P. and Sparks, C., eds.: *Journalism in Popular Culture*, London, Sage, 1992.

Denton, R.E.: *The Primetime Presidency of Ronald Reagan*, New York, Praeger, 1998.

Denton, R.E. and Holloway, R.L., eds: *The Clinton Presidency: Images, Issues and Communication Strategies*, Westport, Praeger, 1996.

Engel, M.: *Tickle the Public*, London, Victor Gollancz, 1996.

Fallows, J.: *Breaking the News*, New York, Pantheon Press, 1996.

Ferguson, M., ed.: *Public Communication: The New Imperatives*, London, Sage, 1989.

Franklin, B.: *Newszak and News Media*, London, Arnold, 1997.

Freedland, J.: *Bring Home the Revolution: How Britain Can Live the American Dream*, London, Fourth Estate, 1998.

Gowing, N.: *Real-time Television Coverage of Armed Conflicts and Diplomatic Crises*, Harvard, Harvard University Press, 1994.

Gripsund, B.: 'The Aesthetics and the Politics of Melodrama', in Dahlgren and Sparks, eds., 1992, pp. 84–95.

Habermas, J.: *The Structural Transformation of the Public Sphere*, Cambridge, Polity Press, 1989.

Hallin, D.: 'Sound bite news: television coverage of elections', in Iyengar and Reeves, eds, 1997, pp. 57–65.

Harris, R.: *Good and Faithful Servant*, London, Faber and Faber, 1991.

Harrison, M.: 'Politics on the Air', in Butler and Kavanagh, eds, 1997, pp. 133–56.

Hart, R.P.: *The Sound of Leadership: Presidential Communication in the Modern Age*, Chicago, University of Chicago Press, 1987.

Hartley, J.: *Popular Reality*, London, Arnold, 1996.

Heffer, S.: 'Spinning for a living ... who cares?', *British Journalism Review*, vol. 6, no. 4, 1995, pp. 6–10.

Hersh, S.: *The Dark Side of Camelot*, New York, Little Brown, 1997.

Ingham, B.: *Kill the Messenger*, London, Fontana, 1991.

Iyengar, S. and Reeves, R., eds: *Do the Media Govern?*, London, Sage, 1997.

Jameson, F.: *Postmodernism, or the Cultural Logic of Late Capitalism*, London, Verso, 1991.

Jones, B.: 'The pitiless probing eye: politicians and the broadcast political interview', *Parliamentary Affairs*, vol. 50, no. 2, 1996, pp. 66–90.

Jones, N.: *Soundbites and Spin Doctors*, London, Cassell, 1995.

—— *Campaign 97*, London, Indigo, 1997.

Jowell, R., ed.: *British Social Attitudes*, SCPR, Aldershot, 1997.

Kavanagh, D.: *Election Campaigning: The New Marketing of Politics*, Oxford, Blackwell, 1995.

—— 'New campaign communications', *Press/Politics*, vol. 1, no. 3, 1996, pp. 60–76.

Keane, J.: *Media and Democracy*, Cambridge, Polity Press, 1991.

Kieran, M., ed.: *Media Ethics*, London, Routledge, 1998.

Kilborn, R. and Izod, J.: *Confronting Reality: An Introduction to Documentary*, Manchester, Manchester University Press, 1997.

Kilborn, R.: 'Democratization and Commodification in UK Factual Broadcasting', *European Journal of Communication*, vol. 14, no. 2, pp. 201–18, 1998.

King, A.: *New Labour Triumphs: Britain at the Polls*, New Jersey, Chatham House Publishers, Inc., 1998.

Kurtz, H.: *Spin Cycle: Inside the Clinton Propaganda Machine*, London, Pan, 1998.

Leigh, D. and Vulliamy, E. : *Sleaze*, London, Arnold, 1997.

L'Etang, J.: 'State propaganda and bureaucratic intelligence: the creation of public relations in 20th century Britain', *Public Relations Review*, vol. 24, no. 4, 1998, pp. 413–41.

L'Etang, J. and Pieczka, M., eds: *Critical Perspectives in Public Relations*, London, International Thomson Business Press, 1996.

Linton, M.: 'Was It the Sun Wot Won It?', seventh Guardian lecture, Nuffield College, Oxford, October 30 1995.

Lippmann, W.: *Public Opinion*, New York, Macmillan, 1954.

Livingstone, S. and Lunt, P.: *Talk on Television*, London, Routledge, 1994.

McKie, D.: ' "Fact is free but comment is sacred": or, was it the Sun wot won it?', in Crewe and Gosschalk, eds, 1995, pp. 137–59.

McNair, B.: *Glasnost, Perestroika and the Soviet Media*, London, Routledge, 1991.

—— 'Performance in politics and the politics of performance: public relations, the public sphere and democracy', in L'Etang and Pieczka, eds, 1996, pp. 35–53.

——'Journalism, politics and public relations: an ethical appraisal', in Kieran, ed., 1998a, pp. 49–65.

——*The Sociology of Journalism*, London, Arnold, 1998b.

—— 'Public service journalism in post-Tory Britain: problems and prospects', in Calabrese and Burgelman, eds, 1999a, pp. 159–71.

—— *An Introduction to Political Communication*, 2nd edition, London, Routledge, 1999b.

—— *News and Journalism in the UK*, 3rd edition, London, Routledge, 1999c.

Merck, M.: *After Diana*, London, Verso, 1998.

Michie, D.: *The Invisible Persuaders*, London, Bantam Press, 1998.

Miliband, R.: *The State in Capitalist Society*, London, Quartet, 1973.

Miller, B.: *Media and Voters*, Oxford, Clarendon Press, 1991.

Morris, D.: *Behind the Oval Office*, New York, Random House, 1997.

Negrine, R.: *The Communication of Politics*, London, Sage, 1996.

Newton, K.: 'Politics and the news media: mobilisation or videomalaise', in Jowell, ed., 1997, pp. 151–68.

Nimmo, D. and Combs, J.E.: *Political Pundits*, New York, Praeger, 1992.

Norris, P.: 'The Battle for the Campaign Agenda', in King, ed., 1998, pp. 113–44.

Pilger, J.: *Distant Voices*, London, Vintage, 1994.

Rosenbaum, M.: *From Soapbox to Soundbites: Party Political Campaigning in Britain Since 1945*, London, Macmillan, 1997.

Sabato, L.: *The Rise of Political Consultants*, New York, Basic Books, 1981.

Sampson, A.: 'The crisis at the heart of our media', *British Journalism Review*, vol. 17, no. 3, 1996, pp. 42–51.

Scammell, M.: *Designer Politics: How Elections Are Won*, London, Macmillan, 1995.

Scammell, M. and Harrop, M.: 'The press', in Butler and Kavanagh, eds, 1997, pp. 156–85.

Scannel, P. and Cardiff, D.: *A Social History of British Broadcasting, Vol. 1*, Oxford, Basil Blackwell, 1991.

Schlesinger, P.: *Putting Reality Together*, 2nd edition, London, Routledge, 1987.

—— 'Scottish Devolution and the Media', in Seaton, ed., 1998, pp. 56–75.

Schudson, M.: *The Power of News*, Cambridge, Mass., University of Harvard Press, 1995.

Seaton, J., ed.: *Prerogatives and Harlots: Politics and Media at the End of the Twentieth Century*, Oxford, Blackwell, 1998.

Seymour-Ure, C.: 'Characters and assassinations: portrayals of John Major and Neil Kinnock in the *Daily Mirror* and the *Sun*', in Crewe and Gosschalk, eds, 1995, pp. 137–59.

Shaw, E.: *The Labour Party Since 1979*, London, Routledge, 1994.

Shawcross, W.: *Murdoch*, London, Simon and Schuster, 1992.

Silvester, C., ed.: *The Penguin Book of Interviews*, London, Viking, 1993.

—— *The Penguin Book of Columnists*, London, Viking, 1997.

Stephanopoulos, G.: *All too Human*, New York, Little, Brown and Company, 1999.

Tait, R.: 'The parties and television', in Crewe and Gosschalk, eds, 1995, pp. 59–64.

—— 'Switching off politics', *British Journalism Review*, vol. 8, no. 3, 1997, pp. 19–24.

Thompson, E.P.: *The Making of the English Working Class*, London, Penguin, 1968.

Tunstall, J.: *Newspaper Power*, Oxford, Clarendon Press, 1996.   *P 140*

Wernick, A.: *Promotional Culture*, London, Sage, 1991.

Williams, K.: *Get Me a Murder a Day*, London, Arnold, 1998.

INDEX